CONTENTS

DEFYING THE ODDS

THE RISE OF DALIT ENTREPRENEURS

DEVESH KAPUR | D. SHYAM BABU | CHANDRA BHAN PRASAD

PENGUIN BOOKS
An imprint of Penguin Random House

PENGUIN BOOKS

USA | Canada | UK | Ireland | Australia
New Zealand | India | South Africa | China | Singapore

Penguin Books is part of the Penguin Random House group of companies whose addresses can be found at global.penguinrandomhouse.com

Published by Penguin Random House India Pvt. Ltd
4th Floor, Capital Tower 1, MG Road,
Gurugram 122 002, Haryana, India

Penguin Random House India

First published by Random House India 2014
This edition published in Penguin Books by Penguin Random House India 2021

10 9 8 7 6 5 4 3 2

ISBN 9788184005707

Typeset in Sabon by R. Ajith Kumar
Printed at Repro India Limited

www.penguin.co.in

FSC www.fsc.org MIX Paper from responsible sources FSC® C047271

This is a legitimate digitally printed version of the book and therefore might not have certain extra finishing on the cover.

INTRODUCTION

The deep social hierarchies of caste have been one of India's most pernicious historical legacies and continue to hobble the country. No group has borne the deadening burden of this history as much as Dalits.

But while the past informs and shapes the future, it does not dictate it. Socially stratified societies have not exactly been the exception in human history. From slavery to serfdom, feudalism to patriarchy, structures of social power have transformed, some collapsing altogether and others transmogrifying.

The iron grip of the old order was pried open by a range of forces—civil wars, revolutions, legal and constitutional changes, the rise of democracy and universal franchise. But it was also reshaped by technological and economic forces, in particular the industrial revolution and capitalism.

Over the last century, Dalits have sought to escape their predicament through multiple ways, such as religious conversion and linking themselves to anti-Brahmin social movements. They have sought to leverage the promise of universal franchise in the Indian Constitution, supporting political parties professing an egalitarian ethos and even creating their own political parties, first the Republican Party in Maharashtra and more recently, the (bahujan Samajwadi Party (BSP) in Uttar Pradesh. And they have sought mobility through the state itself, through affirmative action programmes in education and public employment.

These combined efforts have surely made a difference and the relative position of Dalits in Indian society is a far cry from what it was at the time of Independence. Nonetheless, while a long road has been travelled, the journey is far, far from complete. Social hierarchies are extremely resilient and weakening them requires overt opposition, multiple pressures and subtle ambushes. However, the old pathways of change, which centred on politics and public action, need to be augmented. If the state itself is decrepit and venal, the likelihood that it will be a resolute defender of the economically weak and socially marginalized in practice (as distinct from rhetoric) is somewhat low. Dalits need additional arrows in their quiver to advance their interests.

It is in this context that this book is situated. One path that the community's leadership has been wary about is whether markets—and in particular, entrepreneurship—can be an instrument of social empowerment. In part this is because power and privilege are vested in state organs, which makes accessing organs of the state so critical. In addition, a broad intellectual ethos in India, which looked at markets and entrepreneurship with suspicion, seeing it as an instrument of oppression rather than empowerment, further eliminated this option. With the history of many Dalits as landless labourers, penurious and perennially indebted to moneylenders and landlords, this deep-rooted scepticism was hardly surprising. Business meant traders and moneylenders, occupations with ingrained notions of caste. Hence for Dalits, almost any aspiration was better than becoming a *bania*!

But India has been changing—too slowly for some, too unevenly for others—and with it the well-being of Dalits. This is partly the result of a host of legal and constitutional protections, and partly the cumulative consequences of millions of daily struggles as well as the creation of an emerging, albeit small, middle class as a consequence of affirmative action. But it has also been changing as a result of the complex amalgam of forces unleashed by the growth of the Indian economy, the greater role of markets and integration with the global system. India's actions towards its marginalized communities are under scrutiny not just within the country but also without. New pressures and stress points have erupted along with new fissures and opportunities.

Amidst these unprecedented changes, there has been a remarkable growth of Dalit entrepreneurs, defying the odds as the title of this book declares. Several factors explain this. Firstly, Dalit entrepreneurship has grown because entrepreneurship has grown in India, both because the intellectual climate has changed and also because organized sector employment, be it in the private or the public sectors, has stagnated over the past two decades even as the economy and the population have witnessed massive growth. Net employment in India has been growing mainly in the informal sector, whether in transportation, construction and other service sectors outside agriculture. Hence it is unsurprising that nearly half of India's labour force is now self-employed. With nearly two million Dalits entering the labour force annually, and public sector employment stagnant, the need for a new paradigm of social justice is manifest. The experiences of the entrepreneurs in this book make clear that while markets may not transcend caste, they mitigate its *social* salience, while the experience with reservations have only increased its *political* salience.

It is in this context that entrepreneurship offers new possibilities. The stories in this book are a small slice of a thousand medium and large Dalit entrepreneurs that we have identified and surveyed in collaboration with the Dalit Indian Chamber of Commerce and Industry. It is heartening to note that their combined turnover is in the region of a billion US dollars. But they are not 'representative' in any formal statistical sense either of the Dalit community or even of Dalit entrepreneurs. Finding even these thousand Dalit entrepreneurs was a major task, as there are no official records or data on their existence. Curiously, most Dalit entrepreneurs we surveyed said they were never approached by enumerators of the Economic Census, the only official instrument that supposedly gathers information on entrepreneurs in India comprehensively.

There is, of course, no guarantee that these entrepreneurs will continue to grow, let alone become business tycoons. Nonetheless they are a microcosm of large historical changes that are underfoot in India where a dehumanizing social system is slowly but surely giving way. These changes might appear glacial on a day-to-day basis, but we believe they are epochal. Historians are likely to look back and compare the sheer magnitude of these changes to the century plus of struggles for racial equality in the United States, the decline of serfdom and feudalism in Europe and Latin America and the ongoing struggles for gender equality.

Who are these entrepreneurs? What do they do? What were their pathways to success? In which sectors are they more likely to find success? The entrepreneurs are in a wide variety of sectors, from manufacturing to construction to newly emerging services like healthcare and education. They come from across India but their presence in eastern India is decidedly weaker. Is Dalit entrepreneurship more likely to thrive in states with a more favourable environment for entrepreneurship (as in west and south India) or in states where Dalits are more politically empowered—as has been the case in Uttar Pradesh—but which are not economically dynamic? The answer seems more the former than the latter. A thriving economy may not benefit everyone, but a weak economy does seem to hurt everyone, as is evident by the virtual absence of large Dalit entrepreneurs in Bihar and West Bengal.

There are, regrettably, few women entrepreneurs, an illustration of the continued deep gender inequalities in Indian society, including within Dalit communities.

As one reads the stories in this book, some commonalities emerge in the routes to success for these Dalits. Often, their success was nurtured by one or both parents (and especially the mother) who saw the benefit of providing their child with an education. They ensured funds for the child's education by taking on extra backbreaking work that provided the ready cash, sometimes choosing between their children when finances were severely strained and allowed the education of only one child. Often the siblings would also make sacrifices by taking less so that the pooled resources would be above a minimum threshold. This allowed a chosen child to access opportunities that would create a pathway to success for one member, who in time would hopefully 'pull up' the entire family.

A common thread among these stories is the *jugaad* employed by these budding entrepreneurs to find start-up funds for their new ventures. These funds are often provided by family and friends—the wife selling her jewellery, the mother relinquishing her savings, and other family members and well-wishers chipping in. Without this initial capital, it is unlikely that these fledgling entrepreneurs would have made a success of their ventures.

While all entrepreneurs in India face obstacles because of a lack of credit from the formal banking system, potential Dalit entrepreneurs are doubly handicapped because they almost invariably lack collateral and also because of their more limited access to informal credit through community networks. The Indian government set up the National Scheduled Castes Finance & Development Corporation (NSFDC) in 1989 to help entrepreneurs by augmenting their skills, providing working capital, holding executive development programmes, and so forth. Until FY2013 it had disbursed Rs 2,504 crore (cumulative) to 8.6 lakh beneficiaries (approximately Rs 30,000 per beneficiary). Not only are these amounts trivial, there is no evidence of any outcomes. None of the entrepreneurs in our stories had bothered accessing one more official enclave outfit.

The near absence of linkages with a financial system dominated by public sector banks, supposedly enjoined to lend for 'priority sectors', matters even more since Dalit entrepreneurs lack access to the sorts of social networks that are now recognized as critical for success in any walk of life, especially entrepreneurship. Instead of providing access to new networks, these narrow mandate institutions have straight-jacketed Dalit entrepreneurs as supplicants of a governmental bureaucracy. Indeed the fact that the NSFDC is part of the Ministry of Social Justice and Empowerment rather than under the Ministry of Finance or Commerce or Industry reveals the mindset underlying the government's support for Dalit entrepreneurs.

The role of reservations is muted in explaining their success. Reservations in government jobs can be helpful, albeit indirectly. Having a spouse or a relative in a government job can provide access to new networks and an income safety net that allows greater risk taking. However, only a small minority of the Dalit entrepreneurs in our stories benefited from job quotas. They are a new phenomenon, reflecting a shift in the aspirations (or apprehensions) of Sanskritization half a century ago to baniaization across all castes in India today.

Clearly education matters, but in most cases it is not the sort of elite education offered by the IITs or the IIMs but an education in a polytechnic that equips them with real world skills. The experiential school of hard knocks is their true classroom of learning. Indeed, degrees from elite institutions may well make their recipients risk-averse, avoiding the types of occupations or sectors they believe are not 'good enough' for them. But for this group, having so little to begin with and the determination to make something of their lives means that they have fewer inhibitions. They are willing to try entrepreneurial opportunities in areas as wide-ranging as trading in wholesale vegetable markets, construction or recycling, where the working conditions are rarely air-conditioned offices in swank office buildings. Indeed, the same is the case with manufacturing, where the heat and dust, labour issues and inspectors, among other factors, have meant that the scions of more privileged social groups lack the stomach to rough it out, leaving these spaces as opportunities for those willing to roll up their sleeves.

Unfortunately, the policies of the Indian state have been so inimical of large-scale manufacturing, that they have also severely restricted spaces for Dalit entrepreneurs to enter into the supply chains that would have come into being had manufacturing expanded more rapidly. Large firms outsource a range of supplies and inputs creating demand linkages with small and medium enterprises, some of which in turn have the possibility to grow and become large. That path, however, has been stymied.

For many of these entrepreneurs, the path to social mobility offered by entrepreneurship began with spatial mobility, most of all escaping rural India. Seemingly placid from the outside, its rigid hierarchies can suffocate those at its receiving end. The chaos and squalor of urban India provides at least a cloak of anonymity that keeps the possibility of individual initiative alive. Anonymity increases risk taking since failure has less social costs. Dalit entrepreneurs do not mind failing in places where their kith and kin are not around to mock their failed attempts, even though this might mean a weaker social network.

These are rags to riches stories where adversity compensated for disadvantage, seemingly epitomizing the American billionaire Andrew Carnegie's dictum that self-made men have an advantage stemming from being 'cradled, nursed and reared in the stimulating school of poverty.' Although it is certainly the case that in today's world the socioeconomic advantages of birth continue to matter hugely for life chances, for Dalits the odds have shifted from the impossible to the improbable. As our stories illustrate, working their way up from the bottom has instilled a much greater self-confidence and resilience in this group of Dalit entrepreneurs, and a willingness to seize opportunities in sectors and locations eschewed by more privileged business groups. They epitomize Dr Ambedkar's perceptive insight that 'self-respect is the most vital factor in life. Without it, man is a cipher... It is out of hard and ceaseless struggle alone that one derives strength, confidence and recognition.'

How have these entrepreneurs overcome their childhood experiences of social marginalization and the multiple humiliations of poverty and caste? In some cases it surely lingers, but the absence of rancour is striking given the tribulations they faced growing up. Their dreams outweigh their memories. They certainly, occasionally, glance back, but for the most part they are focused on driving forward knowing that one can't drive too far if one is obsessively focused on looking back. While Dalit intellectuals continue to focus on the past to make sense of the present, Dalit entrepreneurs look at the present to create opportunities for new futures.

For a business to succeed, one must deal with anyone and everyone. It is an open question whether blending in matters or if the maintenance of difference can be a cultural resource that can be leveraged for business purposes. It is the practicality arising from their vocations that drives the worldviews of these Dalit entrepreneurs. But it is not just their worldview. In our interviews of the priests in the temples that had discriminated against these Dalit entrepreneurs (and their families) when they were young, there is the recognition that the world has changed and there is a live and let live attitude, in sharp contrast to the images of perennial conflict.

There is, of course, little doubt that for every successful entrepreneur there are countless others who have failed, beaten down by life's impossible odds—and who are not in our book. The possibilities of social mobility in the new India are even today a mirage for most Indians. In Katherine Boo's evocative account in *Behind the Beautiful Forevers* the structural impediments are increasingly 'the system', a callous, dysfunctional and corrupt state, rather than the shackles of Indian society per se. The narrative of *jugaad*—the energy and creativity associated with evading corruption and regulation—overlooks the massive costs that India's weak governance inflicts on the weak and powerless. For too many Indians, Boo notes, the 'system' severs the link between effort and result, engulfing them in deep despair: 'We try so many things...but the world does not move in our favour.'

While powerlessness is pervasive, some transcend it, creating agency by prying open the pores and cracks of the Indian 'system'. This book is about those few who, through a combination of grit, ambition, drive and hustle—and some luck—have managed to pull themselves up by their own bootstraps (although the metaphor does not work for many of them who did not have shoes growing up!). These are inspirational stories that are hopefully also aspirational for the millions of young Dalits—and indeed, other poor and socially marginalized groups—who are trying to make something of their lives and who have to navigate between the Scylla of low aspirations that lead to resignation and the Charybdis of unattainable high aspirations that breed frustration and despair when they are not met.

To make this possible, the leg-up will come not merely from markets, or well-intentioned state intervention in financial handouts and empowerment through legal rights, but through broad structural changes that provide Dalits the essentials of citizenship: social stability, rule of law, and basic services such as health, education and sanitation and physical infrastructure that should be an entitlement for all citizens.

India has until now eschewed the transformational possibilities of entrepreneurship as a tool of social empowerment. These stories are illustrative that this needs to change—soon—not just for the Dalit community but for India itself. This is hardly the end of the multiple struggles facing Dalits in India. It is not even, as Churchill once said, the beginning of the end. But it might, we hope, be the end of the beginning.

THOMAS BARNABAS

The town of Sriperumbudur is most often remembered as the place where former Prime Minister Rajiv Gandhi was assassinated in 1991. But more recently, it has emerged as the epicentre of a manufacturing boom. Located 40 kilometres southwest of Chennai on the Chennai–Bangalore expressway, Sriperumbudur has attracted some of the world's leading companies—such as Samsung, Dell, Mercedes, Nissan, Renault and Tata—which have set up plants there and manufacture products for both domestic and international markets.

The town is part of the upcoming Chennai–Bangalore Industrial Corridor. The project, financed in part by Japan, encompasses parts of Tamil Nadu, Andhra Pradesh and Karnataka. The proximity of these areas to the Chennai port allows companies located in the Corridor easy access to global markets. While world-class companies are busy churning out their well-regarded products, local firms too, have thrived as sub-component vendors and suppliers of a range of goods and services to these companies.

Standing a few hundred metres from the main road and opposite the Nokia plant is a large blue building in which KJN Enterprises is housed. Specializing in recycling and disposing of industrial waste, KJN Enterprises deals with companies like Dell Computers and Nokia.

Dozens of workers, mostly women, work in the company's 15,000-square-foot premises, unloading scrap that includes used cell phone chargers, paper cartons and polythene bags.

The recycling of scrap is undertaken in three phases. After the waste is unloaded from the trucks, it is divided into categories such as plastics, paper cartons, and so on. Plastic waste, for example, can be of several varieties. After separation, the waste material is compressed by machines and packed neatly.

'The heap may have seven to ten types of waste,' explains P. Thomas Barnabas, owner and CEO of KJN Enterprises. The company initials stand for his sons Kevin and Joey and his wife Nishkalavani.

Tall and handsome, Thomas revels in his success—his company has an annual turnover of Rs 15 crore and employs over 200 people. However, Thomas has not forgotten his village roots. His story has every ingredient—grit, hard work, and the luck and good fortune of marrying an intelligent woman.

With the advent of outsourcing in the early 1990s, a large

number of vendors emerged in response to the demand, providing companies with everything from security guards to office stationery. The companies in the Industrial Corridor import most of the component parts—and sometimes the whole product—from abroad and assemble the end product here. Most products arrive well packaged, generating a formidable amount of waste material. These materials are in turn picked up by scrap buyers at negligible cost.

This abundance might suggest that dealing with scrap is an easy moneymaking business. However, issues of logistics, scale, and environmental and health hazards are problems that plague this business, and even more crippling is the intense competition that often leads to strong-arm tactics.

Thomas had an advantage in dealing with these challenges. His in-laws are from Sriperumbudur, and his outgoing personality and leadership skills allowed him to quickly gather a team of a dozen young men to help secure his business.

Thomas was born in 1970 in the village of Mugalivakkam in the adjoining Kanchipuram district. He had a marginally better childhood compared with other Dalits in the village. His father, T. Pethura, is a third-standard dropout who became a child labourer.

The only thing Pethura inherited from his parents was the burden of serving their landlord. His elder brother Wesley, who is now in his early nineties and going blind, gave an emotional recounting of their childhood. In those days Dalit families worked for landlords, an arrangement that spanned generations, with the children and grandchildren of the Dalits serving subsequent generations of the landlord's family.

'That wasn't slavery; it was a sort of serfdom,' explains Suresh, a Chennai-based Dalit entrepreneur in his early thirties, who is also familiar with Thomas's trajectory.

Pethura began working at the age of nine, soon after dropping out of school. In fact, he quit school so that he could work. He would accompany his parents to the landlord's farms and do odd jobs. Even if only one worker was needed, the entire Dalit family would go to work. Landlords provided lunch for the workers.

'We all got to eat lunch,' says Wesley. They were given scooped out ragi balls into which sambhar would be poured. 'We would take it in our palms. It was quite a scene.'

During the growing season, before the crops were ready for harvesting, there was little work on the landlords' farms. At this time, there were no foodgrains left at home, and neither was there any cash.

The Dalits would still go and work at their respective landlords' farms. Instead of wages, they would be given ragi balls. The children eagerly awaited their parents' return so that they could eat.

Although better off than other Dalits in the village, the Pethura family still lived in a house that was just slightly better than a hut. The walls were made of mud and the roof was thatched.

A second-generation Christian, Pethura would attend church regularly. One day the pastor extolled the virtues of education in his sermon. The pastor also cited several examples to motivate Dalit parents to send their children to schools. Pethura was impressed that his pastor spoke English.

That sermon made a deep impression on young Pethura. He was twenty-one when he married Arupatha Mani in 1961, and thought of his family's future.

In those days most landlords paid wages in kind—food and/or coarse grains. The grain that was given as wages couldn't be sold, since there were no takers. To ensure that his children received an education, Pethura needed money.

He would have to find work that would earn him cash, but he didn't know how and where to seek such work. One day an opportunity came calling.

Indian Drugs and Pharmaceuticals Pvt. Ltd (IDPL), a public sector company, set up its offices just 8 kilometres from Pethura's village. While skilled workers were hired from the nearby cities, the company officials wanted to recruit locals for menial jobs. Some of these positions were for security guards. To attract prospective candidates, IDPL officials would display the uniforms and boots that the guards would wear. Pethura applied for the job and he and a few other villagers were selected at a monthly salary of Rs 60 each.

In the village, Pethura's status suddenly jumped.

Pethura's family slowly grew. After the death of his first child, a boy, in 1962, the couple had their second child, a daughter, in 1965. Thomas was born in 1970, followed by a brother in 1973, and three sisters in 1975, 1977 and 1980.

The eight-member family lived in a tiny house that had no amenities whatsoever. The house didn't need a lock and the doors didn't even have latches.

'We all slept on the floor,' recalls Thomas. 'There wasn't even a cot with the family.'

An incident that still pains him took place when he was in the eighth standard. On a hot and humid afternoon, he was walking back home with an upper caste classmate who was Christian as well. Both the boys were thirsty and exhausted. When they reached his classmate's home, which was on the way to Thomas's, the classmate offered him a glass of water.

His friend's mother not only invited him into the house but also gave him sweets. It was an exhilarating experience for Thomas, and he was eager to share the story with everyone at home.

He thought that if he dressed well, even a poor man could be treated with respect. He wasn't sure if his parents would believe that he'd been treated so well in an upper caste house.

As Thomas was about to leave, his friend's father returned home from work. Before his friend could introduce Thomas, the father asked who the young boy was. He was appreciative of this neatly dressed boy who appeared to be his son's friend.

'Pethura's son.'

'Pethura's son?'

The father turned and stormed into the house and Thomas didn't understand what had happened. Moments later, the father came out dragging his wife by her hair.

'Clean the floor at once,' he barked at her. 'Purify it with something.'

'He glared at me,' recalls Thomas. 'I stepped out of his house and hid behind a tree that was metres from his door.'

The man picked up a shovel and smashed the steel tumbler and plate in which Thomas had been served water and sweets.

'He looked threatening,' recalls Thomas. 'He wasn't in control.'

Having recovered from the shock, Thomas hastily ran home and narrated the incident to his elder sister Vidya. Fearing trouble, she took him to hide in the Dalit church that was close to their house.

'Dalit temples and Dalit churches are the safest places to hide,' says Suresh. 'Fearing pollution, the upper castes keep away from them.'

Thomas's village had about 400 upper caste families and fifty Dalit families. A third from both groups was Christian. Up until the incident, Thomas believed that they had separate temples and churches because of poverty and illiteracy. He recalls his school days when Dalit kids were seated separately. The upper caste children didn't play with the Dalit kids.

'We watched them play.'

His parents had an uphill task of educating their six children, four of whom were girls.

Pethura's dream of educating all his children had its consequences. Barring Vidya, who was enrolled in a Christian college and studied in residence, Pethura's other children lived at home and had to work on Saturdays and Sundays in the landlord's fields.

'Pethura had asked his wife and children to earn their own bread,' recalls Wesley. 'He had reserved his salary for education.'

At times, Thomas's mother would take on extra work, which her children helped her with after they came home from school.

In 1989, Thomas cleared his twelfth standard and joined the Government Arts College at Nandanam to pursue a BA in economics.

Vidya, after completing her degree, secured a job with the Church of South India (CSI). No one in the village could believe that she was earning a salary of Rs 5000 a month. 'Even Father wasn't entirely sure,' recalls Vidya. Within six months, she married an army man.

'We realized how correct Pethura was,' says Wesley, who could not send any of his children to school. 'Within one generation, Pethura's family became unrecognizable.'

Pethura's two younger daughters dropped out of school, one after the twelfth standard and the other after the tenth. 'This was only because of the daily transport costs,' explains Pethura. 'It became impossible to pay the bus fare for five children each day.'

'I watched my siblings making way for me and my sister Vidya,' says Thomas. 'It was agonizing.'

In June 1992, Thomas sat for his final year examinations.

What next? It would be difficult to get a government job. The process was tedious and one couldn't be sure of success even after spending a couple of years trying.

'I wasn't the best,' he says candidly of his academic record in college. 'I wasn't even the second best.'

While he kept the option of trying for a government job open, he decided to enrol in a diploma course in printing technology. Located on the outskirts of Chennai, the Madras Christian College (MCC) ran a reputed course in printing technology. He completed the course in 1994.

Armed with the diploma, he secured a job with Bee Vee Graphics, a pioneer in introducing offset printing technology in Chennai and the publisher of *Chandamama*, a popular children's magazine. He joined the company's marketing division.

Thomas received a monthly salary of Rs 2,500 as well as a decent commission on every order he secured. The company promised him the moon if he crossed Rs 10 lakh worth of orders in one calendar year.

'I took the challenge,' he says.

In a team of fifteen marketing agents, he was the newest recruit and inexperienced. On his very first day at work, he visited MCC. Being a big college, MCC gave a lot of printing jobs to several printers. Moreover, printers would often approach the college, offering their services. He used his contacts at MCC and developed a list of prospective clients.

Within a year, he had crossed the target of Rs 10 lakh. Impressed, the company gave him an office car, a cell phone and an assistant.

Many of Thomas's friends initially mocked him, saying that he had become a driver, but soon realized his worth when many among their relatives and friends began speaking highly of him and his achievements. A Dalit man with a government job approached Pethura with the proposal of marrying his daughter to Thomas. In March 2005, Thomas married Nishkalavani who was five years younger than him.

By his second year with Bee Vee Graphics, Thomas was making waves as a highly successful marketing manager.

'I was re-designated from marketing agent to marketing manager,' he says. 'I was mesmerized by my success.'

While at Bee Vee Graphics, Thomas saw a business opportunity that required very little investment but had the potential for success. He had come across many 'printers' who didn't own printing presses and yet did well as printers. What they leveraged was location—they had offices in busy localities. They would undertake printing jobs for clients in the surrounding area and get the orders printed at Bee Vee Graphics.

Why couldn't he do the same when he knew so many clients? Nishkalavani said he could, and urged him on.

Once his wife gave him the much needed morale boost, he decided to launch himself as a businessman. While still working with Bee Vee Graphics, he rented a 10x10-square-foot shop in Triplicane, a busy locality in Chennai, and got his own business cards printed. He was now the owner of TN Offset Printers.

In early 2006, Thomas quit his job at Bee Vee Graphics.

'My journey had just begun,' recalls Thomas. 'From driving a car, I now walked.'

TN Offset Printers wasn't located in the best area of

Triplicane. Nor was it well furnished. All it had was a large table, two plastic chairs, and a used sofa for guests.

'I was somewhat dishonest,' confesses Thomas. He covered his walls with a large variety of visiting cards, letterheads, calendars and office files, which he claimed were his products.

Thomas' day would start at eight in the morning. Triplicane was his first target. He was determined to convince all the shopkeepers in the area to have their visiting cards printed by TN Offset Printers. He also made it a point to drop off his own visiting card at all the businesses in the area. After a month, he visited other parts of Chennai, where he targeted mostly Christian institutions.

Nishkalavani was bewildered. She had married a man who had a car and a cell phone. Within seven months of their marriage, everything had changed. Not that she missed the comforts that they had enjoyed during his Bee Gee days, but rather she was worried about the way in which her husband spent his days.

'His body would stink,' she recalls, 'because of his clothes. He would be wet all the time, as if he had bathed with clothes on.'

Thomas had no motorbike or bicycle so he would walk more than 10 kilometres a day, leaving his business cards at shops and other facilities.

The meagre savings they had soon started dwindling. After fifteen days in business, TN Offset Printers still awaited an order.

Then came the day when his religious affiliation came to his rescue.

Thomas reluctantly decided to pay a visit to Reverend Milton Jaganathan of CSI. The pastor patiently heard what Thomas had to offer.

'Print my cards,' was the Reverend's reply. However, when he saw Thomas's visiting card, which had no phone number listed, he admonished him saying, 'This is no way to do business.' He advised him to procure a landline and if possible, a cell phone.

'Who is going to take you seriously if you don't have a phone line?' he asked.

Thomas shared the pastor's advice with his wife. She was quick to give him some of the money she had saved. The next day he bought a pager and had new business cards printed.

On the recommendations of Reverend Jaganathan, Thomas met with another Christian leader, Reverend Devakadaksham, who placed an order for printing calendars.

With the blessings of the two pastors, Thomas was able to secure a few orders. Six months after he had opened his business, however, he had yet to acquire a cell phone or a landline. He was unable to hire a peon for the office.

'I was my own office boy, I was my own marketing agent, and I was the face of my business,' he says.

A year later, in 2007, TN Offset Printers was receiving regular orders from a few private schools to print stationery for them. Thomas bought a new bicycle and hired an office boy. By 2008, he was making Rs 5000 a month after paying for staff and other expenses. TN Offset Printers was making moderate progress.

In the summer of 2008 when Nishkalavani visited her parents for a wedding in the family she was amazed to see the extent of the industrial expansion that had taken place in Sriperumbudur over the span of a couple of years. She heard numerous stories of villagers making it big because of the rapid growth.

When she returned from her parents' village, she painted Thomas a picture of Sriperumbudur as a gold mine.

'Dozens of young men from my village have blossomed into businessmen,' she told Thomas. 'People who started small as milk vendors, bottled-water suppliers, even as scrap collectors, have made it big. If you put in even 10 per cent of the time you are investing in your printing business, you will be able to buy a bike within six months,' she advised him.

Initially Thomas was reluctant. He couldn't believe that Sriperumbudur had turned into an industrial hub. He decided to check the facts for himself.

A week later, he paid a visit to his in-laws' home. He spent the day touring the Sriperumbudur industrial cluster. Since the surrounding land had once belonged to the villagers, some of them had easy access to factory premises.

With the help of a villager, he met Vijayakumar, the head of the human resources division of a multinational corporation. He asked Thomas about his background and told him about one of the best business opportunities at the time—the scrap business.

'Scrap?'

'Don't feel offended young man,' Vijayakumar counselled Thomas. He clarified that he was talking about industrial waste, not kitchen waste!

'Tatas began with salt. Dhirubhai Ambani sold snacks in front of his village temple,' Vijayakumar cited several examples of hard work and the dignity of labour.

Vijayakumar explained the economics of scrap. Thomas would buy plastic and cardboard carton waste at throwaway prices. All he had to do was separate the waste into categories. Once segregated, all the categories would turn into money.

'With an initial investment of one lakh, you can earn an income of Rs 25,000 a month,' Vijayakumar assured Thomas.

'Rs 25,000 a month!' Thomas left Vijayakumar, promising that he would be back within a week.

Back home, Thomas narrated what he had learned to Nishkalavani. He could at best arrange for Rs 15,000.

'Where will the rest of the money come from?' he asked his wife. In addition to the money, he would need a place to store and separate the waste.

'I will bring you the money,' assured Nishkalavani. She also assured him that he could use one of her father's thatched houses.

Thomas made up his mind. The couple travelled to Sriperumbudur one Sunday. Nishkalavani persuaded her father to allow them to use one of his thatched houses for segregating the waste.

The very next day Thomas visited Vijayakumar who introduced him to his colleague who was in charge of the marketing division, which also included the waste disposal division.

A deal was struck. Thomas had to collect the scrap from the company premises every day, paying a rate of about Rs 3,500. At the end of the week, he would sell all the the scrap he had collected to a wholesale dealer.

Meanwhile Nishkalavani mortgaged her jewellery for Rs 1.25 lakh.

On the third day in operation, the mini-truck Thomas was using to transport the waste was stopped by men working for the rival scrap contractor. The goons deflated the front tyres of the mini-truck with a warning—'Don't come back tomorrow.'

The word spread in Sriperumbudur's Dalit hamlet that rivals had stopped Thomas' truck. He visited the village in the evening and explained the whole affair. The village youth were up in arms.

The next morning, about fifty to sixty young Dalits invaded the industrial clusters with wooden batons, iron rods and clenched fists. All waste-carrying trucks were stopped, to be released only upon the arrival of their owners.

A police team arrived and a solution was found. The rival group had to pay Rs 1,000 as a penalty for stopping Thomas's truck. Thomas had to assure the police that his boys would no longer stop his rivals' trucks.

'The rival almost fell at the feet of Thomas,' says a villager. The incident established Thomas' reputation as a no-nonsense man with tremendous organizational abilities.'Parties in dispute now come to Thomas before going to the police station.' For Thomas, assertiveness is central to the business of waste collection.

Sure enough, his increasing clout also coincided with a flourishing business. Thomas recently set up a large plant to recycle plastic waste into plastic granules. Trial runs are on. 'This will generate revenue worth Rs 5 crore annually,' explains the plant manager.

Thomas is also set to launch a new plant for making recycled cardboard cartons for packaging. With that, his turnover will cross Rs 20 crore.

'He will be worth a hundred crore by 2020,' predicts Suresh.

'To be honest, Nishkalavani is the entrepreneur and I am her manager,' confesses Thomas. 'She has been the trigger.'

'He is making fun of me,' she replies, downplaying her role.

In addition to giving much-deserved credit to his wife, Thomas is grateful to Reverend Jaganathan, Reverend Devaasirvadham, and Reverend Devakadaksham; they stood by him when it mattered the most.

What's next for Thomas?

His business is on autopilot mode. Expansion plans are in place and he is working to give concrete shape to his hopes of diversification. But he has another passion that he rarely speaks of: taking forward Dr Ambedkar's mission of according equality to all sections of society. It is this dream that led him to earn a graduate degree in law from Kadapa and enrol for a post-graduate degree from Tirupati (both in Andhra Pradesh).

The way to political power passes through the law college. Doesn't it?

Thomas simply smiles.

NAND KISHOR CHANDAN

On a frosty mid-January morning under unusually clear skies, the northeastern edge of Delhi, along the Yamuna, is thronged with people in search of work, driven by their determination to succeed in their quest.

Some might have been heading towards Tronica City, just outside Delhi. This budding manufacturing hub, designed by the Uttar Pradesh government, was built as an industrial town. About 30 per cent of the town's area is earmarked for industrial activity. The rest is given over to the growing, lush green township.

This seemed like just the place for Nand Kishor Chandan, better known as Chandan to his friends, to build his business.

A prominent billboard directs one to Samrat Ashoka Buildwell. Chandan, seated outside its offices, beams and exudes warmth, energizing those frozen to the bone.

Stocky and clad in a black suit, Chandan is the personification of confidence, leaving no question as to who the 'big boss' is. When he calls for 'Anil', five or six boys run out of the building to receive their instructions. Presumably, one of them is Anil. Chandan murmurs some instructions followed by the admonition to 'be careful'. Within no time, an abundance of snacks, fruit, sweets, water and tea appear.

As we partake of the repast, Chandan recounts the road to his current success. He registered his company, Samrat Ashoka Buildwell, with the Uttar Pradesh government in 2011 as a first-class contracting business, building roads and factory sheds. During the first year, his turnover was Rs 2.8 crore.

A motorbike stops nearby, interrupting our conversation. The biker, a man in his late twenties, walks hurriedly into the office. He is Akhthar Khan, Chandan's partner in a real estate business. 'He holds a 25 per cent stake,' says Chandan.

A large car, carrying a man in his early thirties, soon follows. The man waves to Chandan as he walks into the office through the side gate. 'He is a fellow businessman, good at cooking meat,' smiles Chandan. Tall and slim, the man is Raju Gupta, owner of a large printing press that prints medical textbooks.

'These are the businesses I don't take to heart,' says Chandan. 'This is a transition time for me.'

Transition time?

Another car stops in front of the office. A well-built, middle-aged man emerges and walks up to Chandan. Handshakes follow and he is introduced as Sunil Chaudhary. He is in the business of processing sattu from roasted gram. His latest turnover was Rs 20 crore.

Raju Gupta comes out of the building and joins us. We soon realize that Chandan has arranged a lunch for over a dozen business friends. He had recently bought a company, Recon, for Rs 2 crore and his friends had asked for a treat to celebrate the occasion.

Gupta, who belongs to an upper caste, does not eat even eggs at home. Traditionally, the trading castes practise strict vegetarianism. But outside his home, Gupta not only relishes non-vegetarian food but is a master chef when it comes to cooking meat.

'People relish the mutton, the bhuna gosht, he cooks,' Chandan says.

Gupta's recipe calls for a kilogram of onions for every kilogram of goat meat, along with ginger and garlic paste, turmeric, black pepper and coriander. Once the ghee is hot, he fries the onions and ginger-garlic paste. Salt and spices are added later. The meat pieces are placed above the fried onions in a pressure cooker and cooked for two hours on a low flame.

While Chandan continues recounting his 'transition time' story, Anil calls Gupta to inspect the meat cooking in the kitchen. Chandan has built a few rooms for workers, including a kitchen, in the backyard of his office.

'No burnt smell yet,' declares Gupta after sniffing at the pressure cooker.

An hour later, the bhuna gosht is ready and, as if timed to the minute, Anoop Gupta, Chandan's former boss and today's chief guest, enters.

Gupta is nearing sixty but looks a decade younger. He is well-built and full of energy and his body wears his prosperity well. Those gathered stand up, and Chandan introduces his 'mentor' in tones tinged with affection and reverence.

Chandan calls for Anil again, instructing him to serve lunch at once.

The bhuna gosht is delicious. The onion pieces are half-burnt and stuck to the bottom of the cooker and the mutton has taken on a smoky flavour.

'Chandan shocked us when we first met him,' Anoop reminisced. 'He entered the interview room fearlessly. The world has turned upside down in just two decades.'

That might be an understatement. Chandan joined Anoop as his employee in 1992. He has now bought Anoop's company for Rs 2 crore.

In 1992, Anoop owned Global Systems, essentially a trading firm that bought used photocopier machines imported as e-waste, fixed and refurbished them and marketed them to customers in small towns.

A commerce graduate, Anoop didn't have any technical knowhow. Following the loosening of import licence rules in 1991, many electronic goods became fashionable and photocopying was one such activity. Importers in Delhi would buy sub-standard machines from the West and resell them in India's hinterland.

Desperate to succeed, Anoop wanted to build a technical team. Although his staff was able to reassemble the machines, the constantly changing models posed a challenge. 'Most of them were school dropouts from the countryside,' recalls Anoop.

'Every six months, models would change. So we were badly in need of trained hands.'

Chandan had obtained a diploma in mechanical engineering from Delhi in 1990. For eighteen months he ran from pillar to post in search of a job. One day, he learnt of a vacancy at Global Systems.

'I was desperate to land the job,' he remembers, 'but the job must match my taste.'

Of seven siblings, Chandan was number four. His father had retired from a government job in 1987. The family lived on his pension. A marriage had been arranged for his only sister. His two elder brothers had had a limited education and as a result, kept changing jobs while the younger three were studying.

'I had to chip in to supplement the family income,' says Chandan, thinking of those days. His mother had worked as a seamstress for a nearby hosiery firm ever since he was a kid. In fact, barring the three younger sons, the entire family worked part-time for the hosiery firm.

Anoop's Global Systems specialized in Ricoh photocopiers, which used liquid ink. The company had three other partners although Anoop was the majority shareholder.

It was a walk-in interview. Anoop kept asking him about Ricoh photocopiers. Somewhat impatient, Chandan said, 'Your company will be out of business if you persist with Ricoh copiers that use liquid ink.'

'He stunned us,' admits Anoop. Chandan's explanation was straightforward: dry ink machines had started replacing liquid ink ones in the 'home' markets and if Global Systems did not move over to dry ink copiers it was unlikely to survive.

When the interview was over, Chandan was asked to come after lunch for the results of the interview. 'While they went to eat, I waited for an hour over a cup of tea,' recalls Chandan. 'I shouldn't have been that outspoken,' he reproached himself, fearing that it would cost him the job.

Anoop and his colleagues returned from lunch. 'Join us tomorrow,' Chandan was told.

He returned home with sweets. The family invited their

friends and relatives and celebrated the good news over dinner, with fish and meat served liberally. Twenty people were crammed into the three-room house, which had neither balcony nor living area. Luckily, it was winter.

For Chandan, his new job was no less than getting a visa to the United States!

He got up before dawn the next day. While his mother was preparing breakfast, he was busy cleaning his bicycle. 'I oiled all the bearings,' Chandan said.

Global Systems was located in Daryaganj, some 10 kilometres away from Chandan's home. He pedalled as fast as he could, he was so excited.

On his first day at work, Chandan had a brainstorming session with Anoop and other senior members of the company. 'He explained to us how technology was fast changing and we were so convinced,' said Anoop. They had a hearty laugh when Chandan remarked, 'Who knows if colour photocopying is the next thing.'

When Chandan joined Global Systems, Canon and Salex were the market leaders. The company was selling five to six machines a month. 'I was so naïve and knew very little about technology,' admits Anoop. 'I went by whatever my workers said.'

After having observed Global Systems for a month, Chandan figured out what the company's first step towards its continued survival had to be: he advised Anoop to hire an experienced worker from either Canon or Salex, both of which were using dry ink technology.

'Computers and photocopiers were the newest technology that the faculty and students at my engineering college talked about most,' says Chandan. 'I, too, was greatly attracted to the new technology.'

Global Systems hired a man each from Canon and Salex. They came at a price, though. But, thanks to them, the company grew quickly. With the help of some innovative marketing tricks, by the end of 1993, Global Systems was selling a machine a day.

On the completion of his first year at Global Systems, Chandan had bought a used scooter. The company raised his salary every other month.

In 1995, Global Systems was renamed Recon Enterprises, and it was selling 200 machines a month. A machine sold for Rs 60,000 to Rs 70,000.

'We made good money,' says Chandan with a twinkle in his eyes. Anoop nods in approval.

Chandan now rode a motorbike. His work involved going to many towns for repair work. 'Chandan was our best engineer,' testifies Anoop.

While Recon Enterprises was scaling up rapidly, something else happened. Anoop offered Chandan a one-fourth partnership. 'He proved to be too precious,' was Anoop's explanation.

Excited, Chandan sought wise counsel from friends. All encouraged Chandan to launch his own business.

'From a worker to one-fourth owner, that's the maximum you could go,' argued one. 'Be your own Global Enterprises,' said another. 'Be careful of the upper caste partner,' cautioned yet another.

'I got carried away,' Chandan says pensively. 'I was led by passion and not by business calculation.' He quit Recon Enterprises in November 1996 to launch his own business, which also dealt with refurbishing and resale of photocopiers.

Incorporated as National Canon, Chandan launched his company in nearby Ghaziabad. While Recon Enterprises was located 10 kilometres west of Chandan's home, National Canon was 10 kilometres to the east.

Anoop thought Chandan would fail.

'I was so distressed when he quit. Why did he leave me? He was so nice.' Anoop visited Chandan's home along with his wife.

'That's when he came to know that I was a Dalit,' says Chandan. 'There were portraits of Ambedkar all over the house.'

'He had come to wish me a bright future for National Canon.'

Chandan's venture defied all business logic. He set up shop in a place not known for being a photocopier market.

In 1996, the Internet was not yet popular amongst the business persons who were Chandan's prospective client base. Cell phones, also, were very expensive.

Not realizing that he was inviting losses, Chandan hired engineers at high salaries. He built a state-of-the-art office and hired a storage facility. He bought half a dozen used and imported photocopiers and kept them ready to sell.

All this meant an investment of Rs 10 lakh and a monthly expense of a lakh. The lack of business didn't deter Chandan; he accepted the fact that one couldn't make a profit from day one.

For 500 days, National Canon did not make a paisa. But his company survived those days because Chandan had gained a vendor's code with the central government's energy giant, National Thermal Power Corporation. This enabled him to do a steady business with NTPC.

'I lost all the money I had made,' says Chandan. 'I began pledging properties I had bought during my Recon days.'

'I'm grateful to the Queen that the kitchen was running,' Chandan jokes matter-of-factly, referring to his wife Rani who was a health worker in the Delhi government and drew a decent salary.

Though their husbands had parted ways, Rani and Anoop's wife Ruchika never lost touch with each other.

'Shouldn't we invite Anoop and his family for dinner?' Rani asked one day.

Acknowledging that he had been avoiding invitations from Anoop, Chandan finally agreed. 'He'd invited us on a few occasions but we couldn't go,' he says.

'Chandan probably had a rethink,' Rani adds. 'He had foreseen the future of National Canon.'

The dinner turned out to be the ice-breaker between the friends. Anoop was not only happy but he felt honoured by the dinner invitation. He, however, was clueless about Chandan's business strategy.

'Great! You seem to be doing so well,' remarked Anoop as he and Ruchika were leaving. Generally cheerful, Chandan would always put his best self forward—he hadn't shared his business troubles with Anoop.

'Kya hum phir se ek nahi ho sakte?' ('Can't we be one again?') was Ruchika's parting shot.

Chandan wasn't sure whether this was just a warm sentiment or something premeditated. To his relief, it turned out to be more than just a passing thought—in a few weeks, Anoop broached the idea of joining hands.

Chandan was thrilled. 'Until then, I was seeing a bleak future ahead.'

Anoop, too, needed Chandan as Recon's sales were declining. 'I thought Chandan might devise a turnaround.' Anoop later recalled what was in his mind. 'I respected him a lot when he worked for me. And my respect for him increased after he quit.' What had impressed Anoop most was the fact that Chandan never tried to steal his clients.

Anoop made Chandan a handsome offer. It was early 2000.

The offer included a monthly salary of a lakh apart from one-fourth ownership and a directorship in Recon Enterprises.

After rejoining Anoop, Chandan carried out a market survey. He visited the importer who sold used machines to Recon. The very next week, Chandan gave his verdict: they were going out of business. He cited the experience of the importer who had shared Chandan's concern—that the market for used machines was falling.

Chandan came up with a new business plan. 'That's where I saw virtue in making him a partner,' confesses Anoop.

Chandan understood the market situation. Indians were becoming quality conscious and were opting for new machines. Also, the prices of gadgets were dropping so much that households were buying printers along with PCs. E-mailing was also contributing to the decline in the demand for photocopying.

'I closed my eyes for half a minute,' recalls Anoop. 'What shall we do now?'

Chandan cheered up the dejected Anoop. True, there was no demand for used machines but there were still thousands of them in use. For these, there was no one-stop shop for spare parts to conduct repairs. 'Let us start selling spares as well as used PCs,' was Chandan's prescription.

'I had to go by Chandan's genius,' admits Anoop.

The idea worked. By 2001, Recon's turnover touched Rs 25 lakh. The company had outsourced spare-part making to small units nearby.

'Why don't we manufacture these spares ourselves?' Chandan asked Anoop one day. By doing so, the company's profit margin would increase substantially. By 2002, Recon Enterprises was both selling and manufacturing spare parts for used machines.

The new business needed a new company and thus was born Recon India Spare Parts Pvt. Ltd. The company bought 1,200 square metres of land in an industrial belt. In 2004, Recon shifted from Daryaganj to Tronica City and the company's turnover reached Rs 5 crore.

As technology changed so did the fate of companies like Recon. By the following year, in 2005, Recon's sales crashed to Rs 1 crore. It again fell on Chandan to find out why. A month later, he told Anoop the bad news: the business for photocopier spares had no future. Most of the used machines they had sold in the past had reached the end of their lifecycle. The newer, more sophisticated copiers required equally sophisticated machinery to manufacture their spares.

Recon had to completely switch over to being a used PC business. A Mumbai trader bought discarded PCs from the United States as scrap. The de-assembled PC parts were neatly packed and shipped to India.

Recon would buy them at scrap rates and its workers would reassemble them into usable PCs. Some parts would be replaced, and machines would be cleaned and painted, if required. The PCs would look like new but were sold as 'used computers'. While the cheapest new PC came for a minimum of Rs 25,000, Recon's PCs were available for just Rs 6,000.

'We made Rs 3,000 on each PC we sold,' says Anoop. 'Those were our golden days,' adds Chandan. Some sixty workers would work in shifts and were able to meet the demand.

Chandan bought his first car in 2008. A year later, he acquired two properties worth Rs 1 crore. By March 2009, Recon had registered a turnover of Rs 6 crore.

When things were finally looking up for Recon, it was struck by a debilitating policy thunderbolt. In early 2010, the government issued a blanket ban on the import of computer scrap, terming it as e-waste. The ban rang the death knell for Recon India Spare Parts Pvt. Ltd. With some sixty employees, Anoop and Chandan waited six months, hoping against hope that the ban would be lifted. When no hope was in sight, the company locked its gates in March 2011.

Most of the workers left in search of a new livelihood. Chandan and Anoop had to be imaginative. Their business journey had prepared them to expect catastrophe just when they felt assured of success and money.

Chandan had a plot in Tronica City on which he constructed his present office. A friend advised him to register a construction company. Within months all the formalities had been completed, and Samrat Ashoka Buildwell came into existence at the end of 2010. Chandan says, 'I now looked for some business avenue.'

The work started coming in bits and spurts. He bagged a road-building contract worth Rs 87 lakh.

Meanwhile, Chandan's friend Akhtar approached him with the idea of opening a real estate business. 'Only if you promise to handle the business,' Chandan insisted.

With a one-fifth stake in the company, Akhtar runs the real estate part. 'I just use Chandan's goodwill and the business follows,' he declares.

Not trained in civil engineering, Chandan took in another one of his childhood friends as partner. With a one-fifth stake, Sunil Chaudhary manages the construction of roads and buildings.

'A project for setting up a plastic goods manufacturing unit is in an advanced stage,' says Chandan.

'That will cost Rs 1 crore.'

UMESH CHAUDHARY

Faizabad is a quiet and sleepy town in eastern Uttar Pradesh. Despite its notoriety in the media as a place rife with communal tensions due to its proximity to the temple town of Ayodhya, Faizabad is undergoing a quiet social transformation.

A marker of this change is the state-of-the-art Chiranjeev Hospital, which when completed, will occupy an area of 12,000 square feet.

The three-storey building has a modern and elegant presence amidst the ancient surroundings. An army of workers is engaged in applying the finishing touches to the building. Only the ground and first floors are operational and the rest are either near completion or being used to store new equipment. The hospital will have three operation theatres.

'This will be a hundred-bed "Grade A" machine hospital,' a beaming Dr Jayanti Chaudhary says with pride. She is the wife of Dr Umesh Chaudhary, the CEO of Chiranjeev Hospital.

A Grade A machine hospital is one where all the machines and equipment installed are new, the latest, and branded.

'Dr Umesh Chaudhary is Faizabad's famous surgeon,' says a local.

'Ask for the ventilator hospital,' a chemist advised. Chiranjeev Hospital is indeed equipped with a ventilator, a medical device that helps a patient to breathe.

The stress on these details is important.

It is common for new hospitals in small towns like Faizabad to procure machines and equipment discarded by big hospitals in large cities when they decide to upgrade. Used machines and equipment are bought by agents who refurbish them and sell them to hospitals in small towns.

Seated in his CEO's cabin, Umesh, fair, of medium height and bald, is shy and polite, but also inscrutable. He responds very slowly as if first rehearsing every word he utters.

'Ye sharmatein hain—he is shy,' laughs Jayanti.

Perhaps to prove her wrong, or using her quip as a chance to open up, he says, 'We have to be top class . . . why else would the elite flock to us?'

In partnership with a public sector bank, the doctor couple has invested Rs 5 crore in building the hospital. Being Dalits, they have empathy for the underclass.

'So often I waive my fees,' Umesh says. 'How can I be unmindful of my own humble background? When the elite start using certain facilities, the underclass too flock in.'

While the hospital is still under construction, word has

spread that Chiranjeev is going to be a super-speciality hospital.

'That's not true,' says Umesh. 'Just because we specialize in surgery, people think we are great doctors, making a great hospital.' Perhaps he doesn't want to raise expectations of his hospital too high.

Umesh was born in 1975 in the village of Phidawan, 28 kilometres from Faizabad, but he doesn't remember much of his childhood in the village.

He studied in the village school till the third standard. He remembers his tiny one-room home, which was made of mud walls. It was really just four walls and a roof, no bathroom or kitchen. Neither was there any electricity nor water supply.

All five siblings—four brothers and a sister—loved playing in the narrow lanes of the village.

Umesh's father Sunder Lal was a postman in Faizabad.

'He would keep telling us of the power of education,' recalls Umesh.

In 1983, Lal took Umesh and his elder brother to Mirjapur village where he lived. This is his in-laws' village, located at the outskirts of Faizabad. He chose to live here as it's closer to Faizabad, his place of work.

The two brothers gained admission into the Faizabad Mission School.

'I couldn't really figure out why he brought only two of us to town,' says Umesh. 'We missed our mother and other siblings.'

Umesh passed the tenth standard in the first division. His elder brother, two years ahead of him, pursued his dream of becoming an engineer by gaining admission to a polytechnic institute after high school. Umesh wanted to become a doctor and took biology for his Intermediate specialty.

Around this time, Umesh started noticing that his father would vanish every evening and sleep late into the following morning. He also saw that his father no longer went to the petrol station to read the newspaper, something he had done every day.

'Where does he go?' he asked his mausi (aunt), who took care of Umesh and his brother. His mausi narrated the story:

Mirjapur village, where Mr Lal lived, had a petrol station. He would visit the petrol station daily to read the newspaper and have a cup of tea.

The owner of the petrol station, Mr D.N. Sood, was a well-known businessman in Faizabad. He and Mr Lal would discuss the day's headlines and local politics. As the two became friends, Mr Sood was surprised to learn Mr Lal's story.

Mr Lal knew that there was no way he could afford to educate all his six children in Faizabad. He brought his brightest sons to town so that at least they could benefit from a better education and thus have more opportunities. Mr Sood was stunned to learn that the postman's two sons were studying in Faizabad's best school.

Suitably impressed, Mr Sood offered Mr Lal a part-time job to help further his sons' education.

Mr Lal would return from the post office at half past six in the evening and an hour later would go to the petrol station. By the time he returned home at half past eleven at night, Umesh had already gone to bed. But Umesh would think that his father was away the whole night.

When Umesh was in the twelfth standard, he faced the twin tasks of clearing his Intermediate examination and passing his medical entrance test. The small village of Mirjapur clearly could not be the place for him to chase his dreams.

Impressed with Umesh's dream of becoming a doctor,

Mr Sood offered the father-son duo a room adjacent to the petrol station that he had built as a servant quarter.

'It was heaven,' says Umesh.

'The room had electricity, lights, a fan and an attached washroom.'

'Sood sahib was humane,' Umesh says with gratitude. 'He knew our caste and yet helped us.'

In 1992, Umesh passed his Intermediate examination. Out of the 200 students who cleared the exam, only eleven of them passed in first class and Umesh was the school topper. A month later, he cleared the medical entrance test as well. He got admission in the Sarojini Naidu Medical College in Agra.

Aspiring to be a specialist, he pursued an MS at the King George Medical College in Lucknow. He completed his MS in 1999.

Now that Umesh was a full-fledged general surgeon, he had many options open to him, which was at first confusing. Should he opt for government service by availing of the reservations for Dalits, or seek employment in a corporate hospital in a big city, like most of his classmates did?

While he weighed his options, an old wound concerning reservations kept chafing at him. The incident occurred while he was in medical school. One day in class, there was a discussion on reservations for Dalits and tribals. The discussion was robust and arguments and counter-arguments flew across the room. As the arbiter, the professor was to make the concluding comment.

When everyone had had their say, Professor Gupta declared, 'We end up teaching horses and donkeys alike.' Realizing that his words were too harsh, he tried to soften his statement. 'Amongst horses also, there are black horses and white horses.'

By the evening, the campus was abuzz with the reference to horses and donkeys and white horses and black horses.

There was outrage not only among the Dalit students but also among some upper caste students, who came to console the Dalit students. The professor's comment had shaken Umesh to the core, and as he pondered over his career options, he was determined to be successful on his own steam.

'If the white horse means the best, I will prove to be a white horse,' Umesh told himself. Building a top-notch hospital became his dream and propelled him forward.

'Not all dreams come true,' he thought. 'But dreaming big is no crime.'

Meanwhile, a new chapter began in his life. He married his childhood sweetheart Jayanti who had completed her MS from Ranchi. Jayanti had known Umesh since the time they had both attended the same missionary school in Faizabad.

Jayanti's father was a government employee. He was a social worker and known for spreading Dr Ambedkar's message amongst Dalits. He was also a friend of Sunder Lal's.

Umesh finally opted to pursue a type of medical practice that was rather new. He became a 'Doctor on Call'—a service that combined the need for medical care in under-served small towns and rural areas with the prevalence of cell phone usage.

Healthcare facilities in rural areas are even today next to non-existent. People in villages suffer from ailments such as hydrocoele, hernias, appendicitis and bladder stones that often go untreated, and only in emergencies are they rushed to a nearby town, if transport is available. Many private hospitals, called nursing homes, in these small towns cannot afford specialists in every field.

A combination of factors like rising incomes, availability of technology even for the poor, and a relative surplus of doctors in urban areas created the conditions for the Doctor on Call service to thrive.

Doctors interested in being a Doctor on Call would leave their resumés and business cards with nursing homes, after which they would be called for consulation when required.

The Doctor on Call service was a boon to nursing homes and young doctors alike. Umesh and Jayanti joined the crop of young doctors who were now self-employed thanks to the service.

'City nursing homes were flooded with young doctors,' says Umesh. 'Doctors don't want to serve the rural market. The small-town nursing homes on the other hand benefited from Doctor on Call.'

'They paid better than the nursing homes in cities,' he adds.

For over a year, starting in 1999, Umesh did a brisk business. He would travel to small towns around Lucknow—Unnao, Hardoi, Barabanki, Sitapur and Faizabad, for example.

'Rs 1,000 for a visit meant a lot to me,' recalls Umesh. 'Jayanti made another Rs 1,000 a visit.'

Umesh became more imaginative: What if he put together a team of doctors who would travel together? Jayanti endorsed his idea.

As Umesh was a general surgeon and his wife was a gynaecologist, they needed an anaesthesiologist to complete the team. Most birth-related surgeries in nursing homes require the presence of all three.

'With the team ready, we will be able to bargain better with nursing homes,' encouraged Jayanti.

Their search for an anaesthesiologist began.

'We must have a car,' Jayanti added.

But where would they get the money?

Their savings amounted to around Rs 50,000. They could

raise at best an equal amount from friends. The diesel car they had in mind would cost over Rs 3 lakh. 'We felt so frustrated,' Umesh recalls.

No bank was willing to lend money to them. The couple had no land, house, or property in their names to pledge. Nor did they have any guarantors. All their relatives were equally poor.

A month-long search took them to a Tata finance company that reluctantly gave them the loan, after they agreed to buy a Tata car.

'They took pity on us,' says Jayanti.

Once they bought the car, more than one anaesthesiologist was willing to join them.

'We minted money in those four years,' says Umesh.

'We would be out for over eighteen hours a day,' recollects Jayanti.

'We spent more time in the car than working,' says he.

'We slept more in the car than in our bedroom,' recalls Jayanti.

Cash-rich, the couple could now walk a different path. During this period, Umesh saw how nursing homes grew bigger and bigger, and how their owners changed cars frequently.

'They bought big cars as easily as they would buy a bicycle.'

Umesh would often visit the Akanksha Nursing Home in Bhitaria, a roadside market in the Faizabad district, some 60 kilometres east of Lucknow. Umesh liked its owner, Dr Ramesh Kumar Singh, a local upper caste man. One day, he said to Jayanti, 'Let us understand the grammar of nursing homes.'

Umesh and Jayanti joined Akanksha in 2004 at handsome salaries but with a condition. When not needed at Akanksha, they would be free to do what they liked.

In their third week at Akanksha, Ramesh invited the couple for dinner. A great host, Ramesh behaved more like a partner than an employer.

'That dinner was the most stunning moment in our lives,' recalls Umesh.

While having dinner, Umesh asked Ramesh what made him set up Akanksha in the rural market. The answer Ramesh gave was an eye-opener for Umesh.

'I prefer small-town hospitals,' said Ramesh. As he wasn't a rich man, setting up a hospital in a city was beyond his means. It involved risks as well. He also wanted to avoid competing with established players in the urban healthcare industry.

'Here I have a free run,' Ramesh explained the economy of serving the countryside.

'We made up our minds that night,' says Jayanti. 'We were awake past midnight discussing our future plans.'

Jayanti began to study the workings of Akanksha when she was not on duty. Umesh would work on the economics of building an Akanksha-type facility in the Faizabad countryside.

'I kept thinking of the area,' recalls Umesh. 'My relatives are spread over the Faizabad countryside.'

Within two months of that life-changing dinner, Umesh located a piece of land in Kuchera Bazaar on the Faizabad–Rai Bareli road. It was a tiny roadside market that catered to villagers. The land came cheap.

It took the architect a couple of months to develop a rough design. Meanwhile, Umesh told Ramesh about his decision to set up a small nursing home in Kuchera Bazaar.

'In fact, I took tips from Ramesh,' admits Umesh.

Ten months after that fateful dinner, the Chinmay Surgical Centre (CSC) was inaugurated in November 2004.

The couple employed pragmatism over emotion. They knew that CSC would not make profits from day one. In fact, it would require investments for one whole year.

'We invested all we had into CSC,' continues Jayanti. 'We ran it on loans as well.'

While Umesh decided to keep working at Akanksha and visit CSC during emergencies, Jayanti quit Akanksha to focus on CSC. They appointed doctors and nurses they knew well.

Since the nearest hospital for people living around Kuchera was 24 kilometres away in Faizabad, CSC was expected to do well. Yet the couple had to be imaginative to enhance CSC's credibility and popularity.

'He would close his eyes for long spells as if he was sleeping but, in fact, he was thinking of a new business strategy,' says Jayanti about her husband.

'I saw the light at the end of the tunnel,' recalls Umesh.

Umesh and his siblings were born at home, like most Indians of his generation and earlier. There would be no doctor, no nurse, no hospital, no medical care. An illiterate lady, most likely a Dalit, would carry a sickle and walk barefoot to attend to the woman in labour.

Over the past two decades, women had started going to hospitals and nursing homes to deliver their babies, as the health and safety of the mother and child were well looked after there. But greed led to a new practice that is more deleterious than leaving childbirth in the hands of untrained midwives.

A new industry that catered to the more expensive surgical deliveries, caesarean sections, sprouted up at the expense of normal deliveries, which were much cheaper. If a normal birth cost Rs 5,000 to 7,000, the caesarean method would cost a minimum of Rs 15,000.

The term 'caesarean' became a part of the popular lexicon even in villages. Unfortunately, it came to be viewed as a mark of higher social status. 'My daughter-in-law's baby is a caesarean,' people would boast to relatives and friends.

'I thought I needed to break this popular formula,' recalls Umesh. 'We hoped to make money by selling honesty.'

Within a year, CSC became popular for facilitating normal births. People recognized that caesareans were not always necessary and that the procedure would not be forced on them. 'Aab to asptal mein bhi bachche bina pet fade paida ho ja rahein hain.' (Now even in hospitals, babies are born without tearing the stomach).

The message spread quickly. It followed that if most deliveries were normal at CSC, then the nursing home must be practising similar honesty in other surgeries as well.

The twenty-two-bed CSC with eighteen employees became a brand. Building on their success, Umesh and Jayanti began a new project.

Named the Chitvan Surgical Centre, this nursing home was built at Rampur Magan on the Faizabad–Allahabad road. With eighteen beds and fifteen employees, this Centre was launched in 2006.

Building the two successful nursing homes gave Umesh the confidence to proceed on his own. He quit Akanksha Nursing Home but remained friendly with his former employer.

'Ramesh is a great man. A Thakur himself, he extended his helping hand whenever I needed it.'

With the two surgical centres, Chinmay and Chitvan, operational and busy, Umesh went back to his white horse dream—to launch a hospital in Faizabad.

'He was now a brand name,' says Jayanti.

'We dared to take risks,' Umesh adds.

In early 2009, Umesh and Jayanti visited Faizabad every Sunday in search of suitable land for the hospital of their dreams. It took over two months to finalize the Chiranjeev Hospital site.

By 2011, they had received several design proposals from various architects and the couple made their final selection, giving concrete shape to Chiranjeev Hospital.

Umesh and Jayanti's two young children—a daughter and a son—study at the leading English medium school in Faizabad.

What's the next dream?

'To develop Chiranjeev as the surgery hub in and around Faizabad,' says Umesh drawing a long breath.

'The day the elite view Chiranjeev Hospital as the safest place for surgery, my life's dream would have been fulfilled,' he adds.

'White horse!' Jayanti smiles in affirmation.

'Umesh and Jayanti are both below forty and employ over a hundred nurses, doctors and clerical staff,' notes Ramesh.

'I treasure Professor Gupta's comment for it served as a trigger,' says Umesh. 'His words proved to be a blessing for me. Unknowingly, he threw up a challenge and that's why I am here.'

SANJIV DANGI

Sanjiv Dangi, at thirty-eight, bald and well built, is a rare breed among Dalit entrepreneurs. He is a second-generation businessman, well educated (an IITian to boot) and thanks his stars that he has never suffered overt caste discrimination. He is also particular about promoting a culture of business among fellow Dalits.

Not averse to the good things in life, he bought a three-bedroom flat in Delhi's Commonwealth Games Village, constructed in 2010 for participants in the Commonwealth Games held that year. He bought it at an auction for Rs 4.1 crore, the high cost reflecting Delhi's astronomical real estate prices. Located on the bank of the Yamuna river and surrounded by lush greenery, the 'village' is anything but one. In 2012, the government sold these flats through auctions, and the well-heeled rushed to buy them. Names of successful bidders were published in newspapers, including a full-page report in the *Times of India* on 22 May 2012. The newspaper's story featured Sanjiv, along with his photograph, as one of the highest bidders.

'A TV crew came to my Delhi residence,' he recalls.

Earlier, his mother Kamla had bought a 5,500-square-foot independent house in the posh Civil Lines locality of Jaipur, paying what would have been a small fortune even a decade ago. 'Mother gifted me that house on my birthday.'

Sanjiv also has a picturesque four-acre farm in Pushkar, near Ajmer. The farm is home to some 700 mango, amla and gunda trees and also produces exotic vegetables.

An engineering graduate from IIT Bombay, Sanjiv runs a host of businesses. He, along with his non-Dalit partner friends, set up Chandram Solar Power Pvt. Ltd and built a solar photovoltaic power plant at a cost of Rs 7.5 crore near Bikaner with an installed capacity of one mega watt peak (1 MW). Electricity-generation is not his only business, though. Chandram Solar Power specializes in concept-to-commissioning of solar power plants. It builds solar power plants for private companies as well.

'We undertake turnkey projects,' says Sanjiv.

'As an electrical engineer, I had to do a business that matched my educational training,' he answers when asked why he entered the solar power industry.

He sensed future opportunities when the government made it mandatory for all manufacturers who used thermal power (coal) as energy to source a part of their consumption from renewable sources like windmills or solar power.

'Plants such as the one built, owned and operated by Chandram Solar Power have a great future,' explains Sanjiv. 'Big energy-users either set up solar plants themselves or buy them from solar manufacturers,' he says. In either case, his plants would be required.

'Electricity isn't his first business; he is in the food business as well,' chips in Meghwal, a relative of Sanjiv's and a fellow Dalit businessman. In fact, Dangi is a sub-caste (gotra) of the Meghwal caste.

Before setting up Chandram Solar Power in August 2012, Sanjiv had set up a franchise of a well-known American food chain in Jaipur. The idea came to him after a visit to the United States in 2008.

'Just the thought of partnering with an American food joint,' says Sanjiv, 'Made me feel like I was partnering with America.'

'Not food, but construction was his first business,' recalls Dr Parihar, a veterinary physician and a prolific writer on issues related to Dalits. 'In a way, he inherited his father's business.'

Sanjiv nods in agreement.

'Not that simple,' adds Meghwal.

Sanjiv's simple story appears complex.

'Dangis are a family of experimentalists,' explains Dr Parihar.

Sanjiv's great-grandfather Narsingh was a soldier-cum-cobbler in the army of the Maharaja of Jodhpur. Narsingh had fought in World War I, on the side of Britain as Jodhpur was its ally. Sanjiv's grandfather Buddha Ram replaced Narsingh, and fought in World War II as a cavalryman.

Born in 1946, Sanjiv's father Navin Dangi drifted from the family tradition of serving in the army. After matriculation in 1963, Navin joined the cooperative department as an inspector. It was a state government job but Navin wasn't much enthused by it.

'It was monotonous and had no room for creativity,' he recalls. 'Par biradari mein yah bahut pratistha ka job tha.' (In the community, however, the job had a lot of prestige)

Within five years of joining the cooperative department, Navin became disinterested. He had begun exploring opportunities where he could do what he loved doing most. In 1974, he graduated with a BA from the University of Rajasthan, Jaipur, as a private student.

Family lore has it that Navin hated chairs. 'Chairs are no different from chains,' he says.

'We loved fighting war, chasing enemies, riding horses and playing with camels,' he recalls the spirit of his childhood.

Navin made friends with some people who were in the field of construction and real estate. He had watched their businesses grow. Urbanization was spreading in Jaipur as well.

'Construction mein moti kamai thi,' recalls Navin.

'People owned tracts of land and kept them unused,' adds Navin. 'Within a few years, they would develop those tracts of land and build single-storey houses. Some would just buy plots of land, develop and sell.'

Navin adopted the latter business model. He set up a private company in 1971. He would buy plots of land and after an interval of a year or two, would develop them and sell.

'The barren land once developed would turn into gold,' says Navin.

However, he had to conduct his business secretly as he was still a government employee.

In 1969, Navin had married Kamla who was a matriculate. Her father was also a government employee. Not long after the two were married, Navin was transferred from Jaipur to Kota.

He tried to reverse the transfer but didn't succeed. He was left with two options—either to move to Kota or quit the job.

'Kyon sarkar ki gulami karni hai? (why should one be in servitude to the state?)' asserts Navin on his decision to quit his job in 1972. 'My father and father-in-law were anguished, and my mother was in tears,' he adds.

'It was a heroic decision,' says Dr Parihar. 'A Dalit quitting a government job in those days was unheard of.'

While Navin's real estate business was growing, national politics opened up a new opportunity for him. In the 1977 general elections, the Congress Party was voted out. A coalition of parties, the Janata Party, came to power at the Centre. The socialist wing of the government managed to shut down Coca Cola businesses in India.

But to entrepreneurs like Navin, a new opportunity danced before them. Rajasthan attracts tourists from around the world. Foreigners would be shocked to know that Coke was no longer available in India.

'Khas-kar garmio mein, Coke ke begair white tourists pagal ho jate they (in summer especially, white tourists would go mad without Coke),' smiles Navin.

Many people launched local Coke imitations, including Navin, who launched 'Moz'. He got a beverage trademark registered, purchased land at Bagru, near Jaipur, and started manufacturing soft drinks.

He did brisk business and the success, and more profits, meant a surge in his status.

'Hum supply nahi puri kar pate they (we could not fully meet the demand),' recalls Navin.

Meanwhile, Navin had also secured an LPG dealership in 1982 under the Dalit quota. Managing the LPG dealership gave him a much needed financial cushion. By 1990, he had become a well-known name in business circles in Jaipur. The upward mobility in his social and economic standing in society meant he could send his younger son Sanjiv to the prestigious Mayo College in Ajmer.

Set up in 1875 as a boys-only school, Mayo College was one of the earliest and best residential schools in north India. Set up by Sir Richard Bourke, the fourth Viceroy of India (1869–72), the Sixth Earl of Mayo, Mayo College aspired to evolve into the Eton of India.

Sanjiv joined Mayo College in 1986 as a sixth standard student and lived in residence.

'He, in fact, lived in hostels meant for the elite,' says Dr Parihar.

The 'college' offers classes from the fourth to the twelfth standard. As it was started to educate the ruling elites of Rajputana—which meant upper caste boys—it still remains an enclave of power and influence. The college is run by a trust, which is headed by the Maharajas of Jodhpur and Kota in rotation.

However, the winds of change are slowly weathering the sharp edges of Mayo College. For example, during Sanjiv's stay there, its doors were opened to girls. But, in the late 1980s, a Dalit student at Mayo College was a novelty, if not an unwelcome spectacle. However, since the college didn't implement reservations, there was no reason for anybody there to be aware of this breach of tradition. Nevertheless, Sanjiv enjoyed his time at Mayo and now feels it was more a matter of class then, although this would have been less so if his Dalit identity was widely known.

'I wasn't a king, nor was my son Sanjiv a prince. I just dreamt that my son would grow up playing and studying with princes,' says Navin.

After graduating from Mayo, Sanjiv enrolled in IIT Bombay to study electrical engineering, this time making use of the reservation quota for Dalits to secure a seat. When he finished his BTech in 1998, he returned to Jaipur to ponder his future career plans. Being an IITian, he had plenty of options, and could have joined any public sector company of his choosing.

'IITians didn't have to wait,' says Sanjiv. Like most of his batch mates, he could have moved to the United States. But Sanjiv was not interested in settling outside India. Moreover, during his IIT days, Sanjiv caught the civil services bug.

'I thought a civil services job would take care of my aspirations while enabling me to serve the people,' says he. Civil servants in India, especially as district collectors, enjoy enormous power.

He spent four years pursuing his civil service dream but could not make it. While preparing for the civil services, he completed an MBA from a local university.

Sanjiv married Rakhi Vimal in 2002 when he was still jobless. Rakhi's father belonged to the Rajasthan Administrative Service but he was later promoted to the Indian Administrative Service, and Rakhi was an Indian Revenue Service officer.

Though he was unsuccessful in realizing his civil service dream, he still had good options. He could have gone abroad or entered government service. Either of the two assets he had—his claim to reservations and his being an IITian—would have vaulted him into a decent career. Instead, in 2005, he decided to expand the family business. Their core business, named Dangi Associates Pvt. Ltd, was in real estate and was run by his elder brother Rajiv Dangi. A commerce graduate and an MBA, Rajiv had taken over the company from his father in 1993.

'I am always available for my kids,' says Navin.

'I knew that recasting the real estate business along corporate lines would cause an explosion in turnover,' recalls Sanjiv.

Sanjiv had some knowledge of the family business through time spent on vacations with the family during his IIT days. Though Navin had started buying and selling real estate way back in the 1970s, he did not expand into construction. Rajiv too continued the 'tradition' as he shared Navin's philosophy of hard work, frugality and caution.

'They would spend months preparing the company accounts or personally attending to litigation, which is unavoidable in the real estate business. It's not beyond their means to hire accountants and advocates,' says Sanjiv, referring to his father and elder brother. Boldness is a luxury only younger children enjoy.

'My father and elder brother gave me a free hand to recast the business,' says Sanjiv. 'They were so generous.'

'The real estate business would now become a construction company,' says Sanjiv of his first initiative.

In India, the 'real estate' business is viewed with suspicion and is little respected. Dangi Associates Pvt. Ltd would now be Neelkanth Nirman and registered under the Companies Act.

By 2006 the transformation had already set in.

After renaming the company, Sanjiv took a series of big decisions that became game-changers.

Neelkanth Nirman would now build residential towers.

Financial transactions would be above board. Cheque books would replace cash.

Salaries would be paid by cheque.

Neelkanth Nirman would subject itself to labour laws.

Capital would be raised from the market as well.

Sanjiv did not leave even small things untouched when he

thought they could make a difference. A website came into being, so did a company brochure. He got prior approval of building plans from banks so that it would be easy for prospective buyers to get housing loans from those banks. In less than three years, he had stunned all—family, friends, investors and well wishers. By 2009, Neelkanth Nirman had completed construction of a ten-storey tower in Jaipur.

'I had a twenty-five-floor tower in mind,' he says. At that time, there was a prohibition on building residential towers higher than ten storey in Rajasthan. The project was financed by the Rajasthan Financial Corporation.

Located in the Vaishali Nagar area of Jaipur, the ten-storey tower named Blue Winds was sold during a time when the construction industry was hit by recession. Prices were down, yet the company managed to sell all twenty-eight flats.

Selling at Rs 30 lakh each, Neelkanth Nirman registered a revenue of Rs 8 crore from one project alone. The company sold a few more projects with single- and double-storey housing schemes. The changes Sanjiv had introduced had helped him transform what used to be a family-owned real estate company into a modern corporate entity.

Though he enjoyed the support of his father and brother, it was by no means smooth sailing for Sanjiv. From the very start, relatives, friends and investors were sceptical of the model of building a residential tower.

'People learn only from their mistakess,' they would mock.

'They were sure that I was making a mistake,' he recalls.

What people couldn't understand was how Sanjiv would build a tower without owning equipment. To them, a building contractor needed to own large cranes, earth movers, concrete-mixers, electrical equipment and excavators, and employ an army of engineers, technicians and workers.

'Just watch,' he would keep assuring them.

Having an MBA, Sanjiv knew how to use the outsourcing model effectively. He had been to industrial complexes and saw how big manufacturers outsourced up to 70 per cent of their work.

He began by getting an architect to design the building. He hired a contractor to build the foundation and another to build the tower. One contractor did the wiring and yet another did the woodwork. Services such as plumbing, painting and interior design were all outsourced, with Sanjiv's firm developing a core competency in project management and integration of diverse jobs and services. He achieved this by having a dedicated team of a dozen experts that included engineers and supervisors to keep track of all the work, including quality control. Each hired sub-contractor did his part of the work and left after finishing.

'We earned the tag of being good paymasters and easily got the right people to do the job,' says Sanjiv.

Since the Blue Winds project in 2009, Neelkanth Nirman has completed ten housing/land development projects with a combined value of Rs 25 crore.

'He used his education to take the family business to new heights,' says one friend.

'This is what a second-generation Dalit businessman can do,' says Meghwal.

Future plans?

Sanjiv gets specific. He wants to launch a few more franchises of the food chain and expand the capacity of Chandram Solar Power's plant from 1 MW to 10 MW, for which the Dangis have bought 265 acres of land in western Rajasthan and are in the process of developing them into solar parks—all with the goal of crossing a turnover of Rs 100 crore by 2020.

RAJENDRA GAIKWAD

Rajendra Gaikwad's company, the Pune-based GT Pest Control, provides pest control services to residential properties, industrial sites, storage facilities, and poultry, dairy and agricultural farms. Its clients include the National Defence Academy, Tata Motors and Volkswagen (India).

GT Pest Control has twenty-five locations in India and one in Singapore. It specializes in all kinds of industrial and domestic fumigation and the control of termites, weeds, mosquitoes and cockroaches. Using state-of-the-art equipment, it undertakes fumigation of export containers as well.

Rajendra set up the company in 1986–87; the company's annual turnover in 2011–12 was Rs 10 crore and it provides employment to some 700 workers.

With his boyish looks and full cheeks, Rajendra Gaikwad's fifty-two years sit lightly on him. His smiling face bears no hint of the poverty and destitution that plagued his childhood and youth.

Born in 1962 in a hut in Pune, he has four elder brothers and a younger sister. Rajai Tai, the midwife who helped his mother, Anusayabai Shankar Gaikwad, told Rajendra that his mother used a sickle to cut the umbilical cord during his delivery, and the rich in the village would use shaving blades instead. This was a time when few Indians, Dalit or not, went to hospitals for delivery.

Rajendra's childhood was spent in Pune. Being the youngest son meant he was pampered by his elder brothers and even by his younger sister. Their mother worked as a domestic helper, cleaning dishes in half a dozen houses, so she was able to provide her family with enough food. Maids would take leftover food from the houses they worked in.

It took some years for Rajendra to realize that his mother worked as a domestic helper in order to feed the family, a job that had a stigma attached to it and one which society hardly treated as a profession.

His father, Shankar Bhikaji Gaikwad, was a fourth-standard school dropout. He began working as a construction labourer and went on to become a supervisor. He worked for a contractor who undertook repair works at the Pune railway station.

He was a caring person. Once Anusayabai fell sick after eating spoilt leftovers she had brought back from the house of one of her employers. It was mid-August—the humidity was very high and food spoiled quickly. Anusayabai ate the leftovers, leaving the fresh food for her family. She wept and complained of a body ache. Shankar decided to take the limping Anusayabai to the nearby government hospital. Seeing a sick woman, no auto or rickshaw would stop. Shankar carried his wife on his back and ran, with his two sons following. Anusaya was admitted in the hospital, and discharged the next morning. Shankar along with his two elder sons stayed overnight in the hospital.

By the time Rajendra was in the sixth standard, he began to realize who he was. The first thing a classmate would ask was where he lived and the mention of Nisen Huts would send his classmates away.

He asked his mother one day why this was so and the story Anusayabai told unsettled him. Anusayabai and Shankar hailed from the village Vadhu Budruk in Pune district, some 30 kilometres east of the city. With no farmland of their own, working for landlords was their only option. The practice of untouchability was pervasive—and water would be given to them from a distance.

After their marriage, Anusayabai and Shankar settled in Pune. Shankar migrated first, moving to a slum. A few months later, Anusayabai joined him. All was well until a massive flood swept through Pune and destroyed the slum in 1961. The slum dwellers took shelter on a rocky mound known as Nisen.

Municipal authorities provided shelter for some 200 families. As the ground remained flooded for weeks, authorities built 10x12-square-foot huts for every household. When the flood waters receded, the inhabitants were reluctant to vacate the huts and Nisen Huts became a permanent settlement.

The huts had no kitchens, windows or bathrooms and the settlement soon morphed into a large slum. Nisen Huts came to be associated with outlaws, drug peddlers and rowdy elements. Rajendra was born in one of these huts.

In 1977, when Rajendra was in the eighth standard, Shankar's health, which had been poor for a while, deteriorated further. He visited several doctors.

'Go and serve him as much as you can,' one doctor advised Rajendra. Much later he understood why the doctor had said that.

Shankar probably had tuberculosis. A local doctor recommended that he eat two boiled eggs a day. Anusayabai initially managed to procure two eggs a day, but after a few weeks she could afford only one and after a month or so was unable to buy any eggs at all. The best that Shankar could get was bhakri roti with onion and salt.

Shankar passed away. Anusayabai was crushed by her bereavement and by the prospect of raising the family alone. In a way, she never recovered from the tragedy.

'Why did you leave us?' she asked sobbing into the void. It was painful for the children to watch their ailing mother wash dishes to support them and they wanted to chip in. Rajendra's two elder brothers dropped out of school and joined an army of child workers. His sister, too, stopped going to school. On Sundays, Rajendra would paint walls. In the mornings, he would wash autos for a few paise. He did all kinds of odd jobs.

Anusayabai fell sick in 1980. Doctors in the government hospital could not diagnose her illness and she showed no sign of improvement. She was bedridden for over six months and the entire family watched her wither away slowly. She would look into the eyes of each of her children. She wouldn't speak. Tears would roll down her cheeks every time she looked at Rajendra, as he was the most attached to her. He would often massage her feet. Finally, late one night, she died.

'Money could have saved my mother,' Rajendra kept telling himself.

Money had taken a hold of his thoughts.

Rajendra passed his tenth standard examination in 1980, soon after Anusayabai's death. Now orphans, the children became closer to each other. In a way, the double tragedy had made them stronger and more disciplined. His brothers assured Rajendra of their support in his education. He started the eleventh standard, but things didn't work out as hoped. In 1982 he joined a factory as a worker.

'Shouldn't he be doing something else to make money?'

The question would consume him for a long time.

In less than a year, Rajendra lost interest in factory work. Although he had a high school education, he was treated like an illiterate worker. He began looking for a job that would provide better wages and made use of his education.

For about eight months, he went from house to house buying and selling old newspapers. Once he had gathered a quintal of papers, he would take the bundle to a wholesaler. He was the youngest vendor and the most inexperienced. Often, the wholesalers would withhold payments for weeks while Rajendra would have to pay individual sellers on the spot.

One day Rajendra was feeling particularly dejected as he had no cash to pay the used newspaper sellers. His sister enquired whether all was well. Upon learning that he didn't have the Rs 50 that he needed in order to be able to do business the next day, she gave him a piece of her silver jewellery, which fetched Rajendra Rs 35. He also sold their only pressure cooker for Rs 10 to a neighbour—the pressure cooker had been given by a family to Anusayabai for her service.

Despite all his efforts and the support of his siblings, Rajendra could not sustain the business. The family lived on bhakri roti and salt. Often, they would walk for an hour to a relative's place just for food.

Disheartened, Rajendra went to meet Mandhata Patil, one of his mother's former employers. Mandhata Patil's wife always gave Anusayabai a liberal helping of leftover food. Rajendra had visited their home during the festivals and was known to the Patils.

Mandhata Patil gave Rajendra a patient hearing. He wrote a letter introducing him to his friend R.N. Gadgil and assured Rajendra that he would speak to Mr Gadgil as well. He also gave Rajendra Rs 10.

Rajendra spent Rs 2 on food for the family, gave Rs 5 to his sister to buy food for the entire week and kept the rest.

R.N. Gadgil owned a shop, Veenit Engineering Corporation, in Pune's Shaniwar Peth business hub. He sold and repaired fogging machines used in pest control. Although the shop was about 5 kilometres from Rajendra's house, he walked the distance and reached there by 9.30 a.m.

The shop opened at 10 a.m. but Rajendra waited outside for an hour or so, reasoning that it would probably be a while before Mandhata Patil called and spoke to R.N. Gadgil. He could ill-afford being hasty.

As he was whiling away time, an elegantly dressed man entered the shop. He wore an ironed white dhoti and kurta and wore a Gandhi cap.

'He must be Gadgil sahib,' Rajendra thought. He waited another ten minutes for the man to settle in and entered the shop. He gave him the letter and stood before him like a school kid. Halfway through the letter, Mr Gadgil looked kindly at Rajendra. Mr Patil must have mentioned that the bearer of the letter had recently been orphaned and was in great distress. When he finished reading the letter, R.N. Gadgil called Mandhata Patil to report that he had hired the young man. Overhearing the conversation, Rajendra could hardly speak, he was so excited. He bent and touched the feet of his new employer.

It was 1983. Rajendra was taken in as a trainee in the repairs division, initially for three months, at Rs 120 a month. Upon the completion of his training he was to get Rs 150 a month. His tenth-plus education had come in handy.

Rajendra's job was big news in Nisen Huts. It was unheard of for someone from the slum to be hired for a formal job, anything above manual work.

A day before Rajendra was to start the third month of his training, R.N. Gadgil called him into his office to congratulate him. The instructor had certified him as a trained technician. He had learnt the craft in two months. His salary was raised to Rs 175 a month.

A new job and words of encouragement from R.N. Gadgil were the morale booster Rajendra needed. It was a new experience and way of thinking. Self-worth was until then alien to him.

He was accustomed to being at the receiving end of people's contempt—either because he was small and introverted, or because of his mother's occupation, or because he lived in Nisen Huts or, he suspected, because of his caste.

Receiving a compliment, therefore, was new for him, on top of which his salary had also been increased. Was this a joke?

As an engineer at Veenit Engineering, he had to travel extensively, fixing fogging machines for clients in various locations. He enjoyed travelling and the hospitality of clients, but there came a day when he began to think about the big picture. Although he did not as yet have a grand plan, he did have a vague idea that he could not continue to repair fogging machines forever.

It was the New Year, and the idea of 'New Year' resolutions had taken a hold of Pune's residents. So when a co-worker asked Rajendra what his resolution was, he answered matter-of-factly, 'I will open a business.'

On 2 January 1984, R.N. Gadgil called Rajendra into his office. He wasn't his usual laidback self. He seemed a bit formal.

'I am raising your salary to Rs 300 a month,' he declared and added, 'I know that you no longer want to work for Veenit Engineering.' Rajendra stood as if turned to stone. His co-worker whom he had trusted had revealed his New Year's resolution.

Rajendra then told Gadgil about his hopes for the future. Gadgil was moved when Rajendra told him how his parents died because the family didn't have money. Rajendra's words—'I will become a money-maker'—reflected no action plan but a desire and a dream.

'All right,' Gadgil told him, 'be with us or leave us, the choice is yours. But count on me in case you need some support in your money-making venture.'

'Is he making fun of me?' Rajendra wondered. But he thought of the Gadgil family. R.N. Gadgil's elder brother V.N. Gadgil was a politician and a member of Parliament. He was also a minister in the central government. Political families were known for helping people in need.

It was 14 April 1984, the birth anniversary of Dr Ambedkar, a day of celebration for Dalits the world over. A distant relative of Rajendra's had come from Satara to participate in the festivities being organized. He decided to look up Rajendra and his family. Little did Rajendra know that this encounter would change him forever.

The guest, Lanku Damle, who was thirty years old, was to stay overnight with the Gaikwads. He asked Rajendra to accompany him to the nearby market. He bought a chicken, sweets and half a bottle of rum. The way he spent money amazed his host. His wallet was bulging with 100-rupee notes. He wore good clothes and shoes. He even sported a wristwatch.

During dinner, he spoke about his life as an autorickshaw driver in Satara. He told Rajendra that he would save Rs 100 a day.

'You can save Rs 200 a day in Pune,' he claimed, 'because Pune is a large city.'

Damle lived in a government-approved colony, one of his relatives later told Rajendra, and his house in Satara had a kitchen, bathroom, running water, electricity, fans and a living room.

Rajendra kept comparing his salary of Rs 300 a month with the Rs 3,000 that Damle saved every month. Damle might have exaggerated his savings but, Rajendra reasoned, there must be some truth to his claims. Excited and eager, Rajendra decided to find out more about what working as an auto driver entailed. He befriended an auto driver in his area.

'True, we do save over Rs 100 a day after all the expenses,' confirmed one.

'All the expenses?'

Expenses meant Rs 50 a day on the rent for the auto, another Rs 50 on liquor, and another Rs 10 on food, tea and other essentials.

'Don't enter this profession with a rented auto,' he warned. 'You'll be working for someone else all your life. Also remember we work for twelve hours a day,' he cautioned.

Rajendra now had a good idea about how the autorickshaw business worked. There were people who owned a dozen or more autos, which they would rent out to drivers. They charged Rs 50 for a twelve-hour shift. The driver had to pay for the petrol and take care of minor repairs. At times, the same auto would be rented out to two drivers—one for the day and the other for the night.

The situation was different for those auto drivers who bought their own autos. Some did so with their own money and some took bank loans. The price of an auto was a little over Rs 7,000.

Over the two years that he had worked for Mr Gadgil, Rajendra had managed to save about Rs 1,000, which wasn't enough to buy an auto. None of his relatives had enough money to lend. A bank loan seemed to be the only option.

Having no bank account, Rajendra had no idea who could introduce him to a bank to open an account and, more daunting still, who would stand guarantee against the loan.

Gadgil sahib was his only hope.

Rajendra approached Mr Gadgil who was impressed more with the courage behind the dream to buy an auto than the plan itself.

For the first time, and perhaps to elicit his sympathy, Rajendra told Mr Gadgil that he belonged to a Scheduled Caste.

'Do you have anything to offer as collateral?' asked Mr Gadgil.

'Nothing,' Rajendra replied. 'The house is in the name of my father.'

'Come to my house on Sunday morning,' Mr Gadgil told Rajendra. His elder brother and union minister V.N. Gadgil was expected to be in Pune that day. Rajendra reached the Gadgil residence as directed. R.N. Gadgil introduced him to his brother and explained his plight. Moved, V.N. Gadgil wrote a letter to the Rupee Cooperative Bank in Pune. He offered to stand as Rajendra's guarantor.

While waiting for the credit facility to materialize, Rajendra learnt to drive. A friend helped him get a driver's licence. His bank loan was approved in mid-August 1984 and it took another week for the auto to arrive.

Rajendra drove to Veenit Engineering with a box of sweets. R.N. Gadgil wished him good luck and said, 'Keep dropping in.'

After a year of driving the auto, poverty, as Rajendra had known it, had come to an end. He no longer went to sleep on an empty stomach and no longer had to walk miles to a relative's house for food. The family ate decent food and wore new clothes. Household amenities slowly began to accumulate in their rented one-room house.

The initial exhilaration, however, had abated a bit. He faced issues related to dignity. The traffic police would harass Rajendra for minor infractions. The police would also make use of his auto but not pay the fare. Passengers complained that all autos ran inflated metres. 'Don't cheat' would be the common taunt to auto drivers.

Over the first year, Rajendra developed friendships with fellow drivers. His new profession had no doubt ended his family's poverty and they now led a much better life. But something was amiss.

Rajendra began observing how his fellow drivers lived and found that most of them lived in poor localities. He befriended half a dozen drivers—none owned a two-wheeler, or lived in an apartment or in a government-approved colony. It was unsettling.

On a hot afternoon in late May, Rajendra parked his auto near the railway station, on Tadi Pura Road. He sat under the shade of a tree and while sipping ice-cold nimbu paani, struck up a conversation with another auto driver.

'I have been driving an auto for the past three decades,' the other driver, who looked about sixty, told Rajendra, 'and I have very little savings.'

'Why?' Rajendra himself had saved some money in just over a year of driving an auto.

'Because I have been earning for the auto owner,' he said bitterly.

The fellow driver's answer ignited a spark in Rajendra's mind. After dinner, he considered the possibility of owning and renting out a fleet of autos.

'Why can't I also enter the business of renting autos?' he asked himself.

He realized it would have several advantages. It would spare him from the humiliations he suffered at the hands of passengers and the traffic police. He would make money without actually doing the grinding work! Things looked rosy on the business side as well: An auto could fetch Rs 100 a day if rented for twenty-four hours. Five autos would fetch Rs 500 a day. Ten could fetch Rs 1,000—Rs 30,000 a month, or 3 lakh 60,000 a year. His imagination took flight.

It was a eureka moment for him.

The following week, Rajendra rented out his auto to a fellow driver he knew well. He settled for Rs 75 for twenty-four hours. To ensure that his auto would be well looked after, he decided to forego Rs 25 a day.

After a few days of sitting idle, Rajendra decided to look for a job. Buying another auto was his next target. One day, he strolled into the Vrindavan Nursery on Sinhagad Road, where he washed his auto every Sunday.

While he was chatting with the nursery caretaker whom he had befriended, a businessman walked into the nursery in search of some plants. Having repaired his fogging machines in the past, Rajinder knew him as the owner of a pest control business.

After some negotiations, he agreed to hire Rajendra at a salary of Rs 1,000 a month, with the promise of some extra money for repairing fogging machines. Since he was already making Rs 75 a day by renting his auto, Rajendra didn't bargain much.

Seven months into his new job, another opportunity came Rajendra's way. A poultry farm representative needed the services of someone who could rid his farm of rats, which were wreaking havoc with his business.

Rajendra's boss, however, rejected the job outright. 'We are not in the business of killing rats,' was his response. Rat-killing was considered to be a job for the lower castes, for Dalits. No respectable businessman would take on such a contract. The representative offered Rs 500 for clearing the farm of rats. The owner didn't budge. Disappointed, the man walked out; however, Rajendra followed him.

'Will you pay me the same amount if I killed the rats without involving the company?' he asked him.

'Why not? Do you have logistics?'

'What logistics do you need to kill rats?'

The following Sunday, Rajendra reached ground zero at Osade, 40 kilometres away from his home, on the Pune–Panshet road. A large signboard announced the poultry farm—Vencos Research & Breeding Centre. It was completely mechanized and clean. Today, the farm is a billion-dollar company, known the world over under the name of Venkateshwara Hatcheries Pvt. Ltd. However, back then, the rat menace was threatening the hygiene of the state-of-the-art establishment.

Rajendra struck a deal whereby he would be paid Rs 500 a month to keep the farm rat-free. In his zeal to get more work, Rajendra had overlooked a crucial detail: although it wouldn't hamper his work at the pest control company, he had 'forgotten' to inform his employer that he had taken on an additional job.

Killing rats offered Rajendra an opportunity. The man who hired him at Vencos mentioned two more poultry farms that the group was constructing.

'If you can impress the boss, you will get contracts for the other two as well,' he said.

Given the stigma attached with rat-killing, there would not be many takers for the job, and Rajendra hoped it would easily be his. That evening, with four bottles of beer clanging in his bag, he reached Vrindavan Nursery.

What if a billboard at the nursery announced: 'Rat killer available here'?

His friend at the nursery had no problem if a billboard was put up on the roadside.

Poultry farms need rat-killers, so do food godowns, grocers, restaurants, hotels, farmers, households. His list kept growing. He imagined he would need a thousand workers. He would have a car with a driver and would manage things from an air-conditioned office.

As for telling his pest control employer, Rajendra had a tough time making up his mind and finally decided to walk the middle path: Could he work elsewhere on Sundays?

'Go ahead,' the owner gave his consent with a caveat: 'But

if we need you for emergencies, you should be available on Sundays as well.'

Since killing rats needed only a few hours of work once a week, Rajendra could travel both paths. Four Sundays a month were enough to keep Vencos rat-free.

Three days after the billboard was put up outside the Vrindavan Nursery, Pune's wholesale grain mandi management staff came calling. Rajendra demanded Rs 500 to kill the rats already infesting the mandi and another Rs 500 a month to keep the mandi rat-free. The following week, another poultry farm south of Pune became his customer.

He contemplated quitting his job at the pest control company as he was making a mere Rs 1,000 for working twenty-six days, while killing rats on four Sundays was fetching him Rs 2,000.

Three months after Rajendra first served Vencos, their second poultry farm became operational. He was offered the contract for this farm too, although he did not find any trace of rats there. A third poultry farm was to be operational in another four months.

Impressed with Rajendra's work, the Vencos CEO, Dr B. Venkateshwara Rao, granted him an audience and also gave him a cash reward of Rs 100.

'Well done,' he said. 'Expect more orders from others as well.'

Rajendra feels privileged even now to have met the man who is undisputedly described as the father of the Indian poultry industry.

When he went to Vencos two days later, the manager gave him four visiting cards from four poultry farm owners. They all wanted him to contact them as soon as possible. Apparently, Dr Rao had vouched for Rajendra's rat-killing skills at a meeting of Pune's Poultry Owners' Association.

A new profession, a new identity and the fact that he was wanted by big companies: Rajendra was exhilarated.

He quit the pest control company a week later.

He contacted all the four poultry owners and insisted on an advance of Rs 500 from each to begin the process. Subsequently, he charged them at the beginning of each month to ensure the premises remained rat-free. They easily agreed. He bought a moped, which he could pedal when it ran out of petrol.

In January 1987, Rajendra's operations took the form of GT Pest Control and he hired five workers to train. He tried hard to get a phone connection, but the waiting period was over eight years. V.N. Gadgil again came to his rescue. Within months, he had a phone. Two years later he bought a jeep for Rs 75,000 and employed fifteen trained workers.

Meanwhile, word of his services and success spread and a local paper described him as Pune's Rat Man.

Rajendra was not amused by the new tag. Some Dalit communities killed rats for a living, so he felt as if he had been branded by his Dalit identity. More worrisome still was his apprehension that as a rat man, he would find it difficult to get married.

Business expansion was the only way he knew to shed the identity of a rat man. He entered fumigation work, essentially mosquito control on streets and in housing colonies.

Rajendra got married in 1999. By then, he had about fifty trained workers. He started offering cockroach control, followed by termite control. He bought a car in 2000. By the following year, GT Pest Control was a full-fledged company with over a hundred workers.

Having obtained accreditation from the government in 2005, the company was now qualified to bid for fumigation work in central government organizations. The following year the ISO certification became another feather in Rajendra's cap, and he started giving franchises. He chose his relatives first, and five of them are doing well.

With the launch of the Singapore branch, the company entered the big league in pest control. It was no mere business expansion, as it turned out. During the process of meeting the very high quality and safety standards demanded in Singapore, GT Pest Control ended up upgrading its operations in India as well. Given the high standards the company maintains, it's no surprise that other companies in the sector are keen to join hands with GT Pest Control.

Rajendra is now working towards starting operations in Thailand as well.

What next?

With twenty-five offices in India and the Singapore operations, Rajendra manages 700 workers. Pest control is labour-intensive and managing so many workers and branches is proving difficult. While he savours his success, it is also restricting.

He has plans to enter manufacturing. If he touches the Rs 100-crore mark in turnover, his dream is to produce something that is a household necessity. He is researching the production of a herbal paste to keep homes and facilities cockroach-free. He is also working on a herbal mosquito repellent.

He wants his son, who is currently completing a Bachelors in commerce degree, to take over the commercial side of the business. With his daughter Neha completing a degree in chemical engineering, Rajendra Gaikwad's manufacturing designs are well in place.

'I have no complaints,' he says. 'Society has given so much to me and my family.'

BHAGWAN GAWAI

Bhagwan Dharmaji Gawai is a driven man. Standing five feet ten inches tall and with a well-built physique, it is the intensity of his gaze that catches attention. His eyes penetrate the listener, the weight of his words emphasized by his precise gestures.

Bhagwan is chairman and CEO of the Dubai-based Saurabh Energy. The company is headquartered at Fortune Towers in the Jumeirah Lake Towers complex in Jebel Ali, Dubai. The 1,100-square-foot office was purchased for $350,000 and is staffed by a battery of professionals who churn out profits for Saurabh Energy.

Though primarily in the oil business in Dubai, Bhagwan

has diversified his business portfolio to include ventures in India. He is one of the shareholders of the Mumbai-based Maitreya Developers Pvt. Ltd, which has fifty shareholders from around the world. He set up BNB Logistics Pvt. Ltd with a close family friend. In addition, he has entered the retail businesses of spices, travel and transport.

In 2013 he added business consultancy as another feather in his cap. Bhagwan will also soon start a cotton ginning and pressing plant in his native Buldhana district in Maharashtra. He is also diversifying into agro-industries, mainly concentrated in Aurangabad, Mumbai, Dhule and Pune.

How does he manage so many businesses in so many locations?

'Let the managers manage the show,' says Bhagwan and asks, 'Why should the owner be involved in the day-to-day affairs?'

Bhagwan spends fifteen days in a month in Dubai and the rest in India.

'Let my Dalit brethren see the difference that entrepreneurship can make in our lives,' he says, referring to his social vision. He owns a fleet of cars in India, luxury flats in Mumbai and Pune, and bungalows in Aurangabad and Raipur.

'Yes, I do have a high-end Mercedes,' he says with a shrug when asked about his cars.

In 1991, Bhagwan got a job in Bahrain as a shipping/supply coordinator at Caltex Petroleum Corporation Ltd (Caltex Bahrain), an American multinational corporation. His training as an entrepreneur began on his very first day on the job. He worked in the supply and trading wing of the company, where his job required him to connect with new and existing buyers and profile their business history. His previous nine years of work experience with Hindustan Petroleum Corporation Ltd (HPCL) in supply, shipping, operations, distribution and oil storage terminal operations served him well in his new job at Caltex Bahrain. The experience he gained at HPCL and later at Caltex helped fast-track his career.

By 1998, Bhagwan had moved to the Emirates National Oil Company in Dubai as manager of their supply and logistics division. He had built a comfortable life in Dubai. He lived in a posh locality and drove a Mercedes.

While working in logistics, he saw a potential business opportunity. Owners of small vessels who were in search of furnace oil, also known as fuel oil, and who were largely from countries like India, Pakistan and Bangladesh, were an untapped customer base.

Industries such as textiles, cement, sugar and power that use boilers need furnace oil. When the businesses are small, their fuel oil need is also small compared to larger enterprises. Upon arriving in Dubai, the small customers looking for small quantities of fuel oil would be rebuffed by most of the suppliers who looked to sell only larger amounts.

'They were prepared to pay any price,' Bhagwan recalls. He was puzzled by why established suppliers ignored profits just because they came in small amounts. In the oil business in the Gulf, people are used to dealing in millions and billions.

'Why can't someone tap this market?' Bhagwan would ask himself. He saw an unmet demand and wondered if he should take the plunge into business to meet it.

'Why can't I enter trade when so many small buyers are roaming the streets?' he thought.

'I knew how trade in oil and gas could be launched with zero investment,' he says. Just like in any other trade, here, too, the buyer gives the seller a letter of credit (LC). On the strength of that LC, transactions take place. Though this sounds simple, Bhagwan faced a more basic problem.

Despite his knowledge of the oil trade and being an expert in logistics, Bhagwan couldn't quit his job and take up trading immediately. He needed to have a business history and track record. His bank accounts needed to show regular, large transactions. He was, after all, an employee and money was deposited into his account only once a month.

'Banks will not give me an LC,' he kept telling himself. Something had to be done.

Because he headed the supply and logistics department at Emirates National Oil Company, he knew people who owned tankers. Some of them had become his friends. One of them was a UAE national who owned seven small tankers. Being a local and that, too, a local with a 'hyperactive bank account', he could obtain an LC without much trouble.

'Should I offer him a joint venture?' Bhagwan thought.

Either because the business proposal was very attractive or because Bhagwan's persuasive skills were very effective, his friend came on board sooner than Bhagwan had anticipated.

In July 2002, BFC International FZC was launched in the Sharjah Free Zone. Bhagwan and his partner had a 25 per cent stake each in the company. In its very first trade, the company made a profit of $75,000. In just two years, the company had not only become the largest supplier of furnace oil but reached a turnover of $40 million.

However, this success streak was soon hobbled by bad luck. His partner's mother passed away suddenly. He started losing interest in the business. He was very attached to his mother, and he took her death as an ill omen. He concluded that making money through trade was ruinous and decided to close down BFC International.

Bhagwan had no option but to think of a new venture. He had his Indian and Pakistani clients who were keen to pay in advance.

'They kept calling me,' he remembers. His bank transactions were not large enough to secure him an LC. He had to look for another partner.

'The mounting demand from clients was too much for me to ignore,' he recalls.

With supply orders in hand, Bhagwan entered into a partnership with a company named Alsaa Petroleum & Shipping FZC, UAE. Its owner agreed to allot 50 per cent equity to Bhagwan. In the first year the company hit $100 million in turnover.

'I had kept a close watch on my balance sheet,' recalls Bhagwan. 'By March 2008, it had ballooned.'

He was now comfortable enough to end his partnership with Alsaa Petroleum. He was determined to float his own company, and he was confident that he would get a credit facility from banks.

In February 2009, he launched his own company, naming it Saurabh Energy, and registered it with the Dubai Multi Commodities Centre.

Being the sole owner of the company, Bhagwan would frequently travel to India and Africa. He developed a loyal clientele of small importers. Some of them needed as little as 3,000 metric tons of fuel oil.

On his frequent visits to India, he saw the predicament of small importers. They were small and scattered and hence remained weak in the market. He counselled them that it would be much more economical if they came together and imported fuel oil in larger vessels.

Bhagwan set up an office in India to coordinate with

domestic importers. It turned out to be a great business model as importers were no longer required to send representatives to the Gulf for the purchase of fuel oil and its transportation to India. He grouped together a number of small importers who would now import fuel oil in larger vessels and claim their share at Kandla port in Gujarat.

Saurabh Energy entered trading in sulphur, rubber, process oil and solvents to its business.

Growing the India business enabled him to frequently visit the country. Because he would be in India so often, he started reconnecting with relatives and friends.

In 2009, he decided to visit his native village. He had taken his younger brother along and rode in a Toyota Innova car for the visit.

'The car had the impact of an earthquake,' he smiles. 'People came to watch a large car rolling into a Dalit hamlet.'

No one recognized him, and the local people became curious.

Bhagwan narrated the story his life in Dubai and the businesses he was involved in. The villagers were amazed at the achievements of the son of Mrs Gangubai Dharmaji Gawai, his mother.

His expensive dress and the car he rode in had created a buzz. Some thought he had won a lottery. Others thought a childless sheikh couple had adopted him. Yet others suspected that he might have cheated his employer and had now returned home.

After all, he was Gangubai's son. It's inconceivable to people that a poor Dalit widow's son could become anything worthwhile on his own.

Bhagwan was born in July 1955 to illiterate parents in village Rehari in the Buldhana district in Maharashtra.

A part of the Vidharbha region known for drought and farmers' suicides, Buldhana is a labour basket for the state's construction industry. A cotton hub and millet-producing region, crops would invariably fail every fourth or fifth year. Left with no savings, the poor would flee to urban centres.

Bhagwan's father Dharmaji Gawai had joined the army of construction workers when he was just twelve years old. He graduated to being a mason and married Gangubai when he was sixteen years old.

The Dharmaji clan grew to include five children—four sons and a daughter. While Dharmaji worked as a mason locally, Gangubai would work in the cotton fields.

The house that the Dharmaji family lived in had no windows or running water. The village well was the only source of water for drinking, cooking, washing clothes and bathing.

Like most Dalits in the village, the Dharmaji family slept on the ground. Since Dharmaji worked as a mason, he had easy access to empty cement bags. The family made bedsheets of those jute bags. Because Dharmaji was paid in cash, the family did not go hungry.

'Father bought potatoes for the entire family,' recalls Bhagwan. 'Potatoes were very popular in the Dalit hamlet.'

Opportunity knocked on Dharmaji's door in August 1962 when news spread that a labour agent was visiting the area.

The organized sector has a well-oiled system for procuring workers. They use newspaper ads to hire white-collar workers or recruit from select college campuses. Blue-collar workers are often recruited by word of mouth, usually with the help of the existing workforce who bring their siblings, relatives and friends when the factory they work in needs more hands.

The construction industry, however, relies on middlemen

to recruit workers. These labour contractors scour the villages and regions they have ties to, and recruit workers who move from construction site to construction site.

When a team of labour recruiters arrived in the nearby bazaar, on Gangubai's urging, Dharmaji visited the agent the following day.

Like most of the Dalit recruits, Dharmaji was excited but also apprehensive. The labour agent would take care of their journey to Bombay (now Mumbai), accommodate them on the construction site for free and promised them higher wages. But Dharmaji also knew that promises were often more optimistic than the reality.

Eight Dalits from the village bought into the Bombay dream. Dharmaji chose his eldest son Lakshmanrao, then thirteen years old, to accompany him to Bombay. They reached Bombay in October 1962 and were taken to a construction site in East Kandivali.

A suburb, East Kandivali is home to Mahindra & Mahindra automobile industries, which now manufactures passenger as well as commercial vehicles. A construction company, Alankar Industries, was building the Mahindra & Mahindra factory shed and it was to this site that Dharmaji, his son and his fellow Dalits were taken. After working for a year, Dharmaji lost interest and returned to the village. Lakshmanrao, however, continued to work at the site.

'He could not adjust to the kind of accommodation they were given,' says Bhagwan. 'In the village, he lived in a house that had walls.'

Nonetheless, things looked brighter for Dharmaji's family. Lakshmanrao sent money to his parents every month. Dharmaji and Gangubai earned enough to feed the family. With the rise in the family's income, Dharmaji was able to enrol his children in a government school. He also decided to build a pukka house.

In July 1964, Dharmaji died of a cardiac arrest, leaving behind a young widow with five children. His youngest child was just ten months old.

Lakshmanrao was informed of the tragedy and rushed home. After completing the rituals he planned to return to Bombay. Gangubai, however, pleaded with Lakshmanrao to take the entire family along. He complied, taking his grieving mother and four siblings with him.

Lakshmanrao was just fifteen years old then. Gangubai was thirty-five years old. His sister was eleven and Bhagwan was eight years old. His two younger brothers were four years and ten months old, respectively. Bhagwan was in the second standard when Dharmaji passed away.

In 1964, Kandivali was a densely populated suburb and the construction site was surrounded by business and residential properties. The contractor had set up a makeshift workers' colony at the construction site.

'We were given one hut,' recalls Bhagwan.

Bombay is known for heavy rains, and when it rained, the workers at the Mahindra & Mahindra site cursed their fate and the rain god. 'Strong winds and rains would bring the family together,' recounts Bhagwan. 'We all literally held on to the walls to prevent them from falling.'

Since the site had no school, Bhagwan and his siblings stopped going to school. They would play at the site the entire day.

'Kids at the site played and so did we,' he says. 'No one missed school.'

The Mahindra & Mahindra project ended in November 1966 and Alankar Industries began a new construction project in Kholopi in Raigard district. Bhagwan's family followed the company. Just 100 kilometres from Bombay and part of the Konkan belt, Khopoli was an upcoming industrial centre.

At Khopoli, Gangubai pleaded with the site manager to put Bhagwan in school. Lakshmanrao was now seventeen years old. He saw the wisdom behind his mother's pleas and decided to take responsibility for Bhagwan's schooling.

'My mother and brother believed that I would lead the family to prosperity,' recalls Bhagwan. He was enrolled in a private school that was over a kilometre from the site.

'The headmaster at the government school asked all kinds of questions,' he remembers. 'Why did you drop out after the second standard? Why do you want to study further? Where is your father?'

Irked by the questions, Lakshmanrao took Bhagwan to a private school. The site manager had accompanied the brothers. The teachers at the private school asked some basic questions and gave them a form to complete.

'I was the odd man out in the classroom,' says Bhagwan.

At eleven, Bhagwan was tall for his age. He was admitted into the third standard when he should have been in the fifth standard. He suffered all kinds of humiliations at school—barring caste-based humiliation.

'They knew my class, but not my caste,' he says.

At the end of the academic session, the class teacher promoted Bhagwan to the fourth standard.

Just when things were looking bright for Bhagwan, the contractor completed the factory shed project and moved to Nasik. It was in early 1968 that Gangubai led her family to the grape and onion basket of India, following the contractor who would build yet another factory shed.

In July 1968, Bhagwan was admitted into another private

school for his fifth grade. The family could afford Bhagwan's school fees because one more brother and his sister had joined the workforce.

When her only daughter turned sixteen, Gangubai despatched Lakshmanrao to their native village to find a suitable marital match for his sister. He was visiting his village after six years. A month later, he returned with the good news: He had found a boy for his sister, and the marriage took place later in December.

'My mother and elder brother were so relieved,' says Bhagwan. 'In those days girls of fifteen years or above were not expected to be living with their parents.'

By the time Bhagwan completed stying in the fifth standard, the factory shed at Nasik was read. Bhagwan still has fond memories of the Nasik school, and one incident in particular made a deep impression on him.

One day it rained heavily and Bhagwan's school uniform got wet. Their hut had only one wall, which made it hard to protect things kept inside. One of his brothers had taken shelter in the factory shed, but Bhagwan was not so lucky. Since his uniform was wet, he wore other clothes to school.

The school headmaster, a strict disciplinarian, ordered Bhagwan to stand outside the classroom.

'That was the standard practice the headmaster followed when someone broke the school discipline,' recalls Bhagwan.

Outside the classroom, Bhagwan sobbed. 'I cursed my fate,' he says, 'and thought "Why do I live in a hut?"'

One of his classmates knew why Bhagwan had not worn his school uniform. The boy gathered courage and went up to the headmaster and told him the story about the soaked uniform. The headmaster also learnt that Bhagwan lived in a hut on the nearby construction site.

The headmaster summoned Bhagwan and did something Bhagwan did not expect. He asked all the students to donate 12 paisa each. The following week, Bhagwan was gifted two sets of uniforms, a pair of shoes and socks, and a school bag.

Today, Bhagwan selects a private school in a poor locality every year and gifts uniforms to all the students.

After completing the factory shed in Nasik, Alankar undertook a project in Ratnagiri, a port city on the Arabian Sea coast. As it was a large project, Gangubai's family lived there for four years, from 1969 to 1973.

Bhagwan was enrolled for his sixth standard in a private school named Pathak High School. By the time the construction project was finished in 1973, he had completed his ninth standard.

Alankar then secured the contract to build an extension for the Mahindra & Mahindra factory shed that they had originally constructed. Gangubai and her family were back in Kandivali. This time the family was determined that they wouldn't be drifters.

Bhagwan had shown great promise in school. Although the new site had a school, it was a primary school. Bhagwan needed access to a high school. Lakshmanrao was now twenty-four and he had to marry. Another brother was thirteen years old and was already a full-fledged construction worker. The youngest brother was ten. The family decided to buy a house to provide a stable environment for the education of the kids.

'We were not as distressed now as we were in 1964,' recalls Bhagwan and adds, 'and we had a trunk now.' Their dispossession in the past was so complete that they either did not need a trunk or could not afford one.

Following Gangubai's plan, the family would live at the

Mahindra & Mahindra construction site for a few months. Meanwhile, they would locate a house to live in nearby. Bhagwan had been admitted into a private school in Kandivali, the Ram Krishna High School.

Within a few months, the family bought a hut in a slum in Hanuman Nagar in East Kandivali for Rs 250 and shifted to their new home.

'We bought a place in hell,' recounts Bhagwan. 'It was horrible living in a slum.'

For most of his childhood, he had lived on large construction sites with plenty of open space. The huts were not crammed into a small area—there was open space in front of them and the drains were covered.

Compared to that life, the slum was a living hell. The open drains emitted a permanent stench, and congestion and squalor defined life there. Despite these difficulties, Bhagwan focused on his studies and completed his secondary school certificate in 1975.

'I was an instant hero in the slum,' he says. 'I also developed a sense of self-worth.'

He enrolled for a Bachelor of Commerce degree at the Siddhartha College of Commerce & Economics located in Fort, Bombay, a college that had been founded by Dr Ambedkar.

'It was a dream to obtain a degree from Siddhartha College,' says Bhagwan. 'I was so inspired by Babasaheb.'

Soon after joining college, Bhagwan prevailed upon his mother to set up a vegetable stall.

'It was too painful to watch her carry bricks on her head,' he says. 'She was forty-six years old at that time.'

He took an evening job with Yashodham Industries as a junior accountant at a salary of Rs 250 a month. He took the job to help renovate their hut. Within months, another floor was added to the hut.

In 1978, Bhagwan completed his Bachelor's degree and landed a job as an accountant in the Social Service League, a non-profit group.

He joined the college for his Master's in Commerce. While there, Bhagwan made friends with people who came from middle-class families. The father of one of his friends worked for a private bank, Saraswat Bank. In mid-1979, Bhagwan took a loan of Rs 5,000 from the bank to buy a shop near the slum.

He bought the 200-square-foot grocery shop for Rs 6,000 and gifted it to his elder brother Lakshmanrao.

'I had been dreaming of the day my mother and all my siblings would come out of construction work,' he says. His youngest brother does a brisk business in the same grocery shop today.

After graduating from college, he applied for the post of an operations officer in HPCL. As a public sector company, HPCL was required to reserve a certain number of its jobs for historically marginalized social groups (Dalits and tribals). Bhagwan availed of this quota and joined the company as a management trainee in 1982.

'My mother was in tears,' he remembers. She was awestruck by the news that her son would get a salary of Rs 116 a day. 'What a big sahib he has become.' A construction worker would get Rs 20 to Rs 25 a day at the time.

Bhagwan married in 1982 and lived in the slum with the rest of his family until 1987. In 1983, baby Sanjivani was born.

In 1987, he was allotted a two-bedroom flat with a living room, kitchen, two bathrooms and a balcony. Owned by HPCL, the flat was located in upscale Malad West. He moved into the flat and brought his mother and brothers there as well.

'The flat turned into a sort of a monument,' he says. As the news about the size of the house spread, friends from the slum and relatives came to visit just to see the house.

'That's how sahibs live,' Gangubai said after going through all the rooms. 'Why is there an extra bathroom?'

Now that he was earning a comfortable salary, Bhagwan worked on a plan to settle all his three brothers. He also planned to build a career for his brother-in-law. He helped his elder brother Lakshmanrao to settle in the village. Since his parents didn't have farm land, he bought farm land for his brothers. He built a large house in the village to replace the tiny house his parents had lived in. The doorway of his childhood house was so low that they had to bend to enter. His mother had fetched water from a well far away from their house. He now installed a hand pump right inside the house.

Things were going well and Bhagwan was now very much a part of Bombay's middle class gentry.

He bought a house near Kandivali for his mother. He set up agro-businesses for all his brothers. He modernized and expanded the Kandivali grocery shop that his younger brother runs.

As a routine, HPCL promotes its employees every three or four years. Bhagwan got his first promotion in 1986 in his fourth year of service. His second promotion was due in 1990. That year, most non-Dalit officers were promoted to the next higher post; however, the Dalit officers were denied a promotion due to a change in policy. They argued their case with the HPCL management but the company stood firm. Bhagwan was very upset.

'Just because we used affirmative action to get the job, our talent was always suspect,' he recounts. 'It was too humiliating to be treated like second-class citizens.'

Bhagwan filed a case against the HPCL management and quit the job. He vacated the government flat and moved to a private flat in Malad.

'It was a one-bedroom accommodation,' he says.

Gloom descended on Gangubai's family. Relatives and friends sympathized. 'There was despondency all around,' he remembers. 'Family members huddled wordlessly in the flat.'

News spread among relatives and friends that Bhagwan Gawai had been fired from his job and evicted from the company's flat. 'People reached their own conclusions,' says Bhagwan.

'How could a ghumantu (a vagabond or a person from a migratory group) fit into a government organization?' many reasoned.

While people offered words of sympathy, Bhagwan had nowhere to go. He sat on the sofa all day. He was so depressed that he stopped going out to meet friends.

But Bhagwan would find his way back. He was, after all, Gangubai's son. Gangubai passed away in 2010 at the age of eighty-three. She headed the Dharmaji household for nearly fifty years with skill and grace. She had no education and became a widow at thirty-five, with five children to look after. Despite all the deprivations, she had displayed foresight and entrepreneurial spirit. It was she who encouraged her husband to meet the labour agent who was scouting for workers in their area. She was adamant that her husband and eldest son move to the Mahindra & Mahindra factory site in Bombay. She insisted on Bhagwan's education. She built a family and laid the foundation for a brighter future for them.

A few months later, Bhagwan met a friend in Colaba, who told him about a recruitment agency that was looking for young professionals for Caltex Bahrain. Bhagwan visited the agency the very same day. Upon learning that he had earlier worked for HPCL, they asked for his CV.

'I didn't tell them about the HPCL episode,' he smiles. 'I didn't know that HPCL is rated so highly.'

He submitted his CV and was asked to meet with them the following Monday. He was interviewed and selected.

'Friends were so happy for me that I was joining Caltex,' he recalls.

The rest is history.

Bhagwan has three children. His son Saurabh is in the tenth standard. His eldest daughter Sanjivani has a Master's degree in mass communication and media from a college in Pune. She also did a course in film direction from an institute in New York.

Sanjivani became an entrepreneur in 2007 when she established S4 Entertainment Pvt. Ltd. She produced and directed the Marathi film *Foreignchi Patlin*, which was based on a social theme and was a success. She has a few more movies in the pipeline.

Bhagwan's second daughter Sagarika is pursuing her post-graduate degree in interior design from MIT, Pune.

Why is Bhagwan now moving away from the highly profitable oil business to less lucrative businesses in India?

He has the answer ready: to inspire fellow Dalits to launch their own businesses.

Bhagwan Gawai might as well be rewriting his past. All those who had seen or heard of Gangubai's family growing up on construction sites and moving from one site to another would undoubtedly be shocked if they saw how well settled her children are today.

'Who would have imagined that one day Bhagwan will ride a Mercedes on foreign shores,' says a fellow Dalit in Mumbai who has watched Bhagwan's steady rise.

MALKIT CHAND JANAGAL

The headquarters of Janagal Exports impresses at first sight. Abuzz with activity, it is spread over 5,000 square feet of space, with neat displays of T-shirts, kids' garments and denims. The ground floor is reserved for vendors and importers. The many sofas lying about are not enough to accommodate all the dealers who turn up every day. The latecomers have to make do with the plastic chairs.

Early December mornings are generally cool in Ludhiana, a busy town in eastern Punjab, famous for its hosiery industry and the BMWs that are a perk of the trade.

As the morning progresses, a large group of visitors waits outside Malkit Chand Janagal's office; some are restless, others quietly resigned. Strangers to each other, they all vie for Malkit's attention; he'd been away, in London, and just returned.

Malkit tries to answer all the queries directed at him, attending patiently to each of the vendors. But as their number swells, he slips away, promising to come back in an hour.

The third floor of the building is Malkit's home. A large dining hall sits adjacent to a kitchen packed with imported appliances and utensils. Even the electric fittings and paintings seem to have come from abroad. The residence reflects taste and, above all, a desire to acquire the best and enjoy a slice of the good life.

The view outside the Janagal office is quite the opposite. Trucks and handcarts choke the roads. Torn pieces of fabric and other trash are strewn all over. Crowds move along, walking past one another without acknowledging the others' presence.

Everybody recognizes Malkit and his father Mansa though. They are local heroes of a sort, holding out the promise that anyone can gain success no matter where they start from. Theirs is a heart-warming tale of a landless labourer and his son setting up Janagal Exports and turning it into an impressive 70-crore enterprise through sheer industry, without compromising on the old-fashioned virtues of loyalty and integrity.

Their story begins in Bore, a village about 20 kilometres from Ludhiana, where Mansa was born. The son of a landless labourer who worked on a landlord's farm, his father died suddenly when Mansa was two years old. Mansa's mother married him off when he was five, and she died of a sudden illness soon after.

Mansa dropped out of school in the third standard. As

a child, he did odd jobs on landlords' farms and found life uninspiring. He heard stories about the life of a Dalit in his village. 'They begin their lives as farm workers and die as farm workers.' The idea that, being a Dalit, this was the fate that awaited him troubled Mansa.

However, fate dealt him a different hand in the guise of his maternal uncle, Ronki Ram, who visited Mansa's home in 1955. Wanting a better life for his nephew, he took Mansa with him to Ludhiana.

'He felt for me,' Mansa recalls.

Once in Ludhiana, Mansa trained himself to be a tailor, specializing in stitching monkey caps, woollen caps that cover the head on all sides except the face. In parts of Kashmir and the Himalayan foothills, the winter temperatures fall to below freezing, and monkey caps are good protective gear.

Ronki Ram's house was in a village on the outskirts of Ludhiana. 'A dozen members of the family lived in a tiny house,' Mansa remembers. Malkit was born there in 1962.

With the birth of Malkit, Mansa moved to a new house. The house, though, had few facilities. Built on a tiny piece of land, it had no bathroom, kitchen, running water, windows, balcony, fans, or almirah. Another son was born in 1964. As if programmed, a child was born every two years until Mansa had five sons and a daughter. The youngest child, a son, was born in 1975.

As the family grew, so did Mansa's challenges. Schooling the kids was a priority. He had already trained his wife in tailoring. With a sewing machine, she worked from home, stitching clothes for village folk.

But Mansa constantly thought about how to make more money. 'That's how the idea of launching an enterprise was born,' he recalls. He saved some money and bought a couple of manual sewing machines to start making monkey caps.

'It didn't involve any great technology,' he says. A sewing machine cost a few hundred rupees. Mansa was his own designer, cutter and marketing manager.

Mansa eked out a modest living from his cottage industry of cap-making but he had a large family to feed. Also, cap-making was not a round-the-year business—it lasted for just the four winter months.

In 1979, Malkit cleared his twelfth standard examinations. Watching his parents struggle to feed a large family was painful for him and he dropped the idea of going to college. 'College education meant a long wait for a government job. I didn't want that,' says Malkit.

By the time he was seventeen, Malkit knew what he needed to do as the eldest son. He foresaw the future of the monkey cap business and wasn't inspired. The enterprise didn't require extra hands. He realized he would have to find another opportunity. He was desperate.

'I ran around for months,' says Malkit. 'I knew every lane and by-lane of Ludhiana.' Finally, he joined JP Knitwear Company, which specialized in manufacturing T-shirts.

'Nobody in the family liked this decision,' Malkit admits.

'I was shocked,' says Mansa. 'Despite the odds, I wanted to give the best education to my first child.' Within days, word spread that a 'barahvin-pass' (twelfth standard-pass) boy had joined the company as an unskilled worker.

'Most workers were immigrants from Bihar and Uttar Pradesh with very little or no education,' Malkit recalls.

Despite the differences in their backgrounds, Malkit found that he had much to learn from his co-workers. Stories of Malkit's enthusiasm and industry reached the owner of the company, Joginder Jain, who offered him a job in the accounts division. But Malkit had made up his mind: 'I wanted to train myself as a cutter. In the hosiery industry, cutters were paid more and revered most.' Within two years of joining the company, Malkit was promoted to the position of assistant cutter. By 1987, he was a master cutter. 'It was a dream come true,' he says.

A few years later, Joginder Jain met with a series of personal tragedies. His wife passed away and his only son suffered from depression. Struggling under the burden of a host of family issues, Jain allotted some duties to Malkit, who became his deputy.

Malkit now procured fabric and thread from the market, and dealt with buyers who came from all over India. He managed the crucial affairs of the company. At times, Malkit would handle money transactions as well. Impressed by his energy and honesty, the owner raised Malkit's salary to Rs 25,000 a month.

Malkit was now twenty-eight years old and he decided it was time to get married. His father arranged a match with the daughter of a fellow Dalit friend and the two were soon wed.

Malkit oversaw the business operations of the company for almost five years from 1987 to 1992. The experience turned out to be his 'on-the-job' training on every aspect of the business. He knew the price of fabric and thread and the labour cost of making a T-shirt. He could also calculate expenses on power, rent and other overheads. And he figured out that a sewing machine bought for Rs 500 could be used to produce a hundred T-shirts a day and that operating five machines and earning a five-rupee profit per T-shirt amounted to an income of Rs 70,000 a month!

When he first made these calculations, Malkit could hardly believe the numbers—Rs 70,000 per month! 'I calculated the profit margin once again,' he says laughing. Knowing the market inside and out, from sourcing raw material to attracting large buyers, he was confident that he could make a go of it on his own.

He decided to launch his own business-making T-shirts. But despite all his 'feasibility' analyses, he didn't make a move for the next six months or so. 'I was hit by a moral dilemma,' says Malkit. How could he leave his employer who was in such distress? He couldn't, he decided.

Visiting Jain's residence almost every day, Malkit was moved by the circumstances his employer lived in. It was a ghost house. Father and son relied on the maid who cooked their meals and washed the dishes. Once she left for the day, there was no one in the house to be with the son, who was still suffering from depression.

Malkit's family lived in a small house. As the eldest child, he wished to provide a good education for his brothers and sister. The kind of income he needed for this could only come from business. He had to find a way to make it work. Malkit spoke to Mr Jain's relatives and sought their help in finding a bride for his employer's son. His relatives suggested a young woman, and the two were married in March 1991.

The new bride in the Jain household transformed the family. Jain senior regained his footing while his son started on the road to recovery. 'I breathed a sigh of relief,' says Malkit. 'Jain sahib showered praises on me. In return, I asked for the biggest gift he could give. I told him that I wanted to quit the company.'

Jain sahib couldn't believe what he had heard. But Malkit persisted.

'Bhagwan tera bhala kare,' Jain said. He was magnanimous and expressed his gratitude.

Malkit now felt free to embark upon his business quest. He bought a second-hand sewing machine, which he still keeps as a piece of memorabilia. The machine came for a paltry Rs 300. He decided to start working from home and having trained his wife to sew, he now had a partner as well.

But he was faced with another dilemma—whether or not he should compete with Jain by offering his services to Jain's clients. 'I thought for weeks, and decided against it,' says Malkit. 'I didn't want to betray my ex-employer. After all, Mr Jain trusted me when he asked me to deal with his buyers.'

Making T-shirts was not challenging in Ludhiana, but finding wholesale buyers was. For any business, marketing is critical. Malkit, thinking it would be unethical to sell his products to the clients who bought T-shirts from Jain's company, decided to target local buyers.

To compete with existing players, he had to be more imaginative. He had to resolve three critical issues: procuring raw material from the market, making the T-shirts and selling them at a profit. Malkit chose cost competitiveness as his weapon. The first batch of T-shirts was scheduled to be produced on 1 January 1992, but wasn't completed until 30 April 1992. Bringing down the market price was next in his game plan.

Malkit had his way. In those days T-shirt makers bought fabric on a thirty-day credit. But if someone made a spot payment, they received a 5 to 10 per cent discount. Similarly, manufacturers would sell their products to wholesalers on a thirty-day credit and if someone made a spot payment, manufacturers would reward him with a 5 per cent discount.

Malkit decided that his product would be at least 10 per cent cheaper than that of his competition, thus almost eliminating his profit. He kept working on bringing down the prices. 'We decided not to charge labour cost,' he adds. 'I had to succeed.'

Malkit had his business model ready but he would not move unless he secured a buyer. 'Many entrepreneurs perished as they went into production without assured buyers,' he said.

While searching for suitable buyers in the wholesale market, Malkit ran into an old friend—a buyer with whom he had lost touch. Harjeet Singh from Chandigarh dealt in sports goods, including white T-shirts, which were favoured by sportsmen and joggers. Harjeet found Malkit's price structure attractive and placed an order for 1,000 T-shirts. Malkit dipped deep into his pockets to buy the fabric for the order, loaded the material into a rickshaw and headed home.

Malkit and his wife worked well into the night to complete the order. The duo had cut fabric for 100 T-shirts and waited for the sun to rise on 30 April.

'We broke a coconut at the inauguration,' he recalls.

On the first day, Malkit and his wife were able to stitch only fifty T-shirts. Then Malkit's mother joined them with her machine and Malkit borrowed another machine from a neighbour. He finally delivered the 1,000 T-shirts on the fifth day of the launch.

By the fourth month after the launch, Malkit's business hit a plateau, producing only 1,000 to 1,200 T-shirts a week. With a margin of Rs 5 a piece, he was making over Rs 20,000 a month. Considering that Malkit was paid Rs 25,000 a month in his previous job in 1991, the money he was making wasn't a major attraction.

'But the feeling that we worked for ourselves gave us the drive to carry on. We also hoped and felt that something big could happen at any time!' Malkit sold the white T-shirts in the local market as well.

When Malkit's third child was born, he felt ambivalent. Having another child was obviously joyful but he had lost a key co-worker, his wife, who now had to look after the newborn.

In addition, expanding sales was proving to be a daily challenge. In order to attract buyers, Malkit started making multi-coloured T-shirts as well, which he would then distribute among prospective buyers as samples.

Everything changed late one afternoon when Malkit walked into a restaurant. He ran into a buyer who bought T-shirts in bulk from Mr Jain. Hailing from Madurai, he owned a company named Maruti Tex Garments. He had heard of Malkit's journey and his foray into business.

The fledgling entrepreneur took the Madurai man to the shop from where he bought raw material. He saw Malkit's samples and learnt about the price structure.

'He couldn't believe what he heard,' says Malkit. The Madurai man exported T-shirts to the Middle East. He had his own measurements and colour schemes. He wanted to place an order for 25,000 T-shirts to begin with.

'I was once again in a dilemma,' Malkit recalls. 'Wouldn't it mean stealing a client of my former employer?' With the promise to meet the buyer the following day, Malkit left for home. After dinner, he discussed the offer with his wife till past midnight. She raised the question of logistics, to which Malkit had an answer. In those days, if a manufacturer received an order that he himself did not have the capacity to manufacture, he would outsource the production to players who worked with one or two machines from their homes.

Loyalty to Mr Jain weighing heavily on their minds, the couple decided to supply only white T-shirts, which Mr Jain did not make. The following day, the bulk buyer from Madurai was stunned by the couple's white-only decision.

'He developed more respect for me,' says Malkit. By the evening, they had reached a compromise whereby Malkit would drop his white-only stand and instead would manufacture only those coloured T-shirts that Mr Jain did not make.

Malkit had made a breakthrough. In the second week of August 1992 the Madurai man placed an order for 10,000 T-shirts. He had paid 50 per cent in advance. Eventually, Malkit got seven repeat orders from him. He was also able to secure orders from a big buyer from Bhiwani who exported T-shirts to destinations Malkit hadn't even heard of.

His business grew manifold and he shifted his operations to a large facility in the city. A Dubai-based buyer visited his new facility in 1993. Impressed, he placed a huge order. 'Now, I would ship out goods in containers,' says Malkit. By the end of the year, Malkit had launched Janagal Exports. By 1996, the company had hit a turnover of Rs 1 crore. By 2000, the figure had crossed Rs 5 crore.

Price-cutting and outsourcing were Malkit's strengths. He had identified dozens of small entrepreneurs who worked from home with two or three machines. Since most of the stitching was outsourced, workers at Janagal Exports focused on creating new designs. Once demand grew beyond a point, however, automation was the logical next step.

Importers look for consistency, which only comes from using automatic machines. With another bulk order in hand from a Dubai-based importer, Malkit now looked for a used machine to usher in automation. In 2003, he procured a machine imported by a local entrepreneur and installed it in a nearby facility.

But for some reason, the Dubai-based entrepreneur cancelled the order.

'It was a setback,' Malkit says. 'Ten crore meant something in those days.' The machine had passed all trials but Malkit had to wait for a big order before he could start production. It was a chilly January morning in 2005 when Malkit got a call from the buyer from Madurai. After speaking to Malkit, he came to Ludhiana to see the new plant. 'He had a big order from an African market.'

Now there was no looking back. Malkit made his own fabric using the automatic machine he had installed. He would buy yarn in bulk. In 2011, he imported a state-of-the-art automatic machine from Spain, which churned out 14,000 T-shirts a day. Janagal's turnover crossed Rs 50 crore.

Malkit expanded further. In 2012 he opened a bakery in London and imported two more automatic machines from China. Nothing could have been farther from garment-making in Ludhiana than owning a bakery in London. But, for Malkit, grabbing a business opportunity was then more important than debating about the rationale.

Now with Rs 70 crore in turnover, Janagal Exports employs workers directly. Malkit outsources denim trousers to half a dozen vendors in Delhi. He exports men's shirts, children's garments and women's ready-to-wear garments, the production of which is largely outsourced to vendors in Ludhiana and Delhi. The enterprise is truly family-owned—Malkit's brothers are part of it, and his father gives his inputs. His son and daughter have studied in England. The eldest son, a commerce graduate, looks after the plant in Ludhiana. The basement of his home is stuffed with wooden boxes, ready to be shipped abroad. The air is thick with the smell of fabric.

Malkit now drives a Rolls Royce and recalls an incident

from his childhood. His mother had made a salwar-kameez suit for a client, Giano Devi, and asked Malkit to deliver it to her. Giano Devi gave Malkit a one-rupee note as a tip, but Malkit's mother scolded him and asked him to return the money. Giano Devi refused to take it back.

Malkit didn't want another scolding from his mother and had what he thought would be a more fruitful idea to get rid of the one-rupee note. He tore the currency note into pieces and planted the parts, hoping that the note would multiply. 'I had seen garlic being sown,' Malkit Chand laughs. 'But I was caught the next day while watering the plant.'

Money still doesn't grow on trees. But Malkit Chand Janagal sure knows how to make it multiply.

MILIND KAMBLE

Nariman Point, the prestigious business hub in Mumbai, houses the offices of some of the world's leading corporations. Built on reclaimed land from the Arabian Sea, the area was named India's first central business district and has since developed into one of the most coveted addresses for business in the city.

It is a pleasant winter day in 2012, and the Express Towers at Nariman Point display a banner depicting Milind Kamble reading the Marathi daily *Lok Satta*, a sister publication of the venerable *Indian Express*. The tagline reads: 'Shaping the Way Maharashtra Sees the World.'

It is rare for a Dalit to be a brand ambassador for a

mainstream newspaper, an acknowledgement that is perhaps the pinnacle of social recognition. It is no longer unusual to find Dalits making forays into politics and bureaucracy; there are Dalit stars in the arts, literature and academia. However, the 'endorsement' of Milind Kamble, a Dalit business leader, by a mass-circulated newspaper is singular in its recognition of something new in the national consciousness: the rise of the Dalit entrepreneur.

When the *Lok Satta* advertisement first appeared, there was a debate amongst leaders and journalists in Maharashtra on Milind becoming the first Dalit to be a brand ambassador of a cultural product as sensitive as a newspaper.

But clad in dark suits and colourful ties at public events, Milind has been profiled in the national and international media, including the *Washington Post*, *New York Times*, *Wall Street Journal*, *Fortune* and *Time*, and his opinions sought on subjects such as the state of the Indian economy and how the Dalit community is faring economically and socially. He has featured on the cover of the major Indian weekly *Outlook,* which hailed the arrival of the 'Dalit Crorepatis'. In recognition of his leadership, in 2013 the Indian government bestowed upon Milind Kamble one of its highest civilian honours, the Padma Shri. In his mid-forties, Milind is one of the youngest Padma Shri recipients in a non-sports category.

Milind is the founder-chairman of the Fortune Construction Company, which specializes in building roads, commercial and residential towers, tunnels and water distribution systems. The company has completed projects worth Rs 207 crore since it was launched in 2005. With fourteen engineers and 200 employees on its regular payroll, the Fortune group also provides indirect employment to several hundreds more.

Fortune's beginnings were humble and can be traced back

to the village of Chobli, in the Latur district of Maharashtra, an area geographically, financially and socially very far from Nariman Point. It was here that Milind was born on 17 February 1967 to a school teacher father and an illiterate mother.

Milind and his two younger siblings—a brother and a sister—had a decent childhood. Despite being plagued by chronic drought, the modest land the family owned produced enough sorghum, pulses, wheat and vegetables for the family to live on comfortably in a good year and his father's salary ensured a steady cash flow to supplement the income from the farm.

Milind started wearing shoes and socks from the eighth standard onwards in a departure from what was typical for other Dalit boys in the village. Since his father, Prahlad Bhagawan Kamble, was a teacher and respected, Milind didn't suffer much discrimination or exclusion.

'Because we had some money, we didn't have to wait for buffaloes or bullocks to die,' he says. 'Every Sunday, father bought beef from the market.'

After finishing his high school in 1983, Milind joined a polytechnic institute in the neighbouring Nanded district, even though his academic performance was better than what was required to do an Intermediate, before pursuing a BTech in engineering.

The polytechnic earned him a diploma. Given that Milind's family would have been able to provide him with the support and means to pursue a degree, which carried much greater prestige in India, it was surprising that he joined a diploma course instead.

While Milind was preparing for his high school exams, a close relative paid him a visit. Hanumant Waghmare came on a newly acquired Royal Enfield 350 CC Bullet bike, a vehicle as iconic to Indians as the Harley-Davidson is to Americans. Waghmare had joined the Public Works Department immediately after graduating from a polytechnic. Now in his fourth year in the job, he had bought the Bullet.

'Even the village Patils came to see that bike,' recalls Prahlad. Patils are upper caste Marathas.

Waghmare stayed the night in Milind's home and prodded the entire family to send Milind to the Nanded Government Polytechnic. He explained how expensive and time-consuming a BTech degree would be. Milind would first have to do his Intermediate for two years. Although BTech is a four-year course, most students take five years to complete it. If Milind pursued a polytechnic diploma, he would save five years and a lot of money.

Economists would slot Waghmare's analysis as exemplifying the 'opportunity cost of time'. Waghmare simply saw it in very practical terms.

Milind and his parents were grateful that providence in the shape of Waghmare had appeared to guide them and help them save money. 'But he forgot to tell us that a diploma holder would never become a chief engineer,' says Milind now.

After a couple of months, Milind enrolled in the Nanded Government Polytechnic. He opted for civil engineering because Waghmare had studied the same. Like most professional courses, a polytechnic has a two-tier assessment—a written examination and project work. To prepare his project report, Milind was spending a week on a construction site where a factory shed was being built. Having learnt that the students at the site came from Nanded Polytechnic, the contractor, an alumnus of the college, came to meet with the students.

Milind was amazed to learn that the contractor, Vilas Biyani, was so young. Biyani had been in business for just five years but drove a brand new Mahindra & Mahindra jeep. Biyani told his juniors the secret to becoming an entrepreneur. More than money, he said, it is the determination to succeed that is critical in business. But in civil engineering, working for a year or two in a construction company was essential to gain experience, he insisted. He had worked for eighteen months in a construction company as an on-site engineer.

'I bought this jeep after just one project,' said Biyani.

During the conversation, which lasted for more than a couple of hours, Biyani spoke of Pune as being the future hub of the construction industry.

'Mumbai has no more land left to attract industry and construction,' he reasoned. 'Pune has plenty of empty land, it's close to Mumbai and it has excellent weather. MNCs will prefer Pune to Mumbai.'

Buying a new jeep from profits earned from one project? Milind knew immediately that he couldn't ignore Biyani's lessons. Until then his aim had been to finish stuying at the polytechnic and get a government job. He had anticipated that after three or four years in service, he would be able to buy a Royal Enfield 350 CC Bullet, his dream machine so far.

But now he thought his dream too small.

'Could also own a construction company one day?' he wondered.

'Business had just entered my mind,' recalls Milind.

While in Nanded, he was briefly involved in two very different movements. He had joined the Dalit Panthers who championed the Dalit cause and followed Dr Ambedkar's philosophy. He also joined the Akhil Bharatiya Vidyarthi Parishad (ABVP), the student wing of the Bharatiya Janata Party (BJP). These two groups are mutually exclusive and members of one organization are not members of the other.

'But what could I do?' responds Milind, when asked why he was a member of both organizations. 'When I visited my relatives and fellow caste families in Nanded, I found the Dalit Panthers active in the area and I got attracted to them.'

'Inside the collage campus, I found ABVP active and leading the students' movement. I got attracted to them as well.'

And so passed his two years in Nanded, which were comfortable and uneventful—except for his meeting with Vilas Biyani. After obtaining his diploma in mid-1987, Milind was a new man.

Fired up, Milind would discuss his career options with his parents. He would often talk of Pune and the city's potential as a growth centre. For his parents, it was all vague talk, which wasn't leading towards any specific destination.

Prahlad Kamble was sceptical about his son's plans. He would often chide Milind for not applying for government jobs. When Milind laid out his business plans before him, Prahlad was furious.

'How much money do you have to start a business? Are any of our relatives in business?' he asked. 'Don't forget your father is a school teacher.'

Milind's mother Yashoda was ambivalent. Her mind was with her husband but her heart was with her son.

Months passed and Milind hadn't applied for a government job.

'Where are the vacancies?' he would counter his father.

'It was so easy for a Dalit to get a government job,' recalls Milind now. 'Reservations' made it relatively easier for Dalits with academic qualifications, like Milind, to get a government job.

'I had invested in your education so that you would become a sahib,' Prahlad would remind Milind. Differences turned into contentious disputes. The family stopped dining together.

Milind decided to move out of his home. He sought the help of an elderly Panther in Nanded, who wrote a letter to a fellow activist in Pune. 'Hand over this letter to him and he will take care of you,' he assured Milind.

Milind also sought the help of one of his ABVP friends in connecting with their counterparts in Pune.

'I wanted alternate contacts in Pune,' recalls Milind. 'I had to succeed.'

Dreams were in place and some plans, too, were in place. But there was no money. Milind knew his father would never oblige him.

Yashoda felt sorry for her son who was getting increasingly restless day by day. She quietly gave him Rs 500. He packed his briefcase with two pairs of shirts and trousers, a few other essentials and his certificates.

After a ten-hour bus journey from Latur, Milind reached Pune on an August morning in 1988. It took some time for him to reach Tadi Road where one of his contacts lived. Milind had to share a room with another man, an autorickshaw driver named S. Gaikwad. It was just a room with no kitchen or a bathroom. Several families in the three-storeyed building had to share a common bathroom and toilet located on each floor.

Milind now had to find a job in a construction company to gain experience. His encounter with Vilas Biyani remained vivid in his mind. He was desperate to follow Biyani's trajectory.

Milind's roommate knew an accountant who worked for a construction company, Zope Mhalgi Associates. Less than a week after he was introduced to the accountant, Milind got a job with the company at a monthly salary of Rs 700.

'That was too small an amount,' recalls Milind, 'but I lapped it up as it was my first job.'

Less than a year later, Milind joined Maharshi Karve Sanstha, which was also a construction company, as a project assistant engineer at a salary of Rs 1,750 a month.

With his first salary, he rented a modest one-bedroom flat and bought a bicycle on instalments.

Milind enjoyed his work over the next few months. One day, he ran into trouble with the builder. The builder had been procuring a sand-cement-gravel mixture from a plant located at the outskirts of Pune. Milind had doubts, though, when told of the plant's location.

'How long does it takes to cover that distance,' Milind asked the driver.

'More than an hour,' the driver replied.

'I will not use this material,' Milind declared.

Work came to a halt.

The builder learnt of what had happened. 'What's the matter?' he asked Milind.

'The sand-cement-gravel mixture has to be used within half an hour after it is mixed with water,' Milind answered. 'Any delay will weaken the concrete mix and the longevity of the building will be compromised,' he explained to the builder.

'This worksite is no university and you are no professor of building materials,' the builder told Milind.

'Continue,' he ordered his workers and drove away.

Milind could not tolerate the snub and quit the job.

'I didn't even collect my salary for that month,' recalls Milind. 'I had worked three weeks that month.'

On the recommendation of a mason who was working at the project site, Milind met another builder who cared more for quality.

'That's the kind of engineer I am looking for,' said the owner of Mantri Housing Company. Milind was hired for Rs 3,750 a month. He bought a scooter after receiving his first salary.

While still with Mantri Housing Company, Milind registered an enterprise, which he named Milind Kamble Civil Engineers & Contractors. He now looked for work.

He would use his day off, Sunday, to look for work. Soon he got his first break. His friend, the mason, told him about a construction project at Pune's famous Brihan Maharashtra College of Commerce (BMCC). The work being offered was too small and ordinary for big companies to undertake. Milind's friend had witnessed his own employer declining the contract.

In early 1992, Milind clinched the deal with BMCC in less than an hour. He was to build a compound wall at a cost of Rs 97,000. The work had to be completed in a month as the college had a major function coming up. He found the college was more desperate to have the wall erected than he was to get his first contract as a builder.

'I was delighted but tense,' he recalls. He needed Rs 15,000 to start the work. He had to buy tools and instruments. The workers would demand money in advance. The college would provide all the building material needed but pay wages for the workers at the end of the week.

In addition to his personal savings of Rs 5,000, Milind had to quickly raise Rs 10,000.

Should he go to his village and seek his parents' help? Milind ruled out that route. He knew his father would ask too many questions and might not give him the required amount.

He couldn't think of any friends or relatives who might be capable and also willing to help him. He decided to try his ABVP contacts.

Two of his ABVP friends, Joshi and Phadke, both upper caste, shelled out Rs 5,000 each.

Having raised the capital, he signed the contract with BMCC. He hadn't mentioned his new venture to his employer, Mantri Housing Company.

'I wrote a letter of resignation and dropped that in their post box,' he says. 'I didn't want to face them.'

He knew he had made a mistake. He should have informed them of his resignation with a one-month notice. Because he didn't do so, Milind decided not to claim the salary for the eighteen days he had worked.

Working with three different construction companies had helped Milind learn a few lessons that he would successfully carry into his own construction business: complete the project on time, maintain high construction standards, and in addition to wages, provide the workers with free food at the work-site.

Milind Kamble Civil Engineers & Contractors was launched with its first project without any ceremony. When work was nearing completion, an unusual incident occurred. One morning, the college principal was taking a round of the campus when he saw a group of workers trying to pull down a part of the wall that had been constructed the day before. He raised an alarm and guards rushed in. The demolition work was stopped and the workers were held in a room.

When Milind was summoned to the college, he explained to the principal that the section of wall in question had a minor fault and that was why it was being pulled down. The fault would not have been noticed by the naked eye, but was apparent with the appropriate tools.

'The principal smiled and patted me on my back,' recalls Milind. He assured the principal that he wouldn't charge the college for the extra work as his company was responsible for the mistake. The principal also learnt that this was the first project Milind Kamble Civil Engineers & Contractors had undertaken.

'Keep it up,' said the principal and gave Milind a 500-rupee notes.

'What is this for?' Milind asked.

'Because of the kind of business ethics you are practising. You don't have to submit a bill for Rs 500. This is from my pocket.'

While completing the BMCC project, Milind learnt of renovation work being planned in a nearby flat. The shop owner from whom he was procuring materials informed him of the opportunity. He met the flat owner, Rajesh Deshpande, who wanted to redo the house according to his tastes.

Thus, Milind's company got its second business opportunity within weeks after completing work at BMCC.

'I quoted a modest price: 1.57 lakh,' recalls Milind.

One day, while still working on the renovation project, Milind was summoned by the principal of BMCC who told him about an upcoming Maharshi Karve Stree Shikshan Sanstha project—a renovation contract worth Rs 3.8 lakh. Milind was to undertake the renovation of the toilets.

'He even phoned them,' recalls Milind with gratitude. 'I made no profit in the Sanstha Project, either. I had quoted a very low price.'

In its first year of existence, Milind Kamble Civil Engineers & Contractors had a turnover of Rs 6.34 lakh.

Although the company continued getting work, Milind was not excited by the kind of work he was doing. He didn't have the deep pockets to try for big projects. And small projects did not seem to offer a viable growth path.

He pondered over his career. Nothing big was in sight.

Then one morning in March 1994, he went to the cement shop where he bought cement. While he waited for the owner to return from the bank, another visitor arrived.

'He was tall and very fair,' remembers Milind. A.K. Mishra, the visitor, was a regular customer of the cement shop. Both struck up a conversation while waiting for the shop owner's return.

'Milind was the first to speak,' Mishra recollects of that first encounter. Each learnt of the other's business. They exchanged cards.

'I was greatly impressed by Mishraji,' says Milind, 'He was so elegantly dressed.'

As Milind was heading towards his scooter, Mishra called out to him, 'You don't have a phone?'

In those days, there was a waiting period of more than a decade to get a phone connection. Milind had applied for a phone but it would take years to get one.

Glancing at Milind's business card, he asked, 'How do I call you?'

'You can leave a message at this shop,' Milind replied, 'and I will call you back, now that I have your number.'

Mishra was a railway contractor and had his own company, Mishra Associates. His company had a turnover of Rs 10 crore. A migrant from Hardoi in Uttar Pradesh, Mishra valued 'local' friends. His company undertook complete track renewal, construction of new rail tracks and building pathways. Since railways were a central government concern, Mishra did little business with the state government.

Mishra had been on the lookout for lucrative state government projects in road building, water distribution and irrigation. He was also looking for a partner who was a Maharashtrian and had good networks.

'Following our first meeting, I had seen a prospective partner in Milind,' admits Mishra. 'He looked so trustworthy.'

Milind had seen Mishra driving a big car.

'Railways too offer business opportunities?' That was news to Milind. He decided to explore further.

The next day, Milind visited a distant relative who worked for the railways. That visit led to a meeting with a Dalit officer who headed an organization for the welfare of all Dalit officers working in the railways. By that time it had become common for Dalit officers and employees in government departments, barring the armed forces and police, to form their own welfare associations.

Senior engineer K.R. Kamble was excited to finally meet a Dalit who wanted to do business with the railways. He invited Milind to lunch, where he introduced him to a dozen Dalit officers.

'Take as much work as you can do,' said an officer who headed the civil works division. 'But don't compromise on quality, cost and project delivery schedule,' he added.

'Do you have tools and machines to handle large projects?' asked another. 'You can start with small projects,' counselled yet another.

'Register yourself as a vendor,' advised the head of the civil engineering department.

With so much support from fellow Dalits working in the railways, Milind thought he had hit the jackpot. But something was amiss.

Though Milind was dissatisfied with small projects, he was comfortable doing them. They demanded little capital or equipment. But the large projects that he was aspiring to undertake for the railways required substantial outlays of cash, equipment and also experience. He had none of that.

'Find a partner who can bring in all that,' his relative counselled.

Whom else could he go to, except Mishraji?

When he made his offer, Mishra's eyes lit up, knowing that it was a once- in-a-lifetime chance.

'Let's join hands,' he offered straight away.

'You are so valuable,' he said after learning of Milind's contacts in the railways.

For a time, Milind weighed another option: he could secure orders for Mishra Associates and claim his cut. 'But a partnership is better,' he decided. He didn't want to be a commission agent.

He met his relative and other Dalit officers and explained his limitations in terms of capital and machinery. He told them that the only way he could undertake large projects was if he had a partner, which was Mishra Associates.

'Mishra!' exclaimed an officer. They looked at each other in disbelief. Just as 'Kamble' is a Dalit surname in Maharashtra, 'Mishra' is a Brahmin surname in north India.

'Do you mean to say that all orders will go to Mishra Associates?' asked one.

Milind understood their apprehensions. He felt it was natural for his fellow Dalits to question the wisdom of having a Brahmin as a dominant partner in business.

He pleaded with them that money was bigger than caste. 'Let us try him out for a few projects. What would the flip side be? If it doesn't work, we could go alone.'

One in the group saw the big picture and argued that it could be a win-win deal. 'This is the best way to integrate a Dalit into railway contracts,' the officer began. His point was that though it was a worthy endeavour to help a qualified Dalit become a contractor for the railways, non-Dalits in the railways might construe their help as nepotism. But if the contract was awarded to a Mishra, that problem wouldn't arise, and Milind, too, would benefit.

In early 1995, Milind joined Mishra Associates. In the first year, his company had a turnover of Rs 21.5 lakh.

While Milind helped Mishra Associates obtain contracts, his own company supplied the raw materials Mishra required. He decided against forming a joint venture with Mishra. In order to enable Milind to join Mishra as an equal partner, he would have had to invest millions. Instead, he chose to be a supplier of material, which didn't require much investment. He would get supplies on a credit of thirty days from wholesalers, and claim money from Mishra within twenty-one days.

'It was a zero-investment game,' says Milind.

'It was a unique partnership,' adds Mishra.

Milind, on his own feet now, got married in May 1995.

Mobile phones arrived in India around that time. Milind, too, bought one.

'That was my big business investment,' he says. 'With this new weapon, I would be noticed.' Mishra followed Milind and bought a cell phone.

By the end of 1996, Milind was supplying goods and services worth Rs 50 lakh to Mishra Associates.

Mishra had dreamt of doing business with the state government and Milind was expected to get contracts and orders from the government. The formula worked and the first project was for Rs 1 crore. A year later, courtesy of Milind, Mishra Associates bagged another state government project worth Rs 2.7 crore.

In mid-1997, there appeared a newspaper ad seeking bids to lay a pipeline to supply water to Baramati, the town where the well-known national leader Sharad Pawar was born. Mishra Associates pitched for the Rs 25 crore project and won the bid.

'I bought a Mahindra & Mahindra jeep with the profits from just one project,' smiles Milind.

By 2000, the turnover of his company had reached Rs 37 crore.

The Mishra and Milind partnership went from strength to strength. In 2000, they won the Rs 70 crore contract to be the sub-contractors for the Pune–Bombay Expressway project. The following year, they secured a Rs 100-crore roadwork project linking Lavasa to Pune.

It was a turning point in Milind's life. Economic prosperity had brought him social recognition and prestige. He could afford to spend money on social causes. People who had helped him settle in Pune would now seek his support for social causes.

While his company was growing rapidly, Milind became restless. The Dalit Panther in him and his wife Seema would not allow him to bask in the comfort of his success. He realized that he needed to carry forth 'Babasaheb's Mission'. But how he was to do this was not yet clear to him.

Seema's parents lived in Mumbai and Milind would frequent the city. In mid-1999, through her parents, he was invited to attend a conference in West Dadar on the plight of Dalits under the Liberalization-Privatization-Globalization policy, or LPG.

LPG!

In 1991, India initiated economic reforms that sought to replace its decades-old socialist economic policies with market-based policies. It was a tumultuous time. One of the consequences was that many state-owned enterprises were partly or wholly sold to private players. There was a de facto freeze on recruitment. Articulate India was vertically divided into two camps—one in defence of the new direction and the other for the status quo. One of the expressions used in reference to the new economic policies was LPG. Though pejorative, the term caught everybody's imagination.

Dalits across the spectrum were apprehensive. Constitutional safeguards for their protection and welfare were intrinsically linked to state activism. In the new setting wherein markets would replace the state, the reasoning went, Dalits would again be marginalized, which naturally was an issue of critical concern for the community. Several Dalit groups and scholars were assembling in Mumbai to deliberate on these issues.

About a month before the Mumbai conference, Milind had received a letter from a friend who had migrated to the US. The friend had sent him a newspaper article about the Black Entertainment Television (BET) channel and its founder-CEO Robert Johnson, who led BET to become, in 1991, the first African—American-owned company to be listed on the New York Stock Exchange (NYSE).

At the Mumbai conference, speaker after speaker railed against the government for selling off public sector enterprises, thus reducing job opportunities for Dalits. None of the speakers mentioned that new opportunities were available to Dalit businessmen just as they were available to everybody else.

Milind wanted to say a few words during the Q&A session. When his chance came, he narrated the success story of BET and Robert Johnson.

'Brother Johnson has become the pride of all the Blacks,' he declared.

'Brother Johnson!' The words resonated with Milind.

The Dalit movement had sought inspiration from the civil

rights movement in the US. The Black Panthers, founded in 1962, became the template for the Dalit Panthers in 1972. Dalit capitalism received its inspiration from African-American capitalism.

Amidst applause, Milind asked the gathering, 'Is there a Dalit company listed on the Bombay Stock Exchange (BSE)?'

There was pin-drop silence.

'Please introduce yourself,' someone from the dais asked. Milind introduced himself as a businessman and the owner of Milind Kamble Civil Engineers & Contractors. More applause followed.

'My company has a turnover of Rs 50 crore,' he said.

More applause.

He was called on to the dais. The chair presented Milind with a bouquet of flowers, saying, 'Sorry, I am presenting a used bouquet to you. I hope a day will come when a Dalit Johnson will shine on BSE.'

Milind realized that he was the sole businessman at the conference and felt gratified that, rather than brickbats as he had feared, he had received a bouquet, used or otherwise.

The experience was an eye-opener for Milind.

Travelling back to Pune the same evening, he kept asking himself a question: how come there were no business leaders from the community, though there were many Dalit leaders in other fields like politics and religion?

'The idea to create a business body for the community was born before the train reached Pune,' he recalls.

Milind was hoping to find at least a dozen Dalit businessmen who would share his vision. He became more active in community matters. He asked all his contacts if they knew of any Dalit who was in business. It took him months to put together a team of Dalit businessmen.

Finally, on 14 April 2003, on the occasion of the birth anniversary of Babasaheb, Milind along with his colleagues launched the Scheduled Caste/ Scheduled Tribe Chamber of Commerce and Industry.

Being the first elected president of the first Dalit business body meant he had stepped out of his comfort zone. More importantly, his public leadership role began taking precedence over his personal business interests. At times he would feel overwhelmed by doubts and challenges.

While Mishra was happy for Milind, he would remind him that too much social activism would stunt his growing business.

Almost a year later, while reading a news report of a function organized by the Federation of Indian Chambers of Commerce and Industry (FICCI), Milind was troubled. As the oldest industry body in India, FICCI is a household name. It appears prominently in media reports. Top national leaders grace its gatherings and its leaders are invited to comment on policy matters.

He couldn't find any parallels between FICCI and his fledgling Scheduled Caste/ Scheduled Tribe Chamber of Commerce and Industry, a mouthful of a name without an acronym.

As months passed, it was becoming clear to him what had to be done. He would assiduously follow any news related to FICCI.

'I maintained a huge file that had newspaper clippings related to FICCI and the Indian economy,' says Milind.

On the first anniversary of the chamber on 14 April 2004, Milind and his team spent the entire day brainstorming on its name.

'SCSTCCI'!

It was too long, and he didn't like it.

He had to rename SCSTCCI. And he also had to come out of Mishra's shadow. Though they remained friends, Milind had concluded that he would need a free hand to do business while working for the community. He had to take advantage of the construction boom that Pune was then witnessing. Since Mishra Associates didn't specialize in buildings, Milind looked for opportunities in this segment.

One day, he was seated with his former colleagues from the Mantri Housing Company, where he had worked in 1989–90. 'They opened my eyes,' he recalls.

Milind dreamed of becoming a big builder but did not have the required capital or equipment. Most new buildings had a basement, which would be dug by earth-movers. The old practice of making bamboo staircases was replaced by the installation of temporary elevators. A crane was now an essential element in constructing tall buildings.

He was unsettled by the investment that would be required to purchase all the heavy equipment.

His friends from Mantri showed him the way out of his predicament—outsourcing.

'It was a revelation,' he recalls.

Every service could be sourced out. There was no need to raise capital to acquire heavy machinery. There were basement diggers who would come with their own machines. There were entrepreneurs who would install elevators on rent. There were crane operators offering their services for a price.

Milind saw a new window of opportunity.

By the second anniversary of SCSTCCI, some imaginative thinking by Milind and his core team resulted in the renaming of the chamber as the Dalit Indian Chamber of Commerce and Industry (DICCI).

DICCI *à la* FICCI!

'After FICCI, it's the turn of DICCI,' a newspaper captioned its story about the launch of the Dalits' own business body. The name gamble worked. DICCI got some media attention.

The next task was relatively easy. Milind agreed with the suggestion that Milind Kamble Civil Engineers & Contractors, too, needed a modern name. On 14 April 2006 it became the Fortune Construction Company. Following the change in the company's name, he also hired a few more employees.

'Being a role model businessman was on my mind,' says Milind. 'I had to give a corporate look to my business.'

His forays into the construction business would prove to be successful. With Mishra Associates, he had worked mostly as a sub-contractor. With the government, payment was linked with work progress. In other words, for a large part of the work, payment was made after the work had been completed.

However, now that he was working mainly in the private sector, the customer would provide all the raw material—steel, bricks, cement, sand and gravel—in advance. In other words, Milind had zero investment on raw materials. He could also seek some payment in advance, which he would use to pay the daily-wage construction workers; his vendors could wait for payment.

Fortune began with single-storey buildings. The breakthrough came when Milind won the contract for a private engineering college, MIT, in Pune. Spread over 57,000 square feet, the project was worth Rs 9.95 crore.

In 2008, the company secured its first contract for a residential tower. Spread over an area of 74,000 square feet, Silver Dale had 102 flats and was built at a cost of Rs 16.2

crore. This was followed by Peony, a residential tower with 170 flats.

Till 2013, Fortune Construction completed eight projects, worth a total of over Rs 170 crore. Other ongoing projects are worth another Rs 50 crore.

In a way, Fortune's office in Pune personifies Milind Kamble. It doubles as DICCI's office as well, just as the man is both a businessman and a Dalit leader. Distinguished visitors to his office include members of Parliament, ministers, leaders of India Inc., and even Bollywood superstar Aamir Khan, who spent an hour with Milind learning how entrepreneurship was gaining ground among Dalits.

What next?

'I want to enter trading,' says Milind. 'That's where the money lies.'

He has set up a joint venture with a Dalit-owned company based in Mumbai. Together, they plan to trade in coal and fertilizers.

'DICCI requires plenty of travelling. With trade as the new enterprise, I would get time for DICCI,' says Milind.

Milind's fourteen-year-old daughter Maitreyi, his only child, is often seen accompanying her father and sitting at the front-desk during DICCI events in Pune. She wants to go to a school in the US and after that become a hotelier.

Milind's family life, his business and his community work mingle so neatly that it would appear as if he wrote the script of his dreams and the gods blessed him to enact it.

ASHOK KHADE

The village of Rohini lies about 175 kilometres southwest of Mumbai on the shores of the Arabian Sea in the district of Raigad in Maharashtra. Though the area gets plenty of rainfall, the rocky soil doesn't encourage much vegetation. The land, dotted with spare balls of shrubs, looks as though it were blanketed by an old, faded rug. This sparse, though not unfriendly, terrain is home to nearly a hundred fisherman families, who find their succour not from the land, but the sea.

Nearby, the famous Janjira Fort looms out of the sea, drawing visitors to its ramparts. Their attention may also be drawn to the nearby Rajpuri Creek where a massive offshore fabrication facility is under construction. Built by DAS Offshore Pvt. Ltd, the Rohini Fabrication Yard will be Asia's second largest fabrication facility when it is completed. The company has already spent Rs 45 crore on this project with the commitment of further investment.

For Ashok Khade, the head of DAS Offshore, working on this project has been like flying in turbulent weather. Battling through the storms, the gods have smiled on this cobbler's son, bestowing name, fame and fortune. But Ashok's story is not one of chance, of winning a lottery. It is like that of the Janjira Fort that lies in the distance—a life built bit by bit over decades.

Set up in 1992, DAS Offshore undertakes fabrication work for oil well rigs at Bombay High. Located some 160 kilometres west of Mumbai, the region has oil fields with large reservoirs of crude oil. Public sector oil giant, Oil and Natural Gas Corporation (ONGC), has 1,800 oil wells that spew out 10,000 barrels of crude oil every hour.

DAS Offshore constructs oil platforms, helipads and their accessories. The company also manufactures jackets or legs on which oil platforms or helipads rest. For Ashok, fabricating these jackets is his first love. Weighing about 1,200 metric tons apiece, it is difficult to transport a jacket by road—the jackets have to be manufactured at a yard that has a port and a well-organized jetty. The jetty serves a port in the same way that a platform serves a railway. Thus far, Ashok has been making jackets at a government-owned port, paying a hefty rent for its use.

'Port authorities would make more money per jacket that we produce than our company,' says P.B. Bhosle. A hydrographic surveyor by profession, Bhosle oversees the construction of the Rohini facility. 'That's why Khade sahib is building this port,' he says. 'A pair of jackets can fetch Rs 10 crore,' he continues, 'and our turnover from this yard alone will shoot up manifold.'

In 2012, DAS Offshore expanded its reach and opened an office in Dubai. To begin with, the company invested Rs 40 crore and hired fifty employees.

'Once fully functional, the Dubai office will have a turnover many times bigger than the India office,' says Bhosle. 'Dubai has countless oil wells.'

Apart from making oil well platforms and helipads, Ashok's company also undertakes large-scale civil works, like the well-known skywalk in Bandra, Mumbai. It is building a large residential complex for the National Thermal Power Corporation at Sholapur in Maharashtra.

DAS Offshore also won the contract to build a road around the famous Pandharpur temple. The most visited Hindu temple in Maharashtra, it receives over half a million pilgrims during June–July, the month of Ashad in the Hindu calendar.

Housing the deity Vitthal, an incarnation of Lord Krishna, the temple did not allow untouchables to enter. 'I prayed to the god the day we won the bid,' Ashok says, getting emotional. Ashok was quick to add, 'It was from this temple that Gandhiji launched his anti-untouchability movement.'

Now an employer of over 4,500 workers including 150 engineers, Ashok says, 'It's God's gift.'

Khade was born in 1956 in the village of Ped some 400 kilometres northwest of Mumbai. His father worked as a cobbler and his mother was a farm labourer—both were illiterate.

'I remember her leaving for work in the morning without even drinking water,' recalls Khade.

'As per tradition, farm workers have their first meal around eleven in the morning on the farm itself,' adds B.B. Joshi.

Aged eighty-nine, Joshi, a Brahmin, graduated from high school in 1952 but didn't take up a government job. Highly respected for his simplicity and encyclopaedic knowledge of the local society, Joshi has known Ashok's family since Ashok was a baby.

Born in a house that had two rooms, each 15x8 square feet, Ashok loved playing under the open sky.

'Our house was too crowded,' he laughs, 'and the floor, walls, and roof were all made of mud.' The house had no almirah, trunk, window, kitchen, running water, or bathroom. Ashok's mother and sisters would fetch water from a well a kilometre away.

'Achhuton ka kuwan door tha (the well for untouchables was far)' says Joshi. 'Chhuwachhut ka jamana tha. (It was still the age of untouchability.)'

Ashok was not allowed to enter the village temple, which he renovated recently at a cost of Rs 14 lakh. 'I would pray standing outside the temple gate, while my upper caste friends prayed inside,' he recollects.

For Ashok and his five siblings, life was hard during summer. The temperature could often reach over 40 degrees Celsius and people stayed indoors, which meant little work for cobblers on the roadside. Winters were better and Ashok's father, the late Dagadu Tayappa Khade, would do brisk business in those months.

'There were occasions when he made Rs 5 a day,' says Ashok.

'But most of the time, our mother would decide what we'd eat once our father was back with the day's earnings.'

One day it rained all day, stopping only briefly. 'The sky was thick with dark clouds,' he recalls, 'and I was sent to the market to buy some sorghum flour. In childhood, we grew up eating sorghum bread with red chilli sauce.'

Half an hour had elapsed for an errand that should have taken about five minutes and little Ashok wasn't back. When after another fifteen minutes he still hadn't shown up, anxious family members spread out in the village to find him. They spotted him hiding behind some bushes.

'I had slipped and fallen,' Ashok recalls, 'and the flour was spilled in muddy rainwater. I feared facing my family members.'

Because of the heavy rain that day, Ashok's father did not go to work as usual and his mother Tanubai couldn't get any work on the farm either. Ashok had taken all the money that was at home to buy the flour.

'We all went to bed with empty stomachs,' says Ashok, his eyes moistening.

In the midst of adversities, however, Ashok continued his studies. He did well in the SSC (Secondary School Certificate) examinations, scoring a 100 per cent in maths.

'I wrote the maths paper on an empty stomach,' he says. It is difficult to gauge his emotions. He is pensive, recalling the experience and thankful that he can now not only meet all his needs but also indulge in luxuries that his wealth can buy.

Ashok cleared his SSC examinations in June 1972 and hoped to become a doctor. His elder brother Datta Khade was working at Mazagaon Dock. After passing his SSC examination the previous year, young Datta went to Mumbai in search of a job. He joined Mazagaon Dock as a welder-apprentice at a salary of Rs 70 a month.

'We were hard pressed for money,' recalls Datta.

Ashok could think of continuing his education because Datta was employed, earning a regular salary.

Khade reached Mumbai in July 1972 for further education. It was six in the evening. 'I was blown away,' he recalls. 'Tall buildings, cars, and fancy showrooms!'

'What a world this is,' he wondered.

'I, too, will become part of this world.'

On the way to his new home he kept asking his brother, 'When will we reach Kurla?'

'Chalte raho (keep going),' was the reply.

As they approached the suburb of Kurla, the streets started getting narrower.

Datta was still a trainee, and didn't have his own home. He was a guest of his father's sister Shantabai, who lived in a room hardly 10x10 square feet, with her three children and her husband, who was a driver. Factory owners had developed this apartment-type building with one-room accommodation and a kitchen as low-cost housing for workers. A dozen or so such accommodations shared a common bathroom and a toilet. Next to the room was a large open area, a verandah, with a concrete roof, to be shared by all the inhabitants.

As Ashok approached Shantabai's chawl, his idea of Mumbai had taken a beating. 'This is another Mumbai,' he told himself.

Datta slept under the staircase in a space that was not big enough for him to stretch his legs. Still, he was considered lucky because the space was covered on two sides. Ashok was allotted a spot on the verandah that was open on three sides. He was given an old bedsheet that he would spread out on the ground. He would have to fold the bed sheet every morning and keep it inside Shantabai's house. Both the brothers, however, kept their personal belongings inside the house.

'What a life is this?' Ashok thought after his first day at the chawl. By the evening, however, he reconciled to the reality. He saw a few more people unfolding their bedsheets. As he learnt their stories, his respect for Shantabai went up.

'This is what Mumbai is. People start their lives on the ground and end up owning tall buildings,' a sleep mate told him.

Ashok was amazed to learn that many families living in such chawls staggered their working hours so that there would be enough space to accommodate everyone.

'That's why Mumbai never sleeps,' Datta had reasoned to his younger brother.

'Bambai mein naukari mil jati hai, chhokari bhi mil jati hai, par rahne ke liye ghar milna mushkil ho jata hai (In Mumbai, you easily get a job and even a girl to marry. But getting a house to live in is difficult)' a neighbour told Ashok one day.

Within months of reaching Mumbai, the young Ashok enrolled in Siddharth College for his Intermediate in science.

But commuting to and from college became a challenge for him. Siddhartha College is 45 kilometres from Kurla. He would take local trains and spend more than an hour getting to college. It would take him another hour or more to return home in the evening. Seeing his brother's troubles, Datta requested the college principal for a hostel seat. Luck smiled on Ashok and he got admission to the hostel where he was to share a room with another student.

'I could not control my joy,' he says recalling that day.

Once in the hostel, his joy didn't last long. As it didn't have a mess, hostellers ate at roadside eateries. Some would get their food supplied to their rooms. Khade did not have enough money to buy food every day. Datta was supporting the family back home as well. If Khade was to eat outside, he would need a minimum of Rs 10 a day.

Datta's salary was less than Rs 100 a month. 'He still gave me Rs 7 a month as pocket money,' says Khade.

He came up with a unique but punishing routine. He would sleep and study in the hostel, take classes at the college and eat his meals in Kurla. Kurla was 10 kilometres from the hostel. He would take a bus in the morning to eat his first meal at Kurla and then go attend classes and study. He would return to Kurla for dinner in the evening, and then go back to the hostel.

'I hardly remember a day when I got to eat three meals,' he says.

Poverty meant that he needed to be inventive. Good in maths, he gave tuition to junior students and soon became popular. He partly supported himself this way, but lost interest in his own studies. He failed his twelfth standard examination.

'My dream of becoming a doctor came to an end,' Ashok says now.

It is difficult to fathom his feelings—whether he regrets not becoming a doctor or thanks the heavens that that failure paved the way for greater success in life.

With no other options available, Datta helped Ashok land a job at Mazagaon Dock as an apprentice in 1973.

Impressed by his work, his superiors gave him a position in the quality control division in 1975. That was the year their father passed away. Taking care of the entire family fell upon the two brothers' shoulders. Their mother, two unmarried sisters and a younger brother lived in the village.

'It pained me that my mother worked for landlords as a farm labourer,' he says. 'My sisters took care of the household chores.'

Ashok focused on his work and became a favourite of his bosses.

'I had no hobbies that required time, had just one relative, and gave all my time to the company I worked for. The dock was a better place than the chawl at Kurla.'

In 1976, the brothers moved into their own rented accommodation. Datta had gotten married.

Then in 1983, Ashok was sent to West Germany to oversee a ship being built for India.

'My eyes opened,' he says. A year-long stay in Germany transformed him. He saw the quality of life the Germans led. He was mesmerized by their cars, their food and drink. Shopping malls opened up a new universe to him.

'This is heaven,' he would tell himself. 'But this heaven is made of money.'

He returned to Mumbai in 1984, but his experiences in Germany remained with him. He would narrate tales of his German sojourn to his colleagues. To many, his stories sounded incredible.

A German who went by his first name, Ludwig, worked at Mazagaon Dock. He was an expert in underwater welding. Because Datta was a welder too, Ashok knew Ludwig well. He even took tips from him before leaving for Germany.

After his return, Ashok developed a greater admiration for Ludwig. 'I had seen his country and people,' he notes.

One evening, tired of listening to Ashok's continual refrain that Germany was a paradise on earth, Ludwig blurted out, 'The rich in Mumbai live more lavishly than the rich in Germany.'

'I couldn't make anything of what Ludwig said,' recalls Ashok.

'How many German households have maids?' asked

Ludwig. 'Can Germans afford drivers? How many Germans have private security guards? Rich Indians have multiple maids for washing clothes, dish-washing, cleaning floors twice a day, cooking, and even babysitting.'

'I was astonished,' Ashok remembers. One day, Ludwig took him out for dinner to a five star hotel. That was Khade's first glimpse of luxury in Mumbai.

'If you have money, there is a Germany in Mumbai too,' he muttered to himself as he stepped out of the hotel.

'Money got into his brain,' recalls Govind, who held a senior position in Mazagaon Dock.

Ashok's outlook on life was further influenced when he was invited for a dinner that Datta's friend had organized in honour of a colleague who had just retired from Mazagaon Dock. After a couple of pegs, the man who had retired, spoke of his experiences. Khade was moved to learn that the man had spent thirty-six years working for Mazagaon Dock. He was happy and satisfied with his accomplishments. His two daughters were married. His only son was employed at Mazagaon Dock. The dinner of fish curry carried on till midnight.

'I couldn't sleep that night,' Ashok says. He wondered why the retired man was so happy with what he considered his 'accomplishments'.

After working at the dock for thirty-six years, one of the retired man's daughters was married to a bus conductor and the other to a bank clerk. Neither had received a good education; nor had his son, who somehow managed to get a low-paying job at the dock. All he could manage was to build a house in his village in Satara district and buy a second-hand scooter.

'Will I also follow the same trajectory and end up in my village after serving Mazagaon Dock for decades?' Ashok asked himself.

'I pitied myself,' he says, shaking his head.

The next day, he shared his concern with a colleague.

'Look at those who work in private factories and live in slums.'

'We are fortunate to have landed a job at Mazagaon Dock,' replied the colleague.

Meanwhile, his younger brother Suresh, too, had joined the dock as a trainee welder.

Ashok kept thinking about his future. Suddenly he was reminded of what his sleep mate at the Kurla chawl had told him, 'Yahi hai Bambai. Log jamin par so kar jindagi shuroo kiye, aur toweron ke malik ban gaye'!

While he dreamed about the prospects of becoming a tower-owner in Mumbai, weighing them against the option of going back to his native village after retirement, his youngest sister got married in May 1992. The Khade brothers had fulfilled a major family duty. Only their mother was still to be taken care of.

'Now something should be done,' Ashok told himself.

'The day after our sister's marriage, Ashok started talking about business,' recalls Datta.

Back in Bombay, the three Khade brothers met at Datta's home. Ashok had discovered that Mazagaon Dock was to open a new centre in Nhava, some 40 kilometres away from Mazagaon. He realized that this was just the opportunity that he and his brothers needed to strike out on their own. He explained his plans to his brothers.

'Nhava unit sone ka sagar hoga (The Nhava unit will be an ocean of gold),' he told his brothers. 'If you dive, you get gold in abundance.'

Set up in the early eighteenth century on the shores of south Mumbai, Mazagaon Dock is a public sector company that builds and maintains ships and submarines for the Indian Navy as well as merchant ships. It also manufactures large offshore structures, including oil rig platforms, offshore helipads and other accessories related to oil and gas exploration rigs. The 1,800 oil fields in Bombay High need parts for replacement and maintenance, a business worth several hundred crore rupees every month.

'In salt water, iron rusts very fast,' says Datta to explain why Bombay High offers so much business.

In 1989, Mazagaon Dock authorities decided to set up an extension unit at Nhava.

The practice of manufacturing a complete product under one roof was now outdated. Also, the concept of public–private partnerships (PPP) was gaining ground. Both private companies and government undertakings had started outsourcing the production of ancillary parts and services to smaller companies. The Mazagaon Dock authorities launched the Nhava unit not only because the existing facilities were unable to meet the needs of Bombay High, but also to promote the PPP model.

Within months after setting up the unit at Nhava in 1989, the dock authorities opened the doors for private players, just as Ashok had predicted. Datta and Suresh now came to appreciate Ashok's business mind.

The Khade brothers were ready to test the business waters. Ashok had been exposed to the technical nitty-gritty of oil rig platforms, having worked in the quality control department. Datta and Suresh were master welders—welding is a key part of this industry, be it on ships or oil rig platforms.

'Ashok had sensed a goldmine at Nhava,' says Govind. The three brothers would meet frequently over dinner, exploring business opportunities.

'This industry relies on welders,' explains Datta.

With India having launched its economic liberalization programme in 1991, change was afoot and the Khade brothers decided they wanted to be players rather than mere spectators. They had plans. The year was 1992 and the company, DAS Offshore Private Limited, was launched. The name, DAS, had its own story—D stood for Datta Khade, A for Ashok and S for Suresh.

'On the advice of Ludwig, I bought a book on how to name a company,' says Ashok. He resigned from the dock shortly after they received a work order at Nhava. DAS Offshore began its business as a sub-contractor. They accepted whatever work came their way. Meanwhile, Datta had been granted his request for a transfer to Nhava.

'We roamed around like vultures for big business opportunities,' Ashok smiles.

'A friend broke the news,' says Datta.

The ONGC (Oil and Natural Gas Commission) had slapped a huge penalty on the Nhava management for not delivering a job on time. The Nhava management had given a contract to a Chennai-based firm to manufacture a jacket. For some reason, the company had been unable to deliver the jacket.

'A first-timer, the company in Chennai didn't appear to have technical knowhow,' says Ashok. As the Nhava authorities put pressure on the company, its owner packed up his bags one day.

It was mid-January 1993 when the CMD of the Nhava facility asked Ashok, 'Can you deliver it?'

With ONGC slamming a penalty on the Nhava unit, the dock's prestige was at stake. More than that, the very reason for creating the Nhava unit as an experimental PPP was going to fail.

'The Nhava authorities prayed that some private party would deliver the jacket,' recalls Govind.

The three brothers went into a huddle that evening. A consensus was reached. If the Nhava authorities could pay in advance and allow the Khades to use their equipment, why not? The Khades would be happy to complete the jacket project.

The authorities were too happy to accept these terms.

Within a week, DAS Offshore received the project, worth Rs 1.4 crore, which was to be completed in five months. The company got 10 per cent of the total cost as advance.

The brothers took just over three months to complete and hand over the jacket.

'They had surprised the entire dock authorities,' says Govind.

'The word spread like wildfire—a private party has manufactured a jacket in just three months,' says Ashok.

For their part, the Khade brothers would stay at the worksite sometimes for over eighteen hours a day. They often slept at the site itself. Seeing the owners so focused on their job, the workers were motivated to put in their best.

'They were consumed by their mission,' says Govind. 'It was as if the men had turned into machines.'

While the Khade brothers stole the limelight, many questioned the quality of the jacket manufactured so quickly. Once the manufactured jacket passed through the quality control department with a green light, Ashok heaved a sigh of relief.

A repeat order followed in less than a month and now Datta also resigned from his job at the dock.

Over time, a division of labour has taken place. Ashok

looks after the Dubai office and Datta the India office, while Suresh focuses on the construction site.

In her eighties, Khade's mother looks after the eighty-acre farm that her sons have purchased in their native village of Ped.

'I take care of these,' she says, pointing to mango trees. Mangoes, grapes, sugarcane, and turmeric grow on the farm along with wheat and rice.

Any dreams left?

'I wish my children had taken up oil and gas exploration,' says Ashok, looking out of his luxury car, which is, not surprisingly, a BMW.

RATI BHAI MAKWANA

Ranpur is a small town 130 kilometres southwest of Ahmedabad, on the way to Bhavnagar. With a population of 25,000, it is a typical Gujarati town, dry and with sparse vegetation but abundant in commerce and industry. The town grew out of a village, which a century ago had barely a tenth of its current population.

It was in this village, at the turn of the last century, that Gala Bhai Makwana was born. Although as a child, he along with his five younger brothers worked as child labourers, they eventually became successful businessmen. What made this transformation possible was not good luck or intervention from the gods, but Gala Bhai's foresight and tenacity. The achievement is all the more staggering when one realizes that thirteen of his descendants are currently business persons, with turnovers ranging from Rs 1 crore to Rs 750 crore.

	Name	*Company*	*Turnover (Rs crore)*
1.	Rati Bhai Makwana	Gujarat Pickers	750
2.	Devjibhai Makwana	Suraj Filaments	100
3.	Dilipbhai Makwana	Anand Industries	25
4.	Amrutbhai Makwana	Pankaj Plastics	10
5.	Monabhai Makwana	GE Enterprise	5
6.	Vasantbhai Makwana	VGM Industries	5
7.	Nandabhai Makwana	Millennium Industries	5
8.	Rambhai Makwana	Manhar Pickers	4
9.	Lalbhai Makwana	Bhavnagar Pickers	3
10.	Natbhai Makwana	Anand Ropes	3
11.	Jetbhai Makwana	Janta Plastics	2
12.	Valajibhai Makwana	Sachin Synthetics	2
13.	Kalyanbhai Makwana	Gemini Plastics	1

'Gala Bhai planted an evergreen tree on which money indeed grows,' says Ahmedabad-based Dalit entrepreneur, Dinesh Rajvansi.

Gala Bhai started working in the cotton fields at an early age. Jethiben recalls, 'Within a week after my marriage, I too, was out working in cotton fields.' She married Gala Bhai eighty years ago and now she is ninety-six years old. The brothers would also occasionally process raw leather when cattle died.

Soon after his marriage, Gala Bhai got a job as a boiler attendant at a cotton ginning factory in Ranpur.

'It was news in the village,' recalls his widow. 'Gala Bhai was the first Dalit from the village to get a job outside the farm.'

Owned by an Englishman, the large, semi-mechanized factory separated cotton fibre from seeds. At that time, the village was a cotton-ginning hub. It was connected by rail to nearby towns and goods trains would stop there more frequently than passenger trains.

The Bhavnagar–Surendranagar rail line, which passed through Ranpur, was constructed in 1879–80 and owned by the princely state of Bhavnagar, and triggered the industrialization of the area that it cut across. Independent of British rule, the Bhavnagar riyasat was the second largest in what is now modern Gujarat, after the princely state of Baroda. Successive rulers of Bhavnagar were relatively progressive. Instead of building large palaces, the maharaja of Bhavnagar built a rail line.

Gala Bhai proved to be adept as a boiler attendant, a fact noticed by the factory management, who transferred him to the commercial division where he would oversee the loading of cotton bales onto rail wagons.

Gala Bhai struck up a friendship with the driver of a goods train that came through Ranpur. The driver would coordinate with the management of the ginning factory to ensure that the wagons were loaded in time. Because Gala Bhai now looked after the loading department, he interacted regularly with the train driver and they socialized in the evenings.

The train driver was fond of good food and drink. One evening after a couple of drinks, he asked if Gala Bhai knew an untouchable family. When Gala Bhai said that he was an untouchable, they hugged each other in mutual acknowledgement.

'The driver was looking for cooked beef,' recalls Jethiben, though she no longer remembers his name. 'Only Dalits ate beef. I remember cooking about two kilos of beef,' she says. 'He ate as if that was his last meal.'

Years later, the train driver invited Gala Bhai to his daughter's wedding. And so when he was thirty-seven, Gala Bhai visited Bhavnagar for the first time in his life.

'It was as if he was going over to Vilayat,' says Jethiben, 'and he was the first in the family to visit Bhavnagar.'

Gala Bhai was the first in the family to ride in a train and visit a city. Although Bhavnagar was just 100 kilometres away, the family busied itself with preparations for the journey, Jethiben packing sufficient food for her husband. Gala Bhai reached Bhavnagar two days ahead of the wedding and helped his friend with some of the tasks for the wedding, such as cutting a large log into firewood.

Gala Bhai was mesmerized by the city of Bhavnagar. He asked a cousin of the train driver if he could find a job for him, citing his experience as a boiler attendant. The cousin agreed to look out for suitable positions and a month later, the train driver delivered the news to Gala Bhai that there was an opening in a rubber factory for a boiler attendant. The family was ecstatic.

In 1937, Gala Bhai quit his job in Ranpur and left for Bhavnagar. He joined a rubber factory, which made soles for canvas shoes. He shared a room with a relative of the train driver. The company did brisk business; canvas shoes were used by army and police personnel. One by one, Gala Bhai brought all his five brothers to Bhavnagar and built huts for them in the slum that was inhabited by workers of the rubber factory.

With all his brothers married, they were now a formidable family amongst the slum dwellers. The entire family lived and ate together, using only one kitchen. With the money earned, they built six small houses in Ranpur. They were all of the same size and similar design.

'They looked like government houses,' quips Jethiben.

Having returned successful, the six brothers made an impact back home in Ranpur. A number of young men working in the cotton fields approached Gala Bhai for an opportunity.

But Gala Bhai's good fortune did not last. In 1940, a dispute arose among the rubber factory, the shoe maker, and the buyer—primarily the British Indian army. While the rubber soles were made in Bhavnagar—an autonomous princely state—the shoes were manufactured in a British territory. The British government clamped a heavy customs duty on the rubber soles. The following year, the rubber factory closed its operations. All six brothers lost their jobs in one stroke.

'It was as if a death had occurred in the family,' recalls Jethiben.

Being the eldest and the head of the family, Gala Bhai had to find a new job.

Near their slum, there was a grass fodder vendor who was going through difficulties. Many people in the town raised cows or buffaloes for milk and bought fodder from the market. Often, women from the villages would bring fodder and hawk it directly to customers. The customers, though, had no guarantee that the women would be selling at the same place every day.

The fodder vendor had trouble since he sourced his fodder from these village women. At times, if the women found buyers upon entering the city, they would sell the fodder they were bringing in and return home. The fodder vendor would inevitably run short of supply.

'Shall we set up a fixed fodder shop right outside the slum?' Jethiben remembered her husband asking his brothers. 'They all agreed.'

It was the winter of 1941 when Gala Bhai launched his first business venture. He assigned duties to each of the five brothers, who would wait at various entry points to the city and buy grass from the rural women. Soon the brothers' operation came to be known as the best fodder shop in town.

The Bhavnagar royal family were fond of animals and kept herds of cattle in the fort. One of their drivers would often come to Gala Bhai to order fodder. While conducting business, the driver and Gala Bhai became friends. Gala Bhai had by now realized that he could not take any business for granted, and he also knew the limitations of the fodder business. He was in search of an alternative.

Being a Dalit, he was familiar with working with raw leather. He had grown up watching his father skin dead animals and learnt the art of processing raw leather. He could set up a leather processing unit in Bhavnagar but needed some land on which to build.

One day, he told the driver his desire to meet the maharaja, Krishna Kumarsinhji Bhavsinhji, who was well regarded.

A well-dressed Gala Bhai stood at the entrance to the palace. As the royal car approached, he folded his hands in deference, and the driver slowed the car.

Gala Bhai had a minute to make his case. He told His Royal Highness that since Bhavnagar didn't have a tannery, raw leather was going out of the kingdom for processing. He made the plea for land so that he could construct a tannery.

Impressed, the king asked him to come to court the next day. He did so, and was allotted 9,000 square yards of land on the outskirts of the city.

By 1944, Gala Bhai's business was so brisk that he had to pay taxes for the first time. In March 1945, he became a father—his son was named Rati Bhai. During World War II when the price of processed leather skyrocketed, Gala Bhai made a fortune.

One day, a relative who worked in a textile mill in Vikramgam near Ahmedabad told Gala Bhai of a business opportunity. Due to the war, European manufacturers had stopped exporting cotton pickers to India. The pickers are small but vital parts in a textile loom. Gala Bhai requested the relative to smuggle out a used cotton picker so that he could figure out how to construct one. After the relative returned with a used picker, it took a year for Gala Bhai to make one that could be used in a loom.

Processing the raw leather so that it could be used to make pickers proved to be a challenge. The brothers consulted many people with experience in textile mills.

Gala Bhai finally made twelve leather pickers. He went to Vikramgam and asked his relative to secretly test the pickers he had made.

But there was no need for secrecy. The industry was desperate as supplies from Europe had stopped. Looms were shutting down due to the scarcity of pickers. The relative took Gala Bhai to the company's management, who subsequently tested the pickers but found that they were not up to the mark.

Gala Bhai kept trying and succeeded on his fourth attempt. By 1946, he was supplying pickers to the Vikramgam mill.

Being the first to manufacture pickers locally, he did a brisk business. In 1948, he registered his company as Bhavnagar Pickers Pvt. Ltd. By 1950, the brothers had stopped their leather work business.

'That job was very demeaning,' says Jethiben. 'With its foul smell, we wanted to exit the business.'

As more players entered the picker-making business,

Bhavnagar Pickers started importing leather from abroad to make an even better product.

In 1956 while visiting Bhavnagar, Union Finance Minister T.T. Krishnamachari wanted to meet a group of business people. His office had asked the district collector to include some Scheduled Caste business people as well. Because Bhavnagar Pickers had earned a name for itself, Gala Bhai was a proud invitee.

While their company was moving from strength to strength, the brothers found it increasingly difficult to do business together as one family. In 1959 they separated into three groups—two brothers in each group. Their assets, business premises and markets were divided equally. The brand Bhavnagar Pickers was put on auction amongst the three groups and it was bought by Laljibhai Makwana.

By 1962 the brothers divided further. 'Each became independent now,' says Kirit, a second-generation Makwana businessman.

Gala Bhai launched Gujarat Pickers as his new brand. It took a couple of years to establish the company. Since his brothers were now occupied in running their own businesses, he needed help from another family member. His son Rati Bhai, who had completed high school in 1963, was promptly inducted into the family business.

'He waited for me to complete my high school,' smiles Rati Bhai. He would manage the production unit and his father would look after marketing. 'He would be travelling all the time,' recalls Rati Bhai. 'He would frequent cities such as Calcutta, Bombay, Ahmedabad and Vadodara.'

When he turned twenty in 1965, Rati Bhai bought a motorcycle. 'The relatives came to see the bike,' he remembers.

'It generated the same kind of wonder as the bicycle we bought in 1961 had.'

He topped the bike purchase when, at twenty-six, he bought an Ambassador car. For a couple of generations after Independence, the car was a symbol of power and pomp. 'Only a Collector rode in an Ambassador,' he recalls. 'There are now two Collectors in Bhavnagar,' some would remark.

By the mid-1970s, the Makwana brothers were doing well in business. They had all built good homes for themselves and their children were enrolled in elite schools. As it happens so often, this proved to be the calm before the storm.

Around 1978 plastic pickers entered the market. Initially, an Ahmedabad-based Parsi business house imported these plastic pickers, which came at a third of the price of leather pickers.

'We were baffled,' recalls Rati Bhai. 'Clients began ignoring us.' It was painful watching the business fail.

One day he read an advertisement in a local daily about the Government of India seeking dealers for polymers, from which plastic products are made.

Rati Bhai was quick to apply. 'Because a plastic product was destroying us,' he says, 'I had a sort of a psychological response.'

In collaboration with the Soviet Union, the government had set up the Gujarat Refinery in Koyali near Baroda, which commenced production in 1965. The growth in domestic refining capacity was driven by the domestic market requirements of kerosene and diesel, while naphtha, a lighter fraction, was projected to be in surplus. Normally, this would be used to produce one of the principal end-products of petroleum—petrol. But that end-market was not projected to grow because cars were deemed to be 'luxury' goods and the Indian government sharply curbed the growth of the automobile sector.

At the same time, there was a surplus of naphtha in the international market; this led to the exploration of alternative uses for naphtha, namely fertilizers and petrochemicals, and resulted in the government setting up the Indian Petrochemicals Corporation Limited (IPCL) in 1969 to process naphtha into plastic. (The complex became operational only in 1978.)

Though Rati Bhai had applied for the dealership of the Saurashtra region, he was told by friends and well-wishers to lobby for the business.

'A government dealership doesn't come just like that,' a friend argued. Bhavnagar was represented by a gentleman-politician named Prassanbhai Mehta. Rati Bhai was well known in town for his business and the Ambassador car, and Mehta promised to help him.

He was confident of getting the dealership because Mehta had written his recommendation on his official letterhead to the IPCL Chairman. While IPCL was still considering the matter, the Janata government headed by Morarji Desai collapsed and IPCL delayed taking decisions.

'I sat for days cursing my luck,' recalls Rati Bhai. He felt all doors had been shut on him.

After a new government came into power in Delhi in January 1980, Rati Bhai had to start his lobbying afresh and finally bagged the dealership in mid-1980.

'I thanked God,' he says.

Rati Bhai's Gujarat Pickers was entitled to lift 100 tons of polymers every month to market in Saurashtra. That meant a business worth Rs 60 lakh a month.

Six months later, Gala Bhai passed away; he might have

been content and also happy that his son was now a successful businessman.

It was a turning point for Rati Bhai and there was no going back. In 1985, he was made a director of the State Bank of Saurashtra, a public sector bank. That same year Gujarat Pickers closed the picker-making business and the company crossed Rs 100 crore in turnover.

Rati Bhai's business had grown in size and reputation. In 1992, he moved to Ahmedabad. While there, the manufacturer in him became active again. Within a year, he formed another company named Rainbow Packaging. Since he was already trading in polymers, he was in an advantageous position to manufacture plastic products.

'I began with milk pouches that the dairy industry uses,' he says. 'I had tears rolling down my cheeks the day a dairy firm packed milk in pouches I had produced.'

Back in the old days in Bhavnagar, none of his family members were allowed to enter the local temple. 'We worshipped Hindu gods, standing outside the temple doors,' recalls Rati Bhai. If he wanted to enter a temple, he would go to one located far away, where he was not known as a Dalit.

Not resting on his laurels and ever a dreamer, Rati Bhai began to think of even bigger ventures. He zeroed in on the steel mills that had begun sprouting up around Bhavnagar.

Alang Shipyard, which lies 50 kilometres from Bhavnagar, is known around the world as the burial ground for decommissioned ships. Around 200 large ships are dismantled annually at Alang, a small ship generating about 10,000 tons of steel.

Rati Bhai watched ordinary people becoming rich in Alang's ship-breaking industry. Excited by the opportunity, he dived into the steel business. In 1993, he invested Rs 20 crore and established a steel rolling mill named Volvo Steel Ltd. Two years later, his group launched the Chaudhary Ship Breaking Company with an investment of Rs 25 crore. They dismantled twenty ships.

A little over a year into the rolling mill and ship-breaking businesses, bad luck once again struck Rati Bhai.

As a consequence of the economic reforms initiated in 1991, the rupee was devalued three times during that year. That meant that the ship breakers bought decommissioned ships at higher prices, thus increasing their input costs. What was lucrative till then became unviable.

Unmindful of what was in store, Rati Bhai launched a public issue of Volvo Steel Ltd. 'That was the first time a Dalit launched a public issue,' says Kirit. Priced at Rs 10 a share, the shares sold well. 'Rati Bhai had that high a rating among the public,' he adds. A million and a half shares were sold.

The ships he bought were expensive. Two years into the business, he realized that the price of the raw material was close to that of the finished product. For each ship he dismantled, he lost crores of rupees. The rolling mill and shipbreaking businesses were shut one after another.

By 2001, Rati Bhai's milk pouch and plastic barrel manufacturing businesses were picking up. Although they generated a relatively modest turnover of a few crore rupees, during crunch times, it was the IPCL dealership that saved Rati Bhai from sure ruination.

However, something far worse was in store. Under the privatization drive, the government was either selling off public sector enterprises to private parties or divesting its share in them. When IPCL landed in private hands in 2002, Rati Bhai lost his IPCL dealership.

He was stranded on the Ahmedabad streets, so to speak,

Since Rati Bhai knew the polymer market and its clients, and was also familiar with the import process from his time importing fine leather for Gujarat Pickers, he saw an opportunity in imports.

Rati Bhai wasted no time after losing the IPCL dealership and launched his import business. The Internet made trading easier. While his fortunes bounced back with the import business, luck also smiled on him. The IPCL loss was made up by Rati Bhai acquiring a dealership partnering with yet another public sector venture—Gas Authority of India Ltd (GAIL).

With the GAIL dealership, Rati Bhai could restore both his business standing and status. In 2010, he secured a dealership for polymers from another public sector company, Indian Oil Corporation (IOC). In 2011–12 his group of companies had a turnover of Rs 750 crore and paid about Rs 34 crore in taxes.

His eldest son Rajesh sits in the group headquarters in Ahmedabad and looks after the IT department. His second son Mukesh is in charge of Rainbow Packaging, which has a turnover of Rs 76.92 crore. His third son Gautam oversees Rishab Packaging with Rs 11 crore in turnover. Finally, his youngest son Chirag manages the Rs 221-crore GM Exports. Rati Bhai himself takes care of Gujarat Pickers whose turnover is Rs 409 crore.

Today, the business impulse that Gala Bhai acted on so long ago is expanding and prospering within the Makwana clan.

With Rs 100 crore in turnover, Devjibhai's Suraj Filaments is the largest fishnet making company in India. The automatic machines that he imported from Canada manufacture fishing nets for the European market.

Dilipbhai's Anand Industries manufactures bag-sealing threads that are sold to fertilizer and sugar manufacturers. His turnover is Rs 25 crore.

Amrutbhai's Pankaj Plastics manufactures ropes used by the shipping industry. His turnover is Rs 10 crore.

The rest of the clan members recycle used plastic goods to manufacture yarn.

'Some of them will surprise all of us in less than a decade,' said a fellow Dalit entrepreneur who has watched Rati Bhai rise and fall and rise again. He is probably referring to Jitender Makwana who is innovative and bubbling with enthusiasm and runs Gemini Plastics. In his twenties, Jeetu holds a degree in business management.

Perhaps Gala Bhai did not anticipate just how well his clan would do, becoming trailblazers for other Dalits to follow. But perhaps he would not be surprised.

MANNAM MADHUSUDAN RAO

The wide road leading to Jubilee Hills is difficult to navigate with its heavy motor traffic and unwieldy dips and turns. The near absence of pedestrians on the road points to its being an exclusive residential area in Hyderabad, sought by those with the means to afford its dramatic hilltop views and discreetly nestled mansions, a luxury anywhere in urban India.

The major artery, Road Number 86, slices through the heart of Jubilee Hills, servicing the numerous mansions and apartment complexes that have mushroomed on its hilltops. The rich and famous of Hyderabad— film stars, politicians, contractors, big-time moneylenders, industrialists and bankers—have laid claim to the hills. Their homes provide a convenient getaway from the heat and chaos of the city below, while remaining close enough to keep tabs on their business preoccupations. So it is with Mannam Madhusudan Rao, known as MMR, who occupies a prized apartment on the hilltop.

In his late thirties, MMR owns and runs the MMR Group of Companies, involved in construction, including infrastructure projects. He is racing to complete an entire township in Rajahmundry, a project worth Rs 250 crore.

MMR's route to his coveted hilltop address began with a dinner party in September 2011 at a country club in Jubilee Hills. 'That's a dinner I didn't relish,' he now admits. 'It was more about drinks than food!'

Several guests drank heavily and a discussion on caste ensued. The previous week, Damodar Raja Narasimha, a Dalit politician, had become the state's deputy chief minister. No one in the party knew that MMR was a Dalit. Mostly an upper caste crowd, some spoke disparagingly of Dalits. 'Good thing Jubilee Hills has no Dalit resident,' said one, with apparent satisfaction.

'Pretending that I too was drunk and tired, I left the club immediately,' recalls MMR. 'Those words had hit me like shrapnel.'

That night he became determined to buy a house in Jubilee Hills. Within weeks, MMR zeroed in on a duplex apartment that stood on a hillock on Road No 86. He purchased the apartment for an undisclosed sum.

'It was certainly worth Rs 2.5 crore when MMR bought it,' says his colleague Sampat. The state's revenue minister is MMR's immediate neighbour.

The apartment's kitchen measures 450 square feet. 'That's

exactly half the size of the house we were born in,' says MMR's eldest brother Peda Mala Kondaiah.

Kondaiah has had a difficult past. Born to illiterate parents, he has seven siblings. MMR is the fifth child of their parents.

Their father Peraiah, now seventy years old, hadn't inherited any land or business from his parents. Instead he inherited his father's position as an indentured labourer, and replaced his ageing father Ramaiah when he could no longer work.

Traditionally, landlords would not plough land or harvest the crops. The hierarchies of feudalism created clear demarcations between those who did manual work and those who lorded over them. Outside the house, in the field, manual labour was performed by Dalits while inside the house the women in the landlord's household would perform the domestic chores. In addition to working on the land, the landlords would need labour to tend the many bullocks, cows and buffaloes, by fetching fodder to feed them and disposing of their dung. In this way a Dalit family would be tied with a landlord's family for generations. Thus, Peraiah replaced his father to serve the landlord for the rest of his life. His work was the only means of feeding his eleven-member family, which included his eight children, his wife and his father. His wife and grown-up children would take up odd jobs elsewhere when the landlord did not require their labour. With the need to earn a living for the family, the three eldest children never attended school.

'Food mattered more than studies,' says Kondaiah. 'More often, the family lived on boiled jowar (sorghum) and red chillies.' A coarse cereal, jowar is eaten by cattle and farm workers. Jowar would be boiled and left in a pot overnight to be fermented. The next morning, the water would be drained and the jowar would be eaten with red chilli chutney.

'Sometimes, the same stuff would be eaten for weeks together,' recalls MMR.

As farm wages were often paid with grain or other items, the family was always short of cash. MMR's mother, Ramulamma, finding it difficult to watch her husband's suffering, decided to chip in. The family lived in Palukuru, a village some 12 kilometres away from Ongole, the headquarters of Prakasam district. As a centre of tobacco production, Ongole city has a booming cottage industry, involving grading tobacco leaves, trading them, and making cigars. Together with her eldest daughter Varalakshmi, Ramulamma would walk to Ongole each day in search of work in tobacco units. Varalakshmi was hardly fifteen when she started working.

'They wore no slippers or shoes and had no tiffin boxes. I never saw them carrying water bottles, either. They ate red chillies mixed with jowar paste and drank water in the morning and in the evening after they returned from Ongole,' Kondaiah narrates with moist eyes. With the mother-daughter duo joining the workforce, some cash flowed in. Together they would make Rs 50 a day.

The cash flow, little though it was, meant an education for Madhavarao and, three years later, for his younger brother MMR.

'Putting us in school was the driver,' says Madhavarao, who did his BTech and later got a job in the government-owned telecommunications company, BSNL. 'Coming out of the clutches of the landlord was also a driver,' adds Kondaiah.

Ramulamma once heard the story of a relative's son who rode a bike. Born in similar conditions as hers, the boy got a college education, which fetched him a government job. 'They saw a spark in education that could uplift the entire family,' says Madhavarao.

After clearing the fifth standard, Madhavarao joined a junior high school some 10 kilometres from Palukuru. He was put in a government welfare hostel in Singarayakonda, where meals were free. MMR, too, followed suit. Both the brothers did well in school.

When Madhavarao was in the tenth standard and MMR in the seventh, they came home to attend the wedding of their eldest brother Kondaiah.

For the wedding, all four brothers wore new clothes. Kondaiah was in the traditional groom's attire. But most surprisingly for the visiting brothers, their father wore a dhoti till the toes.

Dhoti till the toes!

Sampat explains that in those days the upper castes wouldn't allow Dalit men to wear a dhoti till the toes. Dalit women were not permitted to button their blouses; instead, they would tie the two front ends.

'Part of the breasts would go uncovered,' he adds. 'But Dalits were allowed to dress like the upper castes for weddings in the family. That exemption was partial, though.'

As part of the wedding preparations, a structure was erected alongside the house. 'I couldn't quite understand why my parents were putting up shades along the outer walls of the house,' recalls MMR. 'I thought they were building extra rooms,' says Madhavarao.

The day after the wedding Kondaiah returned with his bride and the family had a feast. 'There was so much meat to eat,' recalls Madhavarao.

That night, the purpose of the newly built structure became apparent. Dozens of empty fertilizer bags were stitched together to form a large covering, which was mounted on the outer walls and supported by sticks. A tent-like structure had sprung up—the whole family slept in this tent. The house was reserved for the new couple to sleep in.

'That's when I realized where the family stood,' recalls MMR. 'My brother and I were now determined to make it big in life.'

A week later, Madhavarao and MMR walked back to their hostel. 'We talked through the distance of 10 kilometres,' MMR says. 'We talked really big.'

'We will buy metal pots for cooking. We will buy bicycles. We will buy fishing nets.'

'Education became the answer to all our woes,' says Madhavarao. He had passed the twelfth standard with a first division and got admission in a BTech course.

'My village folk didn't know what BTech meant,' MMR adds. 'My sisters thought that our brother had already become an officer!'

MMR, meanwhile, passed the tenth standard with a first division in 1991. Two years later, he passed the twelfth standard, again getting a first class. He was entitled to admission in a BTech course. But instead he enrolled for a three-year polytechnic course because it was cheaper.

'The very thought of putting two brothers in BTech frightened the family,' says MMR. 'Where would the money come from?'

Of the three sisters, Vijayalakshmi dropped out of school after the fourth standard. Bhulakshmi dropped out after the fifth. The youngest, Chaithanya, studied till the tenth.

'They made big sacrifices for us,' MMR and Madhavarao recall. 'They all worked as farm labourers so that the two of us could complete our studies.'

Madhavarao completed his BTech in 1997 and in the same year MMR completed a diploma in civil engineering.

According to the rules, students needed to vacate the hostel once they had completed their courses. Madhavarao and MMR now had to leave their hostels with no jobs in hand. A government job would take anywhere from one to two years to secure, from the initial vacancy notification to a candidate getting the appointment letter.

Having no recourse, the brothers returned home. As no newspapers were delivered to their village, they would walk to a nearby town to see if any suitable vacancies appeared.

In the village, meanwhile, the two brothers had become the object of curiosity. Having lived for years in a town, they had embraced an urban lifestyle. They wore trousers and shoes. They brushed their teeth and groomed their hair differently. Most villagers thought that the brothers had already become government officers.

'See how government officers look,' the villagers whispered. 'Many came just to see them,' recalls Kondaiah. But months passed and the brothers still lived with their parents.

Soon the villagers began to have doubts. 'Why would the government give them months of leave?' they wondered. Even their parents, brothers and sisters began to get nervous, for their hopes that the duo would get government jobs were fading with every passing day.

The brothers couldn't see a way out. They were overcome by guilt and shame but without knowing what they were guilty of or what they ought to be ashamed of. Unable to face the villagers' inquisitive eyes, they withdrew indoors.

An answer to their joblessness had to be found. MMR took the lead. He had realized that the government job would not materialize if they stayed in the village. They would have to be in a town. But which town?

'Vara was to be the answer,' MMR says, referring to his

eldest sister Varalakshmi. She was married to Heera Laxmiah who was illiterate and landless. After their wedding, they moved to Hyderabad. MMR had an 'idea' of Vara's life there. They would be living in a house with at least a room to spare, he thought.

The brothers took Heera's address from a postcard he had once sent them. Their sister loved them enough, they reasoned, to give them shelter for a few months, or till one of them got a job.

In March 1998 the brothers boarded a train to Hyderabad. As first-timers in the big city, they were lost and had trouble reaching Bhagat Singh Nagar in Kukatpally. There they found themselves in an area with buildings everywhere and piles of sand, cement and sundry construction material lying about. The air was thick with dust.

'We had the address confirmed twice,' says Madhavarao. They wondered how a family could possibly live in that place.

Indeed, their sister lived there. Vara greeted them with all the affection at her disposal.

'She was surprised to see us,' remembers MMR, 'because we had not informed her of our arrival.'

The brothers were astonished by the makeshift hut the family lived in, which was on a construction site where most of the labourers lived. The builder had put up tiny huts for his workers. The roof was made of cheap plastic and the floor was, well, the bare earth. He had made provisions for water.

The help the brothers had hoped to find at their sister's home was not to be found. They were dejected but Vara consoled them, 'Don't worry; you are in the right place.' She also promised to take care of them.

MMR had made up his mind. He told Madhavarao to prepare for the competitive exams and said that he would earn money. 'I knew only he, with his degree in engineering, could become an officer,' recalls MMR, 'and after all, I just had a diploma.'

That evening, both the brothers slept on the sand meant for construction. Helped by neighbours, Heera had quickly got half a dozen bags of sand and spread them out to form a 'bed' near their hut.

'The sand-bed strengthened our resolve,' MMR says. 'We had to succeed.'

Within a few days, the brothers got themselves organized. Vara and Heera had advised the brothers not to reveal their educational qualifications, remembering the unpleasant experience in the village.

MMR took up a part-time job, which entailed splashing water on the newly built walls. That required an hour each in the morning and evening. He was paid Rs 10 a day. Madhavarao would buy two newspapers—one English and the other Telugu—with the hope of finding vacancies advertised.

'We used the newspapers as bedsheets each night,' recalls MMR. 'It was fun spreading newspapers on the sand.'

A week later, MMR got a job as a night watchman at the same construction site. He was earning a salary of Rs 300 a month. Since he was free all day, he looked for extra work. A month later, he became a tutor in a nearby locality. He taught seventh standard students and made another Rs 900 a month.

'I sent my first salary to my father back home,' beams MMR. 'I asked him not to tell anyone.' He didn't want to give the impression that he and his brother had become officers and raise people's expectations.

Meanwhile, Madhavarao had found a vacancy in a central government office. Something was waiting to happen—and it did. A construction worker informed MMR of a lucrative job opportunity.

After the telecom sector was opened up to private players, companies competed for contracts to lay cables. In Hyderabad, a contractor was laying telephone cables for the Tatas.

The job at the construction site was lucrative because the six-foot-deep digging was to be done during nights only. MMR quit as night watchman to work at the cable-laying site.

'They paid Rs 400 a night,' says MMR. Being a diploma-holder in civil engineering, MMR quickly learnt the technical aspects of cable laying. Three months later, he learnt of a vacancy at G. Srinivas Reddy & Company, which specialized in cable laying. They were holding walk-in-interviews at the Hotel Grand Kakatiya in Somajiguda.

While MMR stood in the queue waiting for his turn, he overheard a conversation between two men standing nearby. A contractor, dark, plump and short, was yelling at a lean young man. Speaking in Hyderabadi Urdu, the contractor was scolding him for failing to bring enough workers the previous night.

MMR got involved in the conversation and introduced himself. He offered to bring enough workers, provided they paid some money in advance. 'Workers won't move without some advance,' he told them. As he was not known to them, the contractor was reluctant to give him an advance, so MMR didn't insist on the payment. With a promise to get twenty-five workers by ten o'clock that night, he rushed home.

MMR borrowed Rs 3,000 from his sister. 'It took hours to convince Vara,' recalls Madhavarao. With his first investment, MMR hired a mini-truck, a Tata-407, meant for ferrying workers. He then reached the village Tarapur, some 10 kilometres outside the city. MMR was sure that the workers would respond to him. His hope had a reason.

Digging manually involves risk. In one accident, a worker from Tarapur village was injured. MMR had demonstrated his kindness and had taken the worker to a hospital. He had also persuaded the contractor to pay the medical bills of the injured worker and half the salary till he recovered.

'The workers were fond of me,' he recalls. 'That's the confidence I had.'

MMR then reached Manikeshwara Nagar, close to Osmania University. The villagers were surprised to see a mini-truck rolling into their basti. It was around four in the afternoon, and some workers recognized MMR. After all, he had been working with them the previous night. They welcomed him as most of them knew of how he had helped a fellow injured worker. MMR was heard with patience. 'They all empathized with me,' he says.

But there was a problem. Most of the workers had been booked in advance by another company for a site elsewhere in the city. But luckily, of the fifty workers booked, twenty had not taken any advance. Fifteen agreed to forego the other job and join MMR instead. One suggested that MMR drive to a nearby village where over a dozen workers would surely be found. MMR agreed and upon reaching the village, he was able to hire thirty workers more. With forty-five workers, MMR headed to the site.

'I sat next to the driver,' says MMR. The rest of the workers rode in the back of the truck. The workers were delighted that they were being transported by truck. The contractor came to the site to see how truthful the young man was. He saw dozens of workers waiting for him. He was delighted and bought food for them all.

Overnight, MMR's men dug a 100-metre-long channel, laid cables and covered the trench. The contractor was pleased. He gave MMR Rs 20,000 and asked him to bring a hundred workers the following day. MMR had made a profit of Rs 13,000.

'It was fantastic!' recalls MMR. 'I had never seen that much money before.'

He reached Bhagat Singh Nagar by autorickshaw. He had to pay the driver Rs 100. He requested Vara to get the money from the hut. Reluctantly, she went inside. As MMR was waiting for Vara to return, Heera noticed the auto parked outside his hut. Curious, he rushed to the spot. MMR had meanwhile gone into the hut to find out why his sister was taking so long to get the money.

'Why that much money?' asked his furious brother-in-law.

MMR told him that he had agreed to the huge fare because he was carrying Rs 13,000 in his pocket. He wanted to reach home at the earliest and safely.

MMR's explanation pacified Heera but his brother-in-law was still wary. 'I have been in this city for years but have not seen this much cash,' he confided to his wife. 'Please keep an eye on your younger brother's activities.'

That evening, MMR hired three Tata-407 mini-trucks. The previous day, he had risked lives by putting forty-five workers in one truck. He collected the workers from the two villages that he had visited the day before and reached the site rather early. MMR offered food to all the workers. After their meal, they had at least an hour to relax as work would start at ten o'clock that night.

The contractor arrived at around eight and was thrilled to see a hundred workers at the site. He asked MMR to come to his home early the next morning to collect wages for the workers for that day, and also some advance.

'One lakh,' the contractor whispered into MMR's ears.

'I stood for about half a minute with my eyes shut,' MMR recalls. 'God has heard my cries.'

MMR appointed a worker as supervisor to oversee the work, while he took an autorickshaw back to his sister's place so he could request his brother and brother-in-law to join him at the site the next morning. He wanted them to be with him when he received the large cash payment and also see how legitimate his business was. Both agreed and he returned to the site.

The next morning, as MMR was supervising the boarding of his men into the trucks, Madhavarao and Heera arrived. The three drank tea at a roadside shop and left for the contractor's house.

An hour later, they reached their destination. The contractor came out and complimented MMR on his efficiency. He gave him a bundle of currency and told him it was one lakh!

MMR then took the contractor aside and whispered something to him. The contractor gave a nod of approval immediately.

MMR, Heera and Madhavarao were taken into a room where they 'dressed' themselves in currency notes. They took off their trousers and using pieces of cloth that Heera had brought, tied rupee notes around their waists. Dressed again, they walked 17 kilometres to reach home. They didn't want to take any chances.

'Pickpockets roamed freely in city buses,' explained MMR.

Once inside the hut, they heaved a sigh of relief. Vara had cooked chicken and rice. They relished the lunch and debated where to keep the money. It was a real risk keeping such a large amount in their hut.

'What if the hut catches fire,' Vara feared. Finally, they decided to ask Narahari, the contractor on whose site Heera and Vara worked, to keep the money for them. 'He has known us for over two years,' Heera said. 'He will agree.'

Vara was asked to leave the hut while they 'undressed' the money, which they then placed in ten packets. Each packet contained Rs 10,000. Meanwhile, Heera was sent to seek the consent of Narahari.

Heera was back within half an hour. Narahari had agreed to keep the money.

'Have you all won a lottery?' Narahari asked in a lighter vein.

Before leaving for Narahari's house, MMR showed the money packets to his sister as well. She was allowed to hold the money in her hands for a while.

'With currency packets in her hands, she looked at me with disbelief,' MMR said. The story was overwhelming for Narahari as well. He had nothing but praise for MMR.

That evening, MMR reached the workers' villages with fifty kilos of laddoos. He took three truck-loads of workers to the site.

'All of a sudden, things turned upside down,' recollects MMR. The contractor was virtually in tears because a court had banned the work at the site. Someone had petitioned the court against laying the cables and the court had stayed any activity till further orders.

MMR paid the workers their full wages and sent them back in the trucks. The following day, he took the remaining money from Narahari and headed to the contractor's house.

The contractor refused to take the money back. 'You may have already spent a lot,' he told MMR.

'He wanted to keep me in good humour,' recalls MMR. Work could start at any time.

With the dream run ending abruptly, the brothers returned to their village for the Sankranti festival. They had bought clothes for the entire family. 'We carried a trunk,' says MMR.

Family members and villagers concluded that the brothers had indeed become government officers.

After staying in the village for four days, they returned to Hyderabad and rented a room in the locality where Heera lived. Vara helped them to buy utensils so that her brothers could cook their own food.

In their search for opportunities, MMR met with Colonel Krishnan, under whom he had worked as a labourer for three months. 'Do you want to work?' the colonel asked and offered him a job immediately. MMR explained his experiences as a sub-contractor. Krishnan listened to MMR's full story and educational background.

The colonel gave MMR a contract worth Rs 5 lakh, and was soon impressed by MMR's work. 'Delivering work before time was most rewarding,' MMR says.

The brothers now shifted to a two-bedroom house. MMR hired a separate space to store the digging equipment. He also secured orders from ASTRA Tele Services and ARM Ltd.

Meanwhile, Madhavarao was interviewed by the state-owned BSNL for the post of assistant manager.

The cable-laying business worked on a formula that would be disadvantageous to small contractors. If a contractor laid a cable for 100 metres, he would receive no advance. He would have to meet expenses from his own pocket initially.

MMR had saved Rs 50,000 from his first job with the contractor, and used that money to do business with the colonel. But when he got a contract worth Rs 10 lakh, he needed to borrow money. He went to Heera's employer Narahari and sought a loan of Rs 5 lakh. Narahari gave him the money on daily interest. MMR completed the work in ten days, and cleared the debt with interest.

By July 1999, MMR had completed contracts worth Rs 50 lakh. He was doing well. Still, MMR did not have a company and conducted all the transactions in cash.

Colonel Krishnan advised him to form a company if he had the ambition. MMR approached Narahari who had seen him growing from a night watchman to a successful sub-contractor. He knew MMR to be a man with an exceptional ability to mobilize workers, manage them well and execute work before time. He also respected MMR's integrity.

'Why don't we form a joint venture?' Narahari proposed. 'My wife can be a 49 per cent stakeholder.'

MMR agreed readily. He needed someone like Narahari to mentor him. Narahari was trustworthy. Also, he had plenty of money and MMR had the skill.

'I was so happy,' says MMR. 'We formed a joint venture company.'

With Narahari's wife Lakshmi as a partner, Sairam Constructions came into being. With MMR's efforts, Sairam Constructions got an order from Global Tele Systems (GTS). The task involved laying cables from Kodad to Vijayawada, further extending till Eluru—a 200-km stretch. Billed at Rs 60,000 a kilometre, the whole project amounted to Rs 1.2 crore—MMR's biggest order till then.

'It was a dream coming true,' recalls he.

Sairam Constructions had to manage two sites. One was in Hyderabad, the main office which handled the rountine work and the other at Kodad–Vijayawada. As the team leader, MMR had taken a decision: He had to be on the new site outside Hyderabad, which would have local workers. The experienced ones had to be taken from Hyderabad, as cable-laying is very technical. 'We needed to build a mobile colony,' he says.

MMR moved to the new site leaving the Hyderabad operations in the hands of the staff of Sairam Constructions, who had been newly hired. Lakshmi, Narahari's wife, had no business experience. MMR was executing the work for GTS, which was going well. Every week, GTS would make payments by cheque to Sairam Constructions. Someone from Sairam Constructions would then carry cash to the site to pay the workers who didn't have bank accounts.

When the GTS project was completed in 2000, MMR returned to Hyderabad. Meanwhile, the marriage of his third sister Vijayalakshmi had been fixed. MMR gave Rs 50,000 to his parents.

'It was big news back home,' said MMR. 'An untouchable has spent so much.'

After his sister's wedding, MMR returned to Hyderabad and called a board meeting of Sairam Constructions.

'We are running at a loss,' said the men who were appointed on the recommendations of Narahari. MMR was shocked. Where had all the money gone?

MMR had left signed cheques with the company to take care of expenses in Hyderabad. Who had stolen the cheques worth millions? MMR would not say anything. 'Sure enough, Narahari was not the man.'

After completing his largest project—worth Rs 1.2 crore—MMR was back to zero. 'There was darkness around,' remembers MMR, 'I felt cheated and shattered.'

'He was thoroughly dejected,' said Madhavarao. 'He wouldn't sleep'.

MMR roamed the city aimlessly. He would borrow money from friends and watch movies. 'Sometimes he would watch three movies a day,' Madhavarao recalls. 'He wouldn't feel hungry.'

Good news was in store, though. Madhavarao had got a job with BSNL and joined its office in Bihar. 'With my brother joining BSNL, I felt reassured,' says MMR.

Months passed and MMR continued to live aimlessly in Hyderabad. 'Almost for a year, I did nothing,' he recollects. 'Madhavarao would sustain me.'

One evening, when MMR was at a theatre watching a movie, he happened to meet his old friend Rameshwaram during the intermission.

After the show, MMR told him his story. Rameshwaram asked MMR to meet him in his office the following day. Rameshwaram, along with his friends, had formed a company named Precision Engineering.

The next day MMR was offered a job at a salary of Rs 10,000 a month. His responsibility was to get orders for the company. Using his old contacts, he got orders worth crores of rupees. As a reward, his salary was hiked to Rs 16,000.

One day while perusing a newspaper, MMR glanced through the matrimonial section and found a promising matrimonial ad for a young Dalit woman who was a government employee.

'A working wife would be a great support,' he thought. 'With her assured monthly income, I could take business risks.'

A couple of weeks later, MMR approached the young woman's parents. The young woman, Padmalata, agreed to the proposal on one condition: MMR would never return to business again. 'You are a failed businessman,' she reminded him.

Soon Padmalata and MMR were married. But MMR's love for business hadn't waned. 'He was determined to succeed as a businessman,' says Madhavarao.

'I know it was unethical,' MMR confesses. 'But I still saw enterprise as my career.'

Though he earned Rs 16,000 a month, MMR told Padmalata he earned Rs 10,000, keeping the rest for his future business ventures.

The couple had rented a small house in Hyderabad. One day, a postman delivered a letter for MMR while he was away on a business trip. Padmalata didn't open it as it was addressed to MMR. But she was suspicious as it came from the Department of Industry.

Once back home, MMR had to admit that he had registered a company. It is a testament to his persuasive skills and patience that Padmalata came on board and MMR could openly think of business as his career path.

With his own company registered, MMR approached the managers of GTS once again. They were happy to see him and empathized with the budding entrepreneur.

MMR got an order worth Rs 3 lakh. He went to his employers at Precision Engineering and pleaded with them to relieve him. They were unwilling. To retain him, they even offered him a partnership. Having become wiser on partnerships, he turned down the offer and parted ways.

To complete the GTS project, MMR needed at least Rs 1.5 lakh. He had a third of that and Anasuya, Padmalata's elder sister, gave the rest. She had been a great help since MMR had married her sister.

MMR completed the work within a month and made a profit of Rs 1 lakh. Even his in-laws were impressed!

In 2004–05, MMR had a turnover of Rs 16 lakh. A

Rs 50-lakh contract came his way from Vodafone. He completed the cable laying in a record forty-five days. More orders followed. MMR bought a two-bedroom house in 2006 and a small car the following year.

By 2009, MMR had emerged as a lead vendor for the major telecom firms in Andhra Pradesh, including Vodafone, Airtel and Tata Telecom.

By 2010, the turnover of the MMR Group of Companies had crossed Rs 50 crore.

MMR has now diversified his operations to include power projects and townships, in addition to his core telecom business.

MMR's next dream: to acquire a mansion on Road Number 86! And he did.

MURALI MOHAN

'Victuz Exports! We have reached our destination,' announces Krishna Kumar Gowda, long-time friend of Murali Mohan, owner of Victuz Exports. Krishna is in his thirties and has a cheerful disposition. He manufactures electronic ancillaries used by auto makers, both for the domestic market as well as for exports. Thirty-eight-year-old Murali is mild-mannered and seems more like an academic than a business person.

A dark-blue BMW grinds to a stop in front of the imposing office of Victuz Exports. Krishna is driving because Murali needs to speak to a team member. Raja Nayak, president of the Karnataka state chapter of the Dalit Indian Chamber of Commerce and Industry (DICCI), is also in the car.

Admittance to Victuz Exports is an exercise. Visitors take off their shoes and socks and wear sterilized socks, blue slippers and surgical face masks provided by the staff.

'That's the laboratory,' Murali says by way of explaining the precautions. The laboratory has rows of neatly arranged kits, tools, gadgets and bottles filled with chemicals, like a manicured garden. 'Our products are governed by the rules stipulated by the Food and Drug Administration (FDA) of the United States,' he continues as he leads the group of visitors winding their way through the laboratory to the food processing unit. 'The FDA has high standards for quality control.'

Victuz Exports Pvt. Ltd exports processed gherkins, white onions, green chillies, baby corn, cherry tomatoes and other vegetables to markets in North America, France, Spain and Russia. With three collection centres spread across the Bellary and Kolar districts, several dozen teams fan out every morning to collect freshly plucked gherkins and other vegetables from farmers. 'We engage close to 3,000 farmers who grow gherkins for us,' Murali says.

In less than two years in business, Victuz has exported 200 containers of processed vegetables and hit a turnover of Rs 45 crore. Of the 200 containers that Victuz exported, 70 per cent were pickled gherkins.

'Almost a jackpot,' says Raja Nayak.

'By the end of 2014, Victuz will have crossed Rs 100 crore in turnover,' projects Krishna. 'Up until now Murali didn't have a large enough infrastructure. Importees from US and Europe place bulk orders.'

The first step in processing is cleaning and separating the gherkins. With water flowing at high pressure, brush washers clean the vegetables. Today, over fifty women, neatly dressed in orange uniforms and imported rubber gloves, are sorting the gherkins according to their size. The smaller the fruit, the higher the price!

After the cleaning and separating, the gherkins are never touched by hand. Another machine, a separator, separates the gherkins into groups of identically sized gherkins. Once graded, machines push them to another area where drums and bottles half filled with vinegar await. A few steps later the bottled gherkins are ready for the packaging unit.

The food technologist heading the entire process shows the visitors how the empty drums and bottles are sanitized before being filled with fruits and vegetables, but is reluctant to elaborate on the pickling processes.

On the drive back to Bengaluru, Murali shares his life story. He received his MSc in biotechnology from Mysore University. Determined to become an agro-scientist, he studied hard and stood second in his MSc examinations in his college. In May 1996, while he was waiting for his MSc results, his professor had advised him to join the Central Food Technological Research Institute (CFTRI) in Mysore and pursue a postgraduate programme. With his high marks, Murali was easily admitted.

In 1998, supported by a monthly stipend of Rs 800, Murali completed his two-year diploma course in food technology. He was offered a job at the CFTRI laboratory for Rs 2,500 a month. Friends and relatives celebrated his becoming a scientist.

'After God come doctors and scientists,' says Murali's father Venkatappa. 'We thought like that those days.' In his early sixties, Venkatappa heads the gherkin-collection centre near his village.

Murali specialized in processed vegetables during his diploma at CFTRI, but he specialized in gherkins during his laboratory job. 'I had fallen in love with gherkins,' he says.

One day a senior scientist at CFTRI invited Murali over for a cup of tea: a representative from Koeleman India Pvt. Ltd was looking for a young food technologist.

A subsidiary of Koeleman Foods International, a Netherlands-based company, Koeleman India was set up in Karnataka to source gherkins and vegetables. Gherkins produced and pickled in India are popular all over the world. 'Because of our soil,' explains Murali, 'Indian gherkins are flavourful and foreigners relish them.' Karnataka, with its soil and climate conducive to growing crops, occupies pride of place when it comes to horticulture.

Murali joined Koeleman in March 1999 at a salary of Rs 4,000. 'It was big news back home,' he says. 'My mother didn't believe it. She was earning Rs 25 a day then.'

Assigned to the pickling division of the company, Murali was amazed to see the kind of equipment used for processing. In 2001 he left Koeleman and joined an Indian company, SMS Foods, at a salary of Rs 8,000, a big raise, he concedes.

Murali introduced the hygiene and quality standards that had been practised at Koeleman, adding value at SMS Foods. 'I impressed the CEO of SMS Foods,' he recalls. He was shifted to the outsourcing division, where he would deal with farmers producing gherkins and other vegetables. It was common for companies to enter into contract farming with farmers who would be given seeds, pesticides and sometimes even advance payment, apart from free consultancy. Every morning, dozens of teams riding in transport trucks equipped with weighing scales and registers would fan out in villages to collect freshly plucked gherkins. Farmers would bring their produce to the roadsides where teams would pick the produce.

As the head of the outsourcing division, Murali earned a name for himself. He introduced the system of crop insurance, which farmers greatly appreciated. If the yield fell by 50 per cent, half of that would be compensated by the company. He also introduced a system of rewards for high-quality produce. 'Just a gift of a nice sari would make women farmers so happy,' says Murali. 'The farmers spoke well of me.'

In 2004 Murali shifted to a new company, Vishaal Natural Food Products, at a salary of Rs 10,000 a month. At Vishaal he joined the marketing division, which enabled him to communicate with clients abroad. Fluent in English and interested in the cyberworld, Murali did well in marketing. Within a year, his salary was raised to Rs 12,000.

In October 2006, while at Vishaal, Murali was approached by Cyril Kariyawasan, who was from Sri Lanka but well known in the food processing business in Karnataka, to work with him. Cyril offered Murali Rs 30,000 a month to persuade him to join him. 'I thought he was joking. I earned Rs 18,000 a month then. He was offering me Rs 1,000 a day! I thanked God.'

Murali had worked under Cyril when he was at SMS Foods. At the time, however, Cyril had returned to Sri Lanka after the tragic death of his young son in 2004. He had helplessly watched the tsunami devour his son.

Cyril returned to Karnataka when a builder in Bengaluru decided to start exporting gherkins. The builder was told that only 30 per cent of the world demand for gherkins was met. 'He had enough money to play around,' says Murali of the builder, whose company he is reluctant to name, but who is still in business and competing with him.

Industry insiders advised the builder to invite Cyril to set up his plant, saying that he would bring in business as well. The builder flew to Sri Lanka to meet Cyril, who agreed to work for the new employer and set up his plant.

'He was offered the moon,' recalls Murali.

Cyril landed in Bengaluru and began to build the team. Highly respected in the food processing industry, he picked the best workers. He had set his own conditions, which included hiring Murali at a salary of Rs 30,000 a month.

'You are the most highly educated person in the industry,' he said when Murali asked the reason behind the generous offer. 'I am offering good money to those I hire,' he assured.

'He believed in my abilities,' recalls Murali.

Murali had the plant installed within five months. Building the factory shed and the warehouse had delayed the production. Meanwhile, although the factory had yet to become operational, the first order for pickled gherkins came from Barcelona.

'We had an order worth sixty containers,' says Murali. 'The business came from Cyril's contact.'

Everyone, from the blue-collar workers to the owner, was thrilled with the bulk order from Barcelona. Cyril, however, had become suspicious of the owner and didn't trust him. Apparently, the owner had agreed to pay Cyril a hefty commission on the business orders he generated, apart from his salary and other perks, but was defaulting on these and other promises that he made.

'Angry, Cyril left the company and flew back to Sri Lanka,' recalls Murali.

The owner had invested over Rs 2 crore in the plant and machinery. Lakhs of rupees had been paid to gherkin farmers in advance. An army of over 100 workers had already been hired. And the lucrative order from Barcelona awaited supplies.

'Can you run the factory and fulfil the Barcelona orders?' the owner asked Murali. A thrilled Murali jumped at the offer.

The owner hiked Murali's salary to Rs 45,000. He also offered Murali extra money for overtime, a bonus, a chauffeur-driven car and a two-bedroom flat.

Murali worked on the sixty-container order on a war footing. By November 2007, the company, thanks to Murali's efforts, had completed the order for the Barcelona importer.

'Farmers stood by me,' recalls Murali. 'Incentives to workers had made a difference.'

This order was followed by one from Reitzel International of Brazil, a reputed company dealing in processed vegetables, which placed an order for 400 containers to be supplied by the end of 2008.

However, since this was beyond the limited capacity of the company, it could only supply 150 containers to Reitzel.

'Even a small order of 150 containers was in itself a record for a start-up company,' recalls Krishna. 'The company had crossed Rs 25 crore in turnover.'

Early in 2009, Murali was approached by Murali Sunadar, a Canadian of Sri Lankan origin, whose company is one of the largest in the gherkin business in North America. 'He became our largest client,' recalls Murali. 'We both became friends after his first visit to Karnataka.'

While the first container was being readied to be shipped to the US, Sunadar made a surprise visit to Bengaluru. Over the next three days, he visited plants and checked the ingredients used during the pickling process.

'Sunadar asked us all kinds of questions,' recalls Murali, 'as if we were employing unacceptable practices. He was strict about the issues of hygiene and quality.'

By the end of 2010, the turnover of the company had crossed Rs 100 crore. The owner raised Murali's salary to Rs 1 lakh a month. Murali had total control of the company and was promised a stake in the company. He worked tirelessly.

The owner had promised Murali a 5 per cent stake in the company once its turnover reached a 100 crore.

'Where is my 5 per cent?' Murali reminded the owner gently.

In mid-2012, when the company's turnover reached Rs 200 crore, Murali was shocked to learn that the company had been sold.

One day, three people entered the factory premises. When the receptionist asked for their identities and purpose of their visit, one of the visitors called the owner, who directed the receptionist to grant the visitors entry.

Once inside, the visitors wanted a tour of the facilities. The duty manager called Murali on his cell phone to tell him about the unusual visitors. Within an hour, Murali reached the factory.

'We plan to buy your company, plant and machinery,' they told Murali when he confronted them about why they were inspecting the machines.

Murali learnt later that the owner had sold the company to a large Indian corporation that was in the food business. The now ex-owner of the company told Murali, 'Let us develop a new brand and you will enjoy a quarter stake.'

'It's over,' Murali told the owner.

The owner offered Murali Rs 25 lakh to win him back.

'No thanks,' Murali told him politely, resolving never to trust him again.

Since Murali dealt with farmers who grew gherkins and

other vegetables, he wondered what they should do with their standing crops. He also had to respond to the importers who kept asking him about supplies.

'I was sandwiched between the farmers and importers,' recalls Murali. 'It was a tense time.'

Three weeks after the plant closed, Sunadar phoned Murali to discuss new import opportunities. They spoke in detail and zeroed in on a scheme— Murali would now become an entrepreneur himself.

'Launch your own processing unit,' Sunadar insisted. 'I will pay for forty containers in advance,' he offered.

Murali needed about Rs 3 crore to buy a plant and machinery. He needed another one crore to invest in infrastructure, manpower and advances to farmers.

'Finding a factory shed and a warehouse was another challenge,' he recalls.

Murali and Sunadar conceived of a bold business plan. Sunadar would place a large business order with Victuz Exports Pvt. Ltd, which Murali would form, and pay the money in advance. Murali would use this money to buy critical equipment and use the import order as collateral for banks to get a loan of Rs 2.5 crore.

'I had to make a project report for the bank to obtain the loan,' recalls Murali.

While professionals worked on the project report for Victuz Exports, Murali was engaged in a war of nerves with his former employer, who had learned that Murali was contemplating setting up his own business. Since he was also interested in starting up a new business, he was worried that his entire team of professionals might go over to Murali. 'Farmers might prefer Murali,' the ex-employer told an industry insider.

Murali had set up a team of professionals who would pursue banks for quick loan disbursements, and another team to procure machinery and other infrastructure materials. Meanwhile, Murali went on a search for a factory shed and a warehouse.

By the time Murali received the news that a bank had agreed to the requested loan, he had found a factory shed near Bellary, Karnataka's vegetable basket.

'It was a do-or-die situation for me,' recalls Murali. His team had identified a warehouse as well.

Murali procured two containers of vinegar from the US. This was a top-quality product, which gave the pickled gherkins a long shelf life. It also saved Murali from buying drums from the local market since he could use the drums that the vinegar was shipped in.

With the preparations underway, Murali began procuring gherkins from farmers, who were eager to unload their fruit. 'We took a big decision,' recalls Murali, 'and my rivals were stumped.'

However, once Murali had procured the gherkins he innovated by reversing the gherkin processing. The traditional process involves first washing the raw gherkins in machines, then separating them manually according to their size, and then further by separator machines that group the fruits in precise sizes. After they are separated, gherkins go in drums with vinegar and the pickling process begins.

Since Murali had yet to procure separators and the all-important packaging machine, he began by washing the gherkins manually, keeping a high standard of hygiene, and then placing the fruits in drums that were filled with American vinegar. Once immersed in vinegar, the gherkins would not perish for over three years.

'Rivals wondered what I was doing with the raw gherkins that I was procuring from farmers,' recalls Murali. 'They thought I was mad! But I knew my product was safe.'

Within three months, the Victuz processing plant was set up. With the machines and equipment ready, Murali's workers took the gherkins from the 240-litre-capacity drums and separated the fruits according to their sizes. Once separated, the fruits were put back in the drums to undergo the pickling process.

'No one in the industry knew about our operations,' says Murali.

At present, Murali is setting up a new plant in Chokkapura village, near Narasapura Hobli, 400 kilometres from Bellary. Spread over four acres of farmland that has now been designated as an industrial plot, the new plant is expected to be operational by the end of 2014. The significance of the location becomes clear when one realizes that it is near Murali's native village.

'I want to empower farmers around my village,' says Murali. 'I am not shutting the business at Bellary. I am expanding.'

* * *

Born to illiterate parents in Chowdadena Halli village in Kolar district, Murali had witnessed his parents almost starve at times so that he and his two siblings, an elder brother and a younger sister, could eat. Though a good student, his elder brother had dropped out by the middle of the eighth standard.

The primary school, till the seventh standard, was in the village but the next level school, from standards eighth to tenth, was 5 kilometres away. Murali needed Rs 2 a day to commute to and fro. 'I could not afford it,' repents Venkatappa. 'We were rarely paid in cash.'

Murali's sister had dropped out after her fifth standard.

A nallah divides the village in two—the upper caste area with the big houses on one side and the Dalit hamlet with smaller homes on the other. Not much has changed in the village since the time Murali was born here.

A 10x10-square-foot house set away from the lane is where Murali was born. Now locked and abandoned, the door to the house is so low that one has to bend to enter.

Murali had requested some of his neighbours to host us. Two persons, Parvathamma, aged sixty-five, and Chandrayappa, aged forty-five, arrived and after the initial greeting, vanished only to return minutes later with biscuits and water tumblers.

'Murali was born in this house,' recalls Parvathamma.

Murali's parents and his two siblings—a total of five—and his aged and ailing grandparents lived in the tiny house, with no windows, running water, or electricity. There is a little open space in front.

'Most houses are similar in size,' says Parvathamma. 'Look at the house I live in,' she points to a house nearby.

By early afternoon there was still no sign of lunch being served. The team had requested Murali to arrange for the lunch that he most often ate in his childhood.

'No one ate lunch in this hamlet,' says Parvathamma with a laugh. 'But we have something for you,' adds Chandrayappa.

Parvathamma invited the team for lunch. She served country chicken curry and boiled white rice.

'We don't want to serve food that cattle eat today,' explains Parvathamma. 'No one eats that kind of food any more.'

During lunch, Murali arrives. People from the neighbourhood gather to see the visitors from the city.

'All the upper caste people in the village put together equal one Murali,' says an elderly man. 'He can buy all the farmland in the village.'

The team sits under a tamarind tree. 'Tamarind trees sustained this hamlet,' says Murali. He adds that people in this hamlet didn't need potatoes, onions, or other vegetables—raw tamarind pods were used as a side dish. The ripened pods were used to make delicious chutney.

Murali's father Venkatappa arrives with fruits and sweets.

'I never allowed my kids to starve,' recalls Venkatappa. 'We sacrificed our meals instead.'

The rainy seasons were the worst for Dalits as all farm work stopped. Venkatappa explains how he raised a couple of goats and hens. During times of scarcity, he would sell a goat to raise money. The milk and eggs were sold in the nearby market. 'Upper caste people wouldn't buy our chickens and eggs.'

Though Venkatappa raised chickens, he hardly had anything to eat. 'There was so much poverty,' he recalls. 'We saw currency notes only in our dreams.'

Murali leads the team to the village temple, which is beautiful and kept spotlessly clean. His father draws attention to three stones outside the temple building.

'These three stones are our gods,' says Venkatappa. 'We are not allowed to go beyond these stones. Not even today.'

'These are the symbols of inhumanity,' says Raja.

'All villages have Dalit gods segregated,' Krishna says.

Venkatappa points to a large pond in the distance. 'We fished in the pond,' he says with a laugh, 'entering it when upper caste people had already fished. We fished whatever was left.'

He explains that before the summer set in, the pond would begin to dry up. The upper caste people would be the first to raid the pond to catch fish, before it dried up completely. It was only after the upper caste people had taken their fill, that the Dalits were allowed to enter the pond and catch fish.

'We hunted frogs and a variety of fish that hide in the clay,' says another Dalit.

* * *

Murali showed great promise by the time he was enrolled for his eighth standard in the Bhartha Rathna Mokshagundam Visveswaraya School (BRMV), which was 5 kilometres away. His teacher would often ask him to teach maths and other subjects to his classmates. To get to the school, he would have had to pay for the conveyance.

A few months into his eighth standard, Murali stopped going to school. His teacher A.R. Krishna Rao got anxious. After a week had passed and Murali had still not shown up at school, Krishna Rao got worried. He remembered how Murali's elder brother had dropped out halfway through the eighth standard.

Rao instructed a student who came from the neighbouring village to find out why Murali had stopped attending school. The student reported back that Murali's grandfather had fallen ill and so Murali had been absent.

Rao asked the student to send Murali's father to school.

Venkatappa met Rao at the latter's home. He explained why Murali had dropped out.

'My father is ill,' Venkatappa told him. 'Whatever money

I have is going to his treatment.' He further explained that it cost Rs 2 a day to travel from the village to school and back.

'But your son is a genius,' Rao told Venkatappa. 'He will become a big scientist.'

A humanitarian and a Brahmin, Rao made a proposal that lit up Venkatappa's eyes: Murali could shift to his residence, live, eat, study, take tuitions—all for free, but on the condition that Murali would clean the house, wash clothes and do odd jobs.

'That's what I can do for your son who is so bright and talented,' Rao had told Venkatappa.

'Will Murali be living in a Brahmin house?' Venkatappa asked himself. 'Maybe my son was a Brahmin in his previous birth.'

'I agreed immediately,' recalls Venkatappa.

'Bring your eating plates,' Rao had told Murali.

Excited, Venkatappa took his son to Rao's house the very next day. Murali was assigned a place where he would sleep, keep his bags, clothes and plates.

'It was like being in heaven,' recalls Murali about his first day at Rao's house. 'I got to eat an unlimited amount of rice and sambar the very first evening,' he adds. 'I drank a glass of rasam.'

'He fed me what he ate himself,' recalls Murali. He would get up five in the morning every day and study under a lamp.

Rao ran a tuition centre from his home. Every evening, a dozen students would come to take tuition.

'They all paid Rs 25 a month,' recollects Murali.

Murali shifted to Rao's house in 1987, and lived there for three years, leaving only after he passed his tenth standard in 1990. Murali proved his teacher Rao right when he secured 90 per cent in maths and above 75 per cent overall.

'He passed the tenth standard with distinction,' Krishna recalls. Both students and parents wondered how a servant boy could clear the tenth with distinction in all subjects.

After the results came in, the father-son duo went to meet Rao and thanked him.

'Father touched his feet and so did I,' recalls Murali. Rao talked to Venkatappa in detail about Murali's future.

Venkatappa told Rao that he wanted at least one of his children to continue their education. But sending Murali to Bengaluru was beyond his means. There was no school beyond the tenth standard nearby.

'What property do you have?' Rao asked Venkatappa.

'Some farmland,' he replied, 'that is worth Rs 30,000 or so.'

'Sell that land and send Murali to Bengaluru for his intermediate,' Rao virtually ordered Venkatappa.

A week later, Venkatappa left for Bengaluru to explore the possibility of enrolling Murali in a school. 'I had a relative who lived in the city,' recalls Venkatappa. 'He was a clerk in the postal department. He couldn't believe that my son had passed with distinction,' recalls Venkatappa. '"Are you sure?" he kept asking.'

The relative assured Venkatappa that Murali would get into a college of his choice. A month later, Murali joined Vijaya College for his intermediate. The college offered courses up to the Master's level.

'I was thrilled to wear sandals that my father bought for me,' recalls Murali. 'Until my high school, I never had slippers or sandals.'

Murali secured a seat in a hostel meant for underprivileged students. 'Three meals a day came for free.' The state government had built the hostel. 'They charged no rent and provided food free of cost,' says Murali.

Murali completed his BSc in 1995, securing a first class with 86 per cent and enrolled for an MSc in biotechnology.

Why not a government job?

Since his eighth-standard days, Murali's teacher Rao had all but brainwashed him into becoming a scientist.

'We have this modern world because of science and scientists,' Rao told Murali countless times. 'Go to the district headquarters and you will find officers as numerous as flies.'

'I am an accidental entrepreneur,' smiles Murali. His firm currently exports a hundred drums of gherkins and vegetables each day.

* * *

When they were growing up, Murali's mother Rajamma made sure that the family always had a good goat and milked it to feed her kids. An elderly lady, Faruttma, recalls, laughing loudly, 'She secretly gave both her sons boiled eggs, which she would boil in my house so that others didn't see.'

His eyes moistening, Murali recollects his father trekking 5 kilometres to meet him once a month when he was in high school. Venkatappa didn't own slippers or sandals, leave alone shoes, and the soles of his feet were always cracked. 'His soles often bled,' says Murali. 'My parents lived sub-human lives.'

'What can I gift my mother?' asks Murali wistfully.

Then he smiles. 'My father will be CEO of this plant and ride a Mercedes,' he says. 'This is my tribute to my parents. My mother will supervise the operations at the outsourcing centres.'

What's next?

'I'm planning to set up a plastic drum manufacturing plant,' Murali says. Victuz procures over 3,000 drums a month. A drum costs around Rs 1,000; the company spends over Rs 30 lakh on drums alone.

'Only Sunadar sends me vinegar in drums,' says Murali. For importers in Europe and Russia, Murali buys drums from the market.

'Karnataka has a huge demand of export-worthy drums,' he says. 'If things go according to my plan, the plastic drum business can become bigger than the processed vegetable business.'

RAVI KUMAR NARRA

Ravi Kumar Narra is a satisfied man. He has just been awarded the Padma Shri by the President of India in recognition of his accomplishments as a businessman. He is only the fourth Dalit business person to enjoy this national honour. At fifty years of age, the award is a timely acknowledgement, something Ravi needed. It's not so much to convince himself of his abilities, nor is it to settle some old scores (though he would dearly want his in-laws to realize that their daughter was astute when she fell in love with him). Over and above all else, the Padma Shri award is a shot in his arm to enthusiastically continue in his mission to promote entrepreneurship among Dalits.

With an annual turnover of Rs 10 crore, Ravi's businesses range from construction to digital services, infrastructure and other fields. His two firms, Aditya Nirman Pvt. Ltd and M/s Aditya Communications are at the heart of his business operations. He provides employment to around 200 persons directly and to 2,000 more indirectly. His crusade for a caste-free society has earned him a considerable following in Hyderabad. He is also the south India coordinator and state president of the Andhra Pradesh chapter of Dalit Indian Chamber of Commerce and Industry (DICCI). These are quite impressive accomplishments for the son of parents who were slum dwellers, and who only has memories of poverty and hardship from his childhood.

Today, he has an ensured steady stream of income that keeps the home-hearth burning. Economic independence has meant freedom from worries about providing for his wife and children. His success reflects some of the life lessons Ravi had directly learnt from the late N.T. Rama Rao, one time chief minister of his state and a popular film star.

'My life has been a roller-coaster,' says Ravi with a smile, adding after a pause, 'with the downs lasting longer than the ups.' Sitting in the lounge of Delhi's Ashoka Hotel, he adds, 'But rueing my fate is not in my nature.' He arrived from Hyderabad a couple of days ago along with his wife Vanajakshi and sons Aditya Rithvik and Aditya Rohan—as a guest of the government—to receive the Padma Shri award.

As news of the award spread, Ravi began receiving phone calls and visits from different political parties and 'old' friends in politics. With India gripped by the frenzy of general elections and his state, Telangana, also having state assembly polls, several parties have been enquiring if he has reneged on his 2009 decision to quit politics. And now, given the accolades he's been receiving, more than one political party is keen to give him its nomination to contest the elections. And why not? He has established his reputation as a successful businessman; and with the Padma Shri, his standing within the community has been elevated a few notches. Isn't it then conceivable, logical, and likely to be smart to take one more dip in politics?

'No. It's a firm no to politics,' he says, clenching his right fist to convey his determination.

'My experience during the poll campaign in 2009 was traumatic. I was very despondent as I found myself stuck in a system that had its own logic and momentum. What I had missed for two decades became clear to me,' adds Ravi, 'I had gained nothing from politics, and lost a lot—money, time, relationships.' That was the crunch year when Ravi took the decision to use his considerable organizational skills and drive to excel in his business. A little later, he decided to wholeheartedly embrace Dr Ambedkar's mission.

* * *

Ravi was born on 1 September 1963 in the Boosa Reddy Guda urban slum in West Marredpally, Secunderabad. The locality is close to the Secunderabad Railway Station as well as the government-owned Gandhi Hospital and has a Dalit majority. Both of Ravi's parents were illiterate and roving labourers, spending much of their time away from home eking out a living for the large family.

His father Shankaraiah worked as a daily wage mason and his mother Susheela was a labourer and, when not away from home, a maid servant. It was a constant struggle for the couple to feed their five sons and four daughters.

Ravi still has vivid memories of accompanying his mother when she would sneak into an isolated area in the nearby Secunderabad Cantonment to make cow-dung cakes and leave them to dry. Later she would collect them and sell them as cooking fuel. That experience still haunts Ravi as he had witnessed how painful it was for his mother to endure the insults from jawans who were unwilling to let her enter the cantonment area.

As a kid Ravi learned life's hard lessons from the experiences of his parents. Most Saturdays, he would see his father negotiate his wages with the contractor. It wasn't a nice spectacle. He resented how the contractor would have the upper hand in the bargaining and, more painfully, his condescending attitude towards Shankaraiah. Witnessing his father's experience, Ravi resolved to become a builder. He cherishes his mother's skill and determination to earn a living.

The silver lining of life in the Boosa Reddy Guda slum was that most of Ravi's extended family lived there as well. Though the family lived in a tiny two-room house with mud walls and a tiled roof, it was a joint family. The families of Shankaraiah and his elder brother Anjaiah lived together, which ensured the sense of a community: the families could lean on each other and the kids—for they were legion—had each other for company.

The family was poor but managed to feed itself. When Ravi was only ten, his mother passed away from complications of childbirth. Of the twin daughters she gave birth to at the end, only one survived.

Five years later, the family shifted to Malkajgiri, a mixed locality within Secunderabad.

Though a slum, Boosa Reddy Guda has the advantage of being next to the Gandhi Hospital and Medical College.

Reservations for admission into medical college came in handy for Anjaiah's son Krishna who enrolled in the medical college, which was an easy walking distance from his home. After completing his five-year course, Krishna started a clinic in Malkajgiri, where the joint family moved to once the clinic was firmly established. The clinic did well and soon grew into a hospital. It was a short journey of about 5 kilometres from Boosa Reddy Guda to Malkajgiri, within the city but the shift made all the difference in the world.

'Mobility is also mental,' says Ravi and explains how the move enabled the family to climb the education ladder, though poverty haunted them much longer. He is sad that those fellow Dalits and his relatives who neglected to move out of Boosa Reddy Guda are still mired in poverty and destitution.

* * *

In India, a cousin becoming a doctor—or an engineer or a soldier, for that matter—simplifies things in terms of ascribed aspirations of the younger ones in the extended family. One doesn't have to agonize over what one should do with one's life because a path has been created. Following his cousin's suit, Ravi opted for BPC (biology, physics and chemistry) in his Intermediate as that combination constitutes the minimum qualification to apply for a seat in a medical college.

He narrowly missed the mark to obtain admission in the medical college. His failure, however, paved a new path for him. Since he did not have the luxury to keep on trying year after year for admission, Ravi needed to act and carve a new path. The compulsion to help manage the family's finances weighed heavily on him.

Ravi had already gained substantial experience during his

intermediate days in procuring supplies for the medical stores owned by his brothers. On a typical day, Ravi would get up before five in the morning, fill water in large drums for the whole joint family, have breakfast and leave to take care of the hospital. Once back from college at one in the afternoon, he would bicycle to the wholesale market in Koti to procure supplies and ferry the heavy load on his bicycle.

From 1984 to 1994, Ravi served as the administrator of his cousin's Sri Venkateswara Hospital, Malkajgiri. During his tenure the hospital grew from a small five-bed nursing home into a forty-bed multi-specialty hospital, now renamed as M/s L.K. Hospital. Meanwhile, he acquired numerous degrees, attending evening colleges. He obtained an LLB (1986–89) and LLM (1989–91) from Osmania University. From the Bharatiya Vidya Bhawan he completed two post-graduate diplomas, one in journalism and the other in public relations. He also studied business management at the Dr Ambedkar Open University.

Ravi's punishing routine of work and study continued for more than a decade. During the evenings, classes and exams became his constant companions.

To an outside observer, his academic trajectory may appear incoherent but it has served him well—be it in politics, in business or in the community work he does nowadays.

'I started enjoying evening college life, though it was my circumstances that didn't let me attend a day college. In fact, life is more vibrant and studies more exciting in the evening college,' says Ravi. Unlike in a 'regular' day college where youngsters are expected to attend, evening colleges are populated mostly by working people who 'choose' to study at considerable cost. In this environment, friendships are more enduring, as Ravi experienced.

In 1986 when he was in the first year of the law course,

Ravi happened to meet Vanajakshi and promptly fell in love with her. What attracted him to her is quite evident but her parents failed to decipher their daughter's ready acceptance of the overture. Hence the matter languished for five years in limbo, as they continued a courtship. Finally, in 1991, Ravi and Vanajakshi became man and wife.

Dr Krishna, eighteen years older than Ravi, had unwittingly become a point of reference for Ravi in two crucial areas. One, as already mentioned, was his academic and professional trajectory that became a proverbial beaten path. Second, Dr Krishna plunged into politics by joining the newly formed Telugu Desam Party (TDP) and, in the 1983 polls, he won from the Secunderabad Cantonment assembly reserved constituency. Not only that, he became a minister in 1984 in the government headed by N.T. Rama Rao. He remained a minister for one year but failed to get a party nomination in the 1985 mid-term assembly polls. Although he again managed to get a TDP nomination in the 1989 assembly elections, he was unsuccessful. His subsequent attempts to get the party nomination never bore fruit.

Meanwhile, Ravi split his time between managing the hospital, pursuing his law degree and courting Vanajakshi, and emerged victorious in all three ventures.

Dr Krishna's overseas sojourns for long stretches had created a political vacuum that Ravi ended up filling. Dr Krishna's wife Dr Lalitha, also a doctor, took care of the hospital while Ravi oversaw its administration. Then came the 1994 elections and the TDP was keen to nominate Ravi as its candidate, but Dr Krishna, too, sought the seat. In the end the party ticket went to a third candidate. The differences between the cousins resulted in Ravi leaving the joint family. Since everything is owned jointly in a joint family, Ravi hardly had anything of his own to take with him. This happened just a week after his first son, Rithvik, was born on 27 October 1994.

It was clear to the family what Ravi must do now—continue in politics. He had already been a member of the student/youth wings of the TDP. Six of the family members (four brothers and two brothers-in-law) came forward to help. Each offered to give Ravi Rs 1,000 a month in return for his commitment to practise law, instead of entering government employment. The offer was a tremendous morale booster though Ravi never had to encash it.

* * *

Ravi, now over thirty years of age, began to live his life independent of his joint family, thus getting the chance to live for himself and his nuclear family. His wide circle of friends and his family stood by him in his hour of trial, when he came out of the joint family. Initially, he practiced law during 1994-95. He floated a construction company in 1995, Aditya Builders, which became Aditya Nirman Pvt. Ltd in 2001.

While he was exploring how to build his business, an opportunity knocked at his door. A gentleman by the name Rajalingam, the father of his friend Srinivas, offered to give Ravi his 800-square-yard plot of land to develop. He also put forth two conditions: Ravi must develop it on his own, without any partners, and there should be no compromise on the quality of the building. According to the the arrangement, Ravi would bear the costs of developing the land and constructing an apartment building, and in return for his land, Rajalingam would get 30 per cent of the constructed area as his share, and Ravi would own the rest.

A friend, K.V. Narasimha Raju, came forward and lent

him Rs 25,000, which became the seed money for Ravi's first business venture. Another friend, Rodda Ravi, helped in managing the business. By May 1997, Ravi had completed Harsha Apartments, which housed forty flats. He moved into its penthouse, which became his first house.

Since then he has not looked back. The business went from strength to strength, but his political life was less successful. However, starting from 1995, he occupied several important positions in the TDP, including that of state president of its student body, convenor of its youth wing, state secretary in charge of human resource development and later, its analysis wing.

He unsuccessfully tried for a party nomination for the 1999 elections. In the next round, the 2004 elections, he did manage to get nominated by the TDP but lost the elections. Due to differences over the call for a separate Telangana state, he left the TDP in 2008 and contested the 2009 elections under the banner of the newly formed Praja Rajyam Party but lost again.

In 2009 alone he spent more than a crore of his own money. That was when he vowed to reboot his life in a new direction. As the election results were declared on Vanajakshi's birthday, he calmly celebrated the auspicious event in the evening despite the disappointing outcome of the elections.

* * *

Following the 2009 debacle, Ravi spent a few weeks assessing his options. He could have dedicated himself to his business. However, a friend introduced him to the ideals of Dr Ambedkar, and the ideas led him in a new direction. Shyam Lal, an Ambedkarite from Maharashtra who had settled in Hyderabad, urged Ravi to take on the mantle of 'Babasaheb's

Mission'. As the weeks went by, his ideals and hopes took concrete shape in the form of Shanti Chakra International, which he registered as a non-profit social organization.

Shanti Chakra's motto is: *Know each other/ Help each other/ Grow together/ Become stronger.*

As he looked deeper into the Dalit movement in the state, Ravi realized that there were several organizational and ideational gaps. To a large extent, many Ambedkarite outfits are moribund.

'I was horrified to come across a fifty-two-year old president of an Ambedkar Yuvajana Sangam (youth society),' says Ravi and adds, 'People read Ambedkar, they talk about Ambedkar but they don't follow him.' The mission is personalized, he has concluded, instead of being institutionalized.

He devised two signature activities for Shanti Chakra, which define its existence and mission. One is 'Prabhuddha Bharat Utsav,' a large family get-together, and the other is 'Run for Caste-Free India.' In addition, there are weekly well-attended lectures by prominent intellectuals on social themes and the relevance of Dr Ambedkar's ideas. And finally, as a somewhat sentimental homage, Shanti Chakra ensures that the Ambedkar statue at the Tank Bund in the city gets a fresh garland every day. These activities have been going on uninterrupted for the past four years.

Prabhuddha Bharat Utsav is a mega event organized every year on 26 January which, Ravi asserts, 'is the real Independence Day for Dalits.' Organized at the Leonia Resorts, about 30 kilometres from the Tank Bund, it is a day-long event, tailored for all ages. The unifying theme of the jamboree is Dr Ambedkar.

'By the way, Prabhuddha Bharat means enlightened India. It is also the name of a journal Babasaheb started,' notes Ravi.

In the 2014 event, nearly 5,000 people took part with each adult participant paying Rs 1,000 as an entry fee.

On Dr Ambedkar's birthday (14 April), Ravi arranges 'Run for Caste-Free India' in Hyderabad. In 2014, in the third consecutive run, nearly 8,000 people took part, out of which almost 5,000 were non-Dalits. The run starts at People's Plaza on Necklace Road and ends at the Ambedkar statue at the Tank Bund, a distance of 3.5 kilometres.

With registration, each participant gets a book—*Annihilation of Caste*, a certificate, a T-shirt, a cap and a bottle of water. A thirty-minute warm-up session is followed by an oath-taking by all participants to help eradicate caste. The run has received such traction that even celebrities take part. It also receives corporate sponsorships.

'When we introduced the run in 2012, the non-Dalit participation was negligible. The following year, Dalit and non-Dalit runners were fifty-fifty and this year non-Dalits are a majority,' says Ravi. It is both an indication of changes in societal attitudes towards caste as well as Ravi's organizational capabilities. His campaign expanded from Dalits-only to making eradication of caste a common cause among all. Traditionally, any anti-caste movement is treated as the business of lower castes alone. Those who organize these events wouldn't even bother to invite the upper castes. But Ravi reached out to all sections in a concerted manner. That tweaking has yielded spectacular results.

In 2011 Ravi became DICCI's south India coordinator as well as president of its Andhra Pradesh chapter. His new role has led him to bring together disparate elements of his activism and business. Till 2009, he was a politician also doing other things, and a couple of years later he was primarily a social reformer. But now, thanks to DICCI, he is a business leader who promotes a culture of business among Dalits and leads by his personal example.

In 2013 he organized under DICCI banner a twenty-one-day residential training programme, IGNITE, for 220 Dalit entrepreneurs including forty women from Andhra Pradesh. Funded entirely by the state government, the orientation programme was held at the National Institute for Micro, Small and Medium Enterprises, Hyderabad.

* * *

Has his social activism replaced politics at the cost of his personal growth as a businessman? After all, during the past five years, only Shanti Chakra programmes and DICCI activities appear to have claimed all his time and effort.

'This phase has also coincided with a slump in the economy and consequently, in my business as well,' explains Ravi, indicating how he made use of the market-imposed leisure. He also has a partner, more often a non-Dalit, in every one of his business ventures, which enables him to spend time away from his business concerns. He has made arrangements, through rents earned from his properties, for a steady income to meet household requirements.

Aditya Nirman is building 120 flats in Miyapur, Hyderabad, at a cost of Rs 25 crore. It is also constructing, at a cost of Rs 2.5 crore, two independent houses on a turnkey basis. Once market conditions sufficiently improve, Ravi is keen to start Apna Apna Consumer Products Pvt. Ltd, a chain of stores that will showcase the products of entrepreneurs belonging to marginalized groups.

What next?

'I want to earn big money and also help entrepreneurs

from marginalized groups,' he says with the clarity that only a political mind can have. His elder son Rithvik will complete his engineering degree in a couple of years, and he wants to become a businessman. Vanajakshi, with her Masters in commerce, also appears to have been bitten by the business bug. She wants to open a boutique with her own dress-making factory. Ravi credits DICCI with making business a fashion in his home as well. And his younger son, thirteen-year-old Rohan, is more an Ambedkarite and wants to become a chartered accountant.

It will be interesting to watch how far Ravi is able to make business a fashion among Dalits in his state, and back it up with his success as a businessman.

RAJA NAYAK

The BTM Layout, an upscale neighbourhood in Bengaluru, is fast becoming the chosen residential locale for some of the city's emergent entrepreneurs.

Raja Nayak's home is hidden from view by a row of palm trees bordering the compound. A stately home, surrounded by a lush green lawn and flower beds bursting with colourful and exotic flowering plants lies within. Its large portico is lined with a fleet of luxury cars and three bikes.

Two alert Dalmatians growl as they scan unfamiliar faces, awaiting a cue from their master, Raja Nayak.

'Calm down,' he says firmly, and they step aside.

Inside, the hexagonal living room has two sets of sofas, which can accommodate a dozen guests at a time. Beyond is the dining area with an outsized table surrounded by eight chairs. Adjacent is a fully loaded bar.

The 3,000-square-foot duplex house has four bedrooms plus a guest room on the terrace. It points at deep pockets and marks the journey of Raja, who belongs to the Valmiki community, a sub-caste among Dalits, from abject poverty to his current success.

The Valmiki community has inaccurately been identified with sanitation work, even though the majority does not practise that profession. Nonetheless, Valmikis are amongst the poorest Dalits.

'By building this grand house, Raja has broken through the stereotype,' says Satish, a fellow Dalit entrepreneur in his early thirties who is in the business of event management.

Six feet tall and moustached, Raja has many businesses of which MCS Logistics Pvt. Ltd is the largest with a turnover of Rs 50 crore. The company's operations include freight carriage and transportation services. The company has agents in most industrial towns in India and offices in Mumbai, Chennai and Bengaluru. It also has business interests in the Middle East, Africa, and East Asia.

Raja's other firm, Akshaya Enterprises, manufactures packaging boxes and has an annual revenue of Rs 5 crore. Raja's eldest son Arjun, who has completed an MBA, manages the firm. His second son, twenty-one-year-old Akshaya, has just set up a bottled-water plant that is projected to generate revenues of a few crore rupees in a couple of years.

Tall and magnetic, Raja's wife Anita Raj runs a beauty clinic, which brings in Rs 5 lakh a month. She is planning to open another branch. 'I have been running around looking for space for over a month,' she says. 'I want a location in the upscale Koramangala area.'

Raja was born in 1961. His father, Muniyappa, did his matriculation but his mother is illiterate. The house they lived in was 10x8 square feet in size with no amenities and located in Balepete, opposite the Bengaluru bus station and near the railway station. The family had to move out because the structures had been built on government land and were illegal.

Muniyappa had mixed fortunes. He was relatively privileged at birth—his father was a police constable. But before Muniyappa started school, his father died, leaving his mother to raise him on her husband's pension.

'The pension was too little to support the family,' recalls eighty-year-old Muniyappa.

Muniyappa married, and after Raja was born, the family moved to Wilson Garden near Lal Chowk. The new house was smaller than the one they had vacated in Balepete.

Muniyappa gave tuitions so he could support the family. He became deeply involved in the youth movement and was attracted to socialism. He started an eight-page fortnightly magazine, which was more to advance his politics than to earn a living. Advertisements generated some revenue.

Ideologically charged, Muniyappa didn't have much time to spend with the family. He somehow managed to provide for their bare minimum needs.

'He would leave in the morning and come back after we went to bed,' recalls Raja. 'He would spend time with socialist intellectuals and activists.'

To Raja, growing up with five siblings—three brothers and two sisters—was both joyful and painful. 'We missed something each time we ate food,' he recalls. 'We often gatecrashed at our maternal uncle's place to eat non-vegetarian food.'

Muniyappa managed to secure a seat for Raja in the United Mission High School on Mission Road. Set up in 1935, the school is well regarded for imparting high-quality education. Raja walked the 5-kilometre distance to school each day. He would sometimes get transport money from his mother but would still walk.

The United Mission School had a sobering impact on Raja. The school was English medium but his family and all those around him spoke Kannada. His father knew English but he was too busy tackling far bigger ideological problems and didn't have time for mundane matters.

'During recess my classmates would buy toffees and I would merely look around,' says Raja. 'I wanted to be able to show off sometimes too. "Why was I enrolled in this school when my parents couldn't afford a tiffin box for me?" I would think.'

He couldn't find an answer.

Raja successfully completed his high school but he was a troubled boy with complexes. He compared the shoes and clothes worn by his classmates to his own and envied their grasp of English. He cursed his poverty and perceived himself to be inferior to his friends because of his lack of money.

'Money became my goddess,' admits Raja.

In 1976 he was enrolled in the National College in Jayanagar for his eleventh standard, which is also called the PUC (pre-university course) in Karnataka.

'I realized the worth of money even more then,' he recalls. 'Students came on bicycles.'

The pain he experienced in school, however, was eased by his childhood friend Deepak Dhingra, who shaped Raja's life in many ways.

Deepak's father was a government official and the family

lived across the street from where Raja's family lived, though they were from vastly different socio-economic backgrounds. 'Rich apartments need slums as well,' sums up Raja, explaining how his family lived opposite a well-to-do colony.

However, class differences did not come in the way of Raja and Deepak's friendship. Not only Deepak, but his entire family accepted Raja. Deepak's family belonged to Punjab and their outsider status made Deepak value Raja's company.

On school vacations, Deepak and his family would visit their home near Chandigarh. Since there were no direct trains between Delhi and Bengaluru in those days, the family travelled to Chennai, from where they took the Grand Trunk Express, which connected to Delhi. During the four-hour layover between the two trains, Deepak would roam around Chennai to see the sights. On one such visit, he witnessed 'foreign rejected' shirts being sold briskly on the pavement.

In the years before India opened up its economy, Indians were desperate for quality goods, ranging from fountain pens and nail clippers to clothes and cassette recorders. To meet this demand for foreign ('quality') goods, domestic sellers would use two tactics: either they would label their products with an 'export quality' tag, or they would term them 'foreign rejected'. The latter category was vague, which was to the advantage of the sellers. It could mean either that the goods had been produced abroad but had been rejected on technical grounds, or that they were Indian-made goods that were bound for foreign markets where they were rejected for some reason. Whatever the label, these goods sold well in a consumer-goods-starved market. Deepak saw people buying 'foreign rejected' shirts packed in transparent polythene for Rs 50 a piece.

'Some manufacturers would put a tag of "foreign rejected"

even though those shirts might never have been exported,' explains Raja. 'They would use the tag as a marketing strategy.'

On a hot summer day in June, Deepak returned to Bengaluru after his vacation. He almost ran to meet Raja and told him about the business prospect. Both the friends discussed the matter for a few days and zeroed in on a strategy.

They decided to buy these shirts from Chennai and sell them in Bengaluru, outside the premises of Bosch India. Bosch is a German multinational corporation that manufactures a variety of engineering products and at the time employed thousands of workers in Bengaluru. Bosch India was also conveniently located near Raja and Deepak's homes.

The budding businessmen, however, had to overcome some initial difficulties. While Deepak came from a well-off family that was quite open in its outlook, this was less so the case for Raja. He feared that his father might not like the idea of him selling shirts on pavements. Muniyappa was an intellectual and moved among learned people. Further, for a socialist, making money from business would be anathema.

Raja's mother, Naratha, reluctantly endorsed his business plans. She also pledged all her jewellery and raised Rs 5,000. Deepak, too, borrowed a few thousand rupees from his father. With their funds, the friends travelled to Chennai where they bought 200 shirts at Rs 50 a piece and returned to Bangalore. The next day, they put down a mattress on the pavement opposite the Bosch factory gate and laid out the shirts attractively, enticing prospective buyers.

During the lunch hour when thousands of workers streamed out of the factory, Raja stood up to his full height and with a booming voice yelled, 'Foreign rejected shirts for

Rs 100 each!' Deepak, meanwhile, took care of sales and administration.

They sold 200 shirts within two hours. On the first day of their business venture, the duo made a profit of Rs 9,000, deducting the Rs 1,000 they had spent on travel and food.

Within a week, Raja and Deepak had made three trips to Chennai, earning a good profit each time. By now Raja's clothing had changed and so did the utensils and the food cooked at home. Muniyappa became suspicious of the sudden change, but Naratha explained it away by telling him that her parents had given her some money.

The following week, however, Muniyappa learnt about his son's street business and was furious. Today, neither is comfortable recounting the war that followed. Inevitably, the business caused a rift between father and son, and their lines of communication snapped.

After a few weeks in business, sales began to decline and, by the third month, there were hardly any buyers. By now, most of the people in the Bosch factory had already bought the shirts. Raja and Deepak had to look for other options. They chose Tirupur as their next destination.

Tirupur, in Tamil Nadu, is a manufacturing hub for hosiery knitwear. Known for quality and scale, much of its output is exported. Raja and Deepak would make two trips a week to Tirupur, which is 320 kilometres southeast of Bengaluru, to purchase goods to bring back and sell. They also set up a table to sell their goods in the store-front of a shop in Koramangala, promising the store owner 2 per cent of their sales.

Both Raja and Deepak continued their education alongside their business.

'I was a 35 per cent student,' smiles Raja, referring to how he scraped by in school by getting the minimum score required to move on to a higher class, 35 per cent.

In 1980 Raja rejoined his alma mater, National College, for his BA. A new prosperity was in evidence in his home, and all his siblings—three brothers and two sisters—were in school. Raja also bought a two-wheeler.

In the winter of 1985, a chance acquaintance led to the growth of the business in a new direction. Raja met Nafees Khan, a shoe manufacturer, and the two talked over a beer at a hotel. Nafees was from Mumbai, and supplied shoes to retailers in Bengaluru. As the acquaintance grew into friendship, Nafees invited Raja and Deepak to Mumbai and showed them his manufacturing plant. He appointed Raja and Deepak as his wholesale agents for Bengaluru; their duties involved collecting the consignment from the railway station and distributing the shoes to retailers in accordance with their orders. They also advised retailers about new products. After collecting money from the retailers, they would deduct their commission and send the rest to Nafees. Since their business was expanding, a division of work was needed. Deepak looked after the garments while Raja managed the shoe side of the business.

A year later, they folded up the garment business; the shoe business was more stable and also demanded their complete attention. Moreover, though selling the 'foreign rejected' shirts had given them their real break, it still required hawking on pavements—something they wanted to put behind them.

Raja bought a shop in Wilson Garden, which essentially served as a storage site. He had completed his BA and was now a full-time businessman. Deepak, meanwhile, had dropped out of college. While the two still remained good friends, Deepak also sought business opportunities on his own. His sister was married to a businessman who owned a large showroom of leather goods. Deepak began to spend more time at his brother-in-law's showroom. Nonetheless, Raja still treated Deepak as his full partner and shared the profits equally.

Their business, however, would suffer a setback, not from within but from without. A business dispute in Nafees Khan's family resulted in his closing his manufacturing unit towards the end of 1988.

'We were on the road again,' says Raja.

A silver lining during this time was that Raja married Anita Raj in 1988 and their first child, Arjun, was born the following year. A few months later, Raja launched another business venture; he opened a restaurant. He located a shop in Koramangala as the site and roped in Deepak, who also liked the idea. The restaurant, Tawa, was launched with great fanfare. Serving roast chicken and Afghani bread, the restaurant was a success.

Deepak had meanwhile embarked on an altogether different trajectory. He had always liked the idea of living in the United States, and had tried to land a job there several times without success. He had been involved with a Christian group which led, in 1991, to his conversion to Christianity.

Eventually, Deepak left for Australia and within a few years of his arrival there, he became a preacher. Without Deepak, Raja found it hard to run the restaurant and shut it down.

Now alone for the second time, Raja had to re-examine his options. He purchased a 4,000-square-foot industrial plot in Jigani, a government-promoted industrial cluster about 40 kilometres outside Bengaluru. Spending about Rs 3 lakh, he built a two-storey building and launched Akshaya Enterprises Pvt. Ltd in 1994.

Raja knew a friend who had a packaging company and

did a brisk business in producing cardboard cartons that computer companies needed to package their products. In the mid-1990s, computers were in great demand, and the industry needed a large number of cartons and was on the lookout for suppliers.

'He helped me start the business,' says Raja. 'He agreed to buy back all the cartons I would manufacture.'

By the end of 1995, Akshaya Enterprises employed fifty workers. Raja was a sub-contractor, supplying cartons, with no brand of his own. 'So long as I made money, I didn't bother who owned the brand,' he admits.

In March 1996 Raja caught the train to Chennai with a friend in order to purchase a Honda City car—Bengaluru did not have a Honda showroom at the time.

On their return, Raja and his friend reached the railway station just moments before the train's departure—they managed to jump into the bogey of the moving train after a mad scramble.

Raja did not have the time to buy gutka, the dry chewing tobacco that comes in tiny sachets. In the train compartment, he began to feel the need for a shot of tobacco.

Opposite him was a man who was consuming Raja's favourite brand of gutka. 'I was restless,' he remembers, but he was hesitant to ask a stranger for gutka.

Raja's friend volunteered to ask and the man was more than happy to share. The man, Nataraj Aiyar, introduced his wife Alamelu, who shared some of the home-cooked food that she carried. During the journey, Raja, Nataraj and his wife talked about their businesses.

Nataraj and his wife ran MCS Logistics Pvt. Ltd, a logistics business company. Karnataka was witnessing massive exports of granite to the US, European and Chinese markets. Nataraj offered Raja a deal with his logistics business in Karnataka—he would have a 20 per cent share in all the business that would originate from Karnataka. Raja readily agreed.

Nataraj asked Raja to look for an office space in the Koramangala area and then returned to Chennai. Within a month, Raja had a furnished office. Nataraj had spent Rs 3 lakh to furnish the Bengaluru office and also bought a new Tata Sumo car for office use.

Within the first year, Raja generated a turnover of Rs 1 crore. By the end of the second year, the Karnataka branch crossed Rs 4 crore in annual turnover—a crore more than the combined turnover of Nataraj's business outside Karnataka.

Nataraj rewarded Raja by allotting him a 40 per cent stake in the company in December 1998. In 1999 when Nataraj and his wife moved to Mumbai to open a new office, Raja started looking after the business in Karnataka as well as in Tamil Nadu.

Being an outgoing personality, Raja plays a key role in procuring business for the company. With Rs 55 crore in turnover, the company is now doing well.

Raja never tried to take over the company. 'I will never do that,' he says emphatically. 'After all, they had created MCS Logistics. I do visit the Mumbai office every second week.'

What next?

In association with a major Indian corporation, Akshaya Enterprises is on an expansion drive. 'I want to make this company bigger than MCS,' says Raja and adds, 'for my own satisfaction.'

Raja plans to re-launch his Tawa restaurant. 'I don't want to live with the tag of a man who failed in the food business,' he says, getting a bit emotional. 'Money is not a criterion for me any more. I have made enough.'

Having gone from acute poverty to affluence within a span of two decades, Raja appears content. But is he resting on his laurels too soon? He is only in his early fifties.

His wife Anita has a different take. She is not satisfied with the success they have achieved. She wants to expand her beauty clinic and turn it into a chain.

'When it comes to business, I am separate from my husband,' she says. 'I am a woman and I am on my own.'

Determination is writ large on her smiling face. Akash, their nineteen-year-old second son, is in college, and he, too, wants to chart his own course in business, away from the shadow of his father!

Perhaps Raja does have a reason to be content. He has become a role model not only for his wife and their three sons, all of whom have become entrepreneurs, but for the entire community.

That's no mean achievement.

HARI KISHAN PIPPAL

At sixty-two, when most Indians go into retirement mode, Hari Kishan Pippal manages three businesses—a corporate hospital, a two-wheeler agency and a shoe factory—while keeping up with his investments in stocks and real estate, among other things. A couple of decades ago, he could not in his wildest dreams have imagined the life he enjoys today. But dreaming is not in his nature. His focus on action as well as on the present has served him in good stead, contributing to his current success.

The Heritage Hospital, asserting its presence on the Agra–Delhi highway, is recognized as a quality healthcare provider in a 'panel' of leading companies. Set up in 1999, the hospital has a workforce of 350, including doctors, paramedics and administrative staff, and in 2012–13, recorded a turnover of Rs 45 crore.

A year after starting the Heritage Hospital, Hari acquired a dealership of Honda scooters—People's Honda—in Agra. Honda's largest vendor in the city, it sold an average of thirty scooters and serviced 200 vehicles a day in 2012. With a staff of 246 that includes engineers, People's Honda generated Rs 55 crore in revenue in 2012–13.

Another acquisition of Hari's is People's Exports, which produces 800 pairs of shoes a day. Meant for the high-end Western markets, a pair of its shoes could cost up to $300. Hari employs about 300 workers and made Rs 70 crore in 2012–13.

Hari owns a fleet of cars and is an investor as well, from stocks to real estate. He is fluent in English, German and French, in addition to his mother tongue Hindi. He travels often to North America, Europe, Russia and East Asia.

As a boy, Hari was a good student and loved going to school. He scored 98 per cent in mathematics, very rare in those days. His future seemed to be bright, when family difficulties struck and his education abruptly came to end.

'I failed the twelfth standard,' he says.

Hari's father Ram Singh had married four times. The first two wives died of illness. The third and fourth lived amicably with their husband.

With eight brothers and six sisters, life wasn't easy for Hari. Ram Singh and his brother would make shoes for British officers on special order.

Though illiterate, Ram Singh ensured a good education for his children. His eldest son, a post-graduate, became the chief personnel officer in the ordnance factory in Jodhpur. His second son also completed his post-graduation and became a superintendent in the central ordnance factory in Agra. The third son became a veterinary doctor and the fourth a paramedic in a government medical college. His eldest daughter became a teacher and her younger sister finished her graduation.

With a second division in high school, Hari looked forward to further studies. But suddenly things turned against him. Ram Singh suffered a stroke at the Lucknow railway station in 1966. It was his second stroke and he was seventyyears old. Since he was heading to the cantonment to deliver shoes to army officers when he suffered the stroke, he received immediate medical attention and survived. The family was relieved and grateful for his survival, but Ram Singh would remain paralysed and bed-ridden for the rest of his life.

'Even in bed he was an inspiration,' remembers Hari who was sixteen years old then. Ram Singh would encourage Hari to believe in himself and not in the destiny dictated by the circumstances of his birth.

The subsequent tribulations that Hari faced after his father's illness were beyond anything his age or education had prepared him for. He had three younger brothers and two younger sisters to take care of, as well as two mothers and an ailing father. The immediate challenge was to feed a nine-member household. The long-term one was to send his siblings to school and arrange their marriages. Who would bear all these expenses?

His elder brothers assured him of their support, but the family dynamics intruded and their promised help was somewhat threadbare. As is common in large families, the elder brothers were well-settled with good jobs, but they lived away from home. They also had their own families to look after, and their ability to help was limited.

Hari is cautious when talking about his siblings and his complex relationship with them—after all, the fourteen siblings were born to four different mothers. 'Our elder brothers did help us on critical occasions,' he offers.

Hari's high school results were out in June 1966, and he had enrolled for the eleventh standard. As his father was sick and out of work, Hari needed to earn some money. He had a relative, Heera Singh, who plied a rickshaw. Heera lived in a nearby village and went to Agra to work during the day. The road to Heera's village was so bad that he couldn't pedal his way home. Therefore, he would park the rickshaw in Hari's backyard before leaving for home in the evening.

In early April 1967, the board examinations for twelfth standard students began, which lasted over a month. The eleventh standard students enjoyed a month-long holiday once the board exams commenced. Hari sat at home and weighed his options while his friends were busy playing hockey, football, or cricket. The burden on Hari's shoulders was too great, and would not allow him the luxury of indulging in sports.

One evening, his mind wandered over to the rickshaw that Heera had left behind for the night. An idea took shape in Hari's mind but it was punctuated by doubt and a sense of shame. He sat on the rickshaw saddle and pedalled first a little, then cautiously some more until he covered a distance of some fifty yards. Within half an hour, he was plying the rickshaw comfortably. 'Easier than the bicycle,' he told himself as he pedalled forward.

One day, while he was still on a dry-run, a woman signalled for him to stop. She had a baby and asked him to take her to a nearby hospital. Happy to oblige, and mustering the courage, he took his passengers to their destination in ten minutes. She paid him his first wage, a 25-paise coin, which was also the price of a first-class ticket to a cinema those days. He refused to take the money but the lady forced the coin into his hand.

Hari had now found a way of adding a little bit more money to what he was earning from giving tuitions. During the day, he would give tuitions, which would fetch him a few rupees, and for a couple of hours in the evenings he would ply the rickshaw and add a few more rupees to his monthly income.

But he had to keep his rickshaw-pulling a secret. Given how little respected a rickshaw-puller is even among the poor, his family would not have allowed him to ply a rickshaw. He shared his concern with Heera, and a plan was hatched.

Hari would ply his rickshaw in areas far away from home to minimize chances of an acquaintance recognizing him. He would also wear headgear that partially hid his face. He told the family that he had taken up a part-time job in a transport company, to explain where he went every evening. To complete the deception, the rickshaw would be parked at a friend's place instead of in his home.

Within a month or so, Hari was taking home one and a half rupee a day. Sometimes he would make Rs 2. In the late 1960s, one could buy five kilos of wheat for Rs 1. 'I ran the family,' he says proudly.

One day in 1967, a foreign couple asked Hari to take them around Agra; Pippal took them on a three-hour joyride. They would stop at roadside shops to enjoy snacks or tea. At the end of the journey, Hari asked for Rs 5 as the fare.

'They looked shocked,' says Hari, 'and I cursed myself and thought that I should not have demanded that much.' In fact, they thought the young man had asked for too little, and gave him a 10-rupee note instead.

'They smiled at me,' he recalls. 'Foreigners pay more.'

Back home, he had a tough time accounting for the 10-rupee note.

'Where did you steal this money from?' his mother asked him, fuming. It was naïve of him not to have anticipated the question.

It was not easy to cook up an answer. When he finally managed an explanation, he was hardly convincing, 'My teacher gave me the money to buy books.'

The family was not impressed. Why would he meet his teacher during the holidays?

He continued plying the rickshaw for a few more months. But he knew he couldn't pull it off for long, and called it a day.

'The family pride was at stake,' he admits now. 'What if I was caught?'

But the lessons he learned as a rickshaw puller were to guide him in his future success: Don't let 'what-if' questions and fear impede you. The reward is not only for hard work but also for the willingness to take risks. Also, 'customer satisfaction' is not enough—you have to 'pleasantly surprise'.

Hari continued giving tuitions even after he failed the twelfth standard board examinations in 1968. He made one more unsuccessful attempt.

Being out of school meant he had to find gainful employment. After trying his hand at several vocations, he finally landed a job with a company that made rings and pistons for diesel engines. He started working in its accounts division for Rs 80 a month. 'I was a bit educated,' he says.

A few days into the job, Hari had to change his name. One day a worker called out loudly to him, using his first name,

'Hari Kishan'. The owner came out shouting 'Who is this idiot?' His name too was Hari Kishan.

To avoid confusion, Hari Kishan Pippal became Hari Singh Pippal!

The next logical step for Hari was marriage. The big event was arranged for the summer of 1973. With the help of relatives, he tied the knot with Geeta, the daughter of a prosperous Jatav businessman who owned a shoe factory.

It didn't take long for Hari to realize that marriage was enjoyable only for the well-to-do. For him it meant frustration and humiliation. His poverty took away any fun from the experience. Even four decades after the event, he narrates his predicament as a newly married man with a tinge of irritation.

To begin with, it was an Indian-style arranged marriage. The first time he met his bride was at their wedding, the way one meets a stranger in the market.

'I had not seen Geeta before marriage,' recalls Hari, 'and I wouldn't get to see her in my home either, when she came to live with me.'

Traditionally, after the wedding, when the bride arrives at the groom's house, she is greeted by the family members and relatives, and presented with gifts. After everyone retires for the night, a few women in the family summon the groom. Anxious and excited, he responds eagerly. A playful charade ensues as the women pull the groom into the bride's chamber and the groom, for his part, pretends to be uninterested. The women finally leave the groom alone with his wife. Known as suhaag raat, this is the golden night any new couple dreams of.

But for Hari, nothing of that sort happened. Their small house accommodated not only his big family but also other relatives who had come for his wedding. There was no way a room could have been spared for the couple. 'I would be awake till past midnight and just wait,' remembers Hari. 'Nobody came to drag me in!'

He would spend the day sleeping. Friends and relatives would make fun of him. For him it was a double whammy, humiliation added to frustration.

Geeta left for her parental home on the seventh day. Once again 'what-if' thoughts started troubling him. 'What if she told her mother about not being with her husband all week?'

Hari had received goods aplenty as wedding gifts. His wife must have noticed one relative grabbing a transistor and two others fighting over a bicycle. Yet another took away the cot meant for the newly-weds. 'What if Geeta told her parents all this?'

As the tradition goes, after a few months the husband, or his father, goes to the in-laws' house to bring back the wife. Hari's condition was such that he took more time—almost a year—than was usual. All the while he was waiting he was preparing himself to face his wife, building up his defences. He'd saved money to buy impressive gifts for Geeta. He dressed 'like an officer' and wanted to impress on Geeta that the poverty she had witnessed was a thing of the past. But, once in front of his father-in-law, all his preparations came to naught. He stood speechless at the barrage of shouting and invectives from the old man.

'Why would a man marry if he couldn't even afford a room to live in with his wife?'

'We were fooled by your brothers' success and position.'

His message was clear: 'We will not send our daughter with you.'

Humiliated, Hari left his in-laws' house with a resolve to succeed. But he wasn't sure what 'succeed' meant. After a couple of weeks, he quit his job and headed for Faridabad, an industrial town near Delhi and 200 kilometres away from Agra. A relative who worked in a well-known tractor manufacturing factory helped him find a job in the unskilled category. So in 1974, Hari joined Escorts, India's leading tractor manufacturer.

After a year of focused work, Hari was promoted to the skilled workers category, and he began cutting steel. Though he had vowed not to go back to Agra till he had made it big, he had to visit the city to attend a cousin's wedding. Geeta had an inkling that her husband might turn up for the wedding. Her father, too, had reconciled to the fact that his daughter couldn't live in her parental home forever as remarriage was taboo.

Geeta spotted Hari from a distance. She couldn't believe her eyes—he was dressed like an officer. With the help of an elderly woman, she was able to meet him. 'Don't ignore me… I'm prepared to live with you even on the streets,' she pleaded.

'The tears in her eyes moved me,' he recalls.

Hari's in-laws also realized that they couldn't avoid talking to him for long. They offered him a job in their company, which made high quality shoes.

Hari was keen to join them so that he could start living with his wife. But there was a catch: doing so would hurt his father's ego.

His father, Ram Singh, was a community leader. At each of his four weddings he had ridden a horse. Ram Singh would not like his son to become a ghar jawain—the expression is almost always used with derision. It wasn't acceptable for a son-in-law to be at the beck and call of his in-laws. Hari couldn't even take up any employment with them. That, too, would be looked down upon.

A solution was found. Hari became a partner in his in-laws' company. He was now an equal with them. Within a year Hari proved his worth. But his relations with his father-in-law were—well, like any between an old man and his son-in-law—frosty.

Hari cleaned up the company's operations and showed a corrupt accountant the door. By the end of the second year, he was in complete charge. By this time, Geeta gave birth to a son.

Hari would often ponder over the business model his father-in-law had adopted. Though illiterate, the old man had made it big in business.

But Hari was not convinced that his way was the only way. For example, the company was making footwear for the European markets and delivering the product to a middleman, Mangat Ram, who exported it to Europe. In those days even the export of shoes was regulated by the State Trading Corporation (STC). Those who could manipulate things at the Delhi level, which was the centre of power, were able to secure export orders. The real manufacturers would be at the mercy of people like Mangat Ram. Hari knew that Ram made a handsome profit on the product that Hari's company made. If only his company could export shoes directly.

'Mangat Ram lived lavishly,' notes Hari.

For Hari to find an export market, he would have to approach A.K. Sen, the director of the STC, who also happened to hail from Agra.

In less than six months, Hari secured an order worth Rs 1 lakh. He was given specifications—colour, quality of leather, sizes and price range.

He boarded a train at Delhi and wanted to reach Agra as fast as possible. 'I cursed stations each time the train stopped,' he recalls. 'I just wanted to reach my father-in-law as soon as possible.'

Hari broke the news.

His father-in-law fell silent first before shouting angrily, 'Why do you want to ruin me?' He narrated stories of many shoe exporters going bankrupt due to the rejection of their consignments.

'We fought,' says Hari. He quit his in-laws' company the same day.

He now had to explore other avenues. He had often met a banker, K.B.L. Saxena, at the milkman's shop. Hari would gossip with him whenever the milkman was late in opening his shop. Saxena had once prodded Hari, 'Why don't you open your own shoe-making workshop?'

After falling out with his in-laws, Hari headed straight to Saxena, who explained the basic eligibility criteria for a bank loan. Hari had to show the certificate from the STC stating that the sample he had supplied had been approved, along with a copy of the supply order of shoes worth Rs 1 lakh. Hari would also have to show the bank manager that he had a functioning shoe manufacturing unit in Agra.

Having already obtained the STC certificate, he created a makeshift factory in one room of the house he lived in. He neatly arranged the tools his father had once used and placed a host of shoe frames along the walls. He also arranged for a few workers and a master designer of shoes. He convinced the bank inspector about his ability to make shoes worth Rs 1 lakh.

With an assured bank loan, Hari went to Chennai and bought fine-quality leather for his requirements. He arranged the consignment to be sent by train and came back home. A few days later, he went to the Agra railway station to collect the leather. He returned home dejected. He was told that his leather had not been unloaded at the Agra station and had ended up at the Jammu railway station instead. The bad news spread faster than he feared. Some laughed at his foolhardiness. Others were sceptical of the whole transaction.

'He may never have bought leather in Chennai,' said one.

'He is cheating the bank,' said another.

Hari went to Saxena with the purchase receipts and consignment-booking bills. Upon confirming with the station master of Agra, Saxena gave Hari another chance. This time he dispatched a man from the bank to accompany Hari to Madras. To be safe, Hari booked the consignment on the same train in which he came back.

Within two months, he completed the order and sent the shoes to the STC. It was two weeks before the deadline. His product was accepted and he began to get repeat orders. He would outsource the work to nearby shoe-makers but would monitor quality. He would supply them with leather, designs, threads and high-quality adhesive.

In the early 1980s, Hari got about fifty repeat orders. In 1984, he bought his own plot of land for Rs 800 per square foot. A large manufacturing factory had now come into being on the Agra–Delhi highway.

Hari bought a large house in a posh area of Agra. When he got his first export order in 1982, there were twenty-one Agra-based exporters and he was the twenty-first in terms of business size. By 1991, he had become the second largest exporter.

'I aimed at scaling up to the number one slot,' he says.

His importers were in the Soviet Union and Eastern Europe. He manufactured shoes for the elite there. While he was doing well and dreaming big, the Soviet Union was collapsing, before its final dissolution in December 1991.

Subsequently, Hari's buyers disappeared and he lost some Rs 40 crore. It was a catastrophe few could survive.

Losing money was part of business as usual but what hurt him most was that he had lost the market. In Agra, shoemakers and exporters specialized in different regions. Some would make shoes for East Asia only, some for West Europe and others for Arab countries alone. For Hari, entering into a new market was not going to be easy.

After much thought, he turned to the domestic market.

But turning to the domestic market also proved fatal. 'I was destined to fail,' says Hari of his domestic market gamble.

The shoe factory's shutters came down in 2000. Hari had continued to manufacture shoes for eight years, making losses, with the hope of a recovery. He had even sold his kothi in a posh colony of Agra.

'I was on the street again,' he recalls.

With four growing children, Hari had to think of their education and future. He came up with a plan to convert the shoe factory premises into a restaurant-cum-banquet hall. The 600-square-metre plot was on the Agra–Delhi highway and very close to an upcoming upmarket housing complex.

'Money was a problem,' recalls Hari. He shared his plans with Geeta and by the next morning, he miraculously had plenty of cash in hand.

When he was doing well financially, Hari had given his wife expensive gifts twice a year—on her birthday and on their wedding anniversary. He would give her jewellery on her birthday and gold biscuits on their wedding anniversary. Over the years, Geeta had accumulated over a kilogram of gold.

The following morning, when Hari was drinking tea, Geeta came up to him, holding a bronze vessel. She first shook it twice and then poured the contents out on the table in front of him. A heap of gold and jewellery lay on the table.

'I was taken aback,' he says. 'Did I gift that much of gold to my wife?'

He decided to take only the gold biscuits and didn't touch the jewellery. 'The jewellery I had gifted her was coated with love. How could I sell my love?'

In 2002, Hari's restaurant, Agrawal Restaurant Pure Vegetarian, was opened. It did brisk business.

What was the secret of its success? Location.

Even after meticulously planning the venture, opening the restaurant was still a risky business. Opening it a block away from its current location might have wreaked havoc with his plans.

Hari feels he has been rewarded for taking risks and, as always, for 'pleasantly surprising' the customer.

Meanwhile his younger son saw a newspaper advertisement placed by the Honda scooter company, seeking dealers for Agra. The Pippals applied and got the dealership, and are now one of the biggest Honda dealers in north India. With a degree in business management, the eldest son heads People's Honda.

Running a restaurant requires a lot of personal attention. Hari wanted to hand over responsibility to his sons—but none of them was eager to take charge of the restaurant.

He made yet another decision fraught with risks. He thought of opening a hospital. One of his sons had married a doctor, and the Heritage Hospital project became a reality. Hari's second son, a software engineer, heads the Heritage Hospital.

Did Hari's losses in the shoe export business affect him? His youngest son thinks he knows what disturbs his father the most. 'He hates being a loser,' he says emphatically.

With a degree in animation from Greece, this son joined IBM in Gurgaon. Though he was getting a handsome salary, he quit the job and joined his father in setting up a state-of-the-art shoe factory in Agra.

When the Dalit Indian Chamber of Commerce and Industry (DICCI) took a delegation of Dalit entrepreneurs from north India to the Tata Motors plant in Lucknow in 2012, Hari was a part of the delegation. It was there that he saw Tata trucks being manufactured on an assembly line. Inspired, he installed within months an assembly line in his shoe factory.

'This is the first shoe factory in Agra where shoes are made on an assembly line,' says a fellow shoe-maker.

It is Hari's willingness to change and experiment that brought him out of being a freelance rickshaw puller to a highly successful businessman.

SUKESH RAJAN

Munshi ki Pulia, the bustling commercial hub in the upscale neighbourhood of Indira Nagar, Lucknow, is home to many a thriving business, but few are as promising as the one housed in the Prime Plaza building. The solid five-storeyed structure covers 1,00,000 square feet of space and is valued at around Rs 70 crore. The company, ABS Masale, acquired the building with a 75 per cent stake in 2007.

It is half past nine in the morning, and it has just stopped raining. A blue two-seater BMW pulls into the premises and a tall, slim Sukesh Rajan alights from the car and swiftly makes his way to his first-floor office, where a battery of employees and officers await his arrival.

Slightly reluctantly, the thirty-four-year-old Sukesh discloses how much each of the diamond rings adorning his fingers on both hands cost him. He acquired the ring on the right index finger for Rs 90,000 and paid Rs 50,000 and Rs 20,000 for the two rings on his left hand. The chain around his neck, made of thirty-five grams of gold, is worth over Rs 10 lakh. The bracelet on his wrist weighs forty grams. Altogether, he has almost a 100 grams of gold on him.

Married and with two children, Sukesh owns three budding companies: ABS Masale, which makes spices and sattoo (roasted black gram flour, eaten with salt or sugar; considered good for diabetics, sattoo is a ready-to-eat poor man's health food), ABS Beverages, which bottles water and soda, and Ample Infrabuild, which is building a township.

With a Rs 20-crore turnover, ABS Masale is the mother company. It makes and markets in pouches a variety of spices and condiments, such as red chilli powder, turmeric and coriander. It also produces ten metric tons of sattoo every day.

Every day, ABS Beverages spews out 55,000 one-litre bottles of water, 1,000 twenty-litre jars of water and 2,000 half-litre bottles of soda water.

Ample Infrabuild India Pvt. Ltd is building the Ample Green township on 125 acres of prime property on the Lucknow–Barabanki road. With 800 independent flats and bungalows, the project is worth Rs 450 crore. It will have its own corporate office in the posh Gomati Nagar area of the city.

Sukesh lives in a mansion, with a designer lawn. In front of the house stands a garage, which houses a Ford Endeavour and a Volkswagen Beta Jetta. A BMW E series and a Honda City have been crowded out and might have to weather the elements on this day.

Seated on a sofa embellished with silver plating, Sukesh

loosens his Rado Centrix wristwatch and sips a cup of lemon tea. Once courtesies have been exchanged and confidence gained, he is ready to go down memory lane.

Like most Dalits, Sukesh wasn't born in a hospital. He was born in a mud house with no running water or bathroom. Food was cooked over firewood and a lantern served as the only source of light at night.

His village, Nagra, falls in the Ballia district of eastern Uttar Pradesh. The village is divided in two, with one portion encompassing a roadside bazaar, and the other part lying half a kilometre away from the road.

For baby Sukesh, the bar was raised very high when he was just in the second standard in the village government primary school. One of his uncles had qualified for the Indian Revenue Service (IRS). Part of the all-India civil services, IRS is considered the third most prestigious civil service in the country. Sukesh felt that he had to match the achievements of his uncle and be the pride of his own parents, who would then have a social standing on par with his uncle's parents.

Because they wanted Sukesh to succeed, his parents denied him the usual boyhood pursuits of hunting for field rats or catching fish in the ponds and waterways.

Sukesh missed rat hunting the most.

In eastern Uttar Pradesh and Bihar, Dalit youth relished eating field rats. During the first rains, rats would come out of their waterlogged holes and dig fresh holes at higher elevations.

'It was easy to figure out when a hole was made,' recalls Sukesh. 'It wasn't difficult to catch rats.'

During the summers when wheat was harvested, Dalit youth would spread out in the fields with buckets and digging tools like shovels and spades. Because of flooding, the rats would be forced to come out of their holes and were easy to catch.

Field rats make holes in the ground to store grains such as wheat, barley, and paddy. Besides catching rats, the Dalit boys would dig holes to collect the grain that the rats had stored.

'That's the pocket money they would earn for themselves,' recalls Sukesh.

'I watched my friends doing all that,' he says, 'and rued that I was missing it.'

Sukesh completed his high school in 1992 from the nearby Janta Inter College, which was half a kilometre from his village. In July that year, he joined DAV School on Bilthara Road for his eleventh and twelfth standards. The school was renowned for imparting a good education, but was 23 kilometres away from Nagra.

Sukesh would travel on his bicycle every day for a total distance of 46 kilometres.

'Back home in the evening I would fall asleep immediately after dinner,' recalls Sukesh. 'I would be so tired.'

Sukesh's father Naresh Kumar prepared for the challenge of educating his son. If Sukesh were to pursue his civil service dream, he would have to move to Allahabad. That would mean more expenses. There was no way that Naresh, who had an eighth-standard education, could earn money in his village. He had to migrate to a city.

Using an old contact, Nareshmigrated to Lucknow. After trying out various vocations, he settled on working with a civil contractor as an on-the-site supervisor.

Sukesh, meanwhile, cleared his Intermediate in 1994 and headed to Allahabad. He enrolled in the Hindi department of the Allahabad University. The university was known for producing civil servants. With plenty of coaching centres, civil service aspirants from all over India would descend on the city. Sukesh's immediate goal was to get a college degree so he would be eligible to appear in the civil service examination. He was admitted in Allahabad University in August 1994 but failed to get a seat in the hostel.

He rented a one-room accommodation and cooked his own food—that was how most of the students lived.

For the first six months or so, he faced many challenges. He was new to the city and took time to adjust to city life. Cooking food was the biggest challenge. He ate at local eateries when finances permitted.

Since the syllabus for the civil service examination is aimed at college graduates, Sukesh had to do well in his studies. He also had to learn English as civil service aspirants are tested on their proficiency in English.

Sukesh completed his Masters in 1999. While still a student at Allahabad University, he started appearing for the civil service examination and in 1999 he reached the interview level.

Clearing the civil services examination is a one-year process and is demanding as it serves to select only a few hundred of the most able from among several hundred thousand aspirants. It is a three-level exam.

Sukesh's father would send money every month, but it was not enough to cover all his needs. He started giving tuition classes to support the civil-service examination coaching he was taking. 'I taught school kids throughout my stay in Allahabad,' says Sukesh.

Despite his repeated efforts, he failed to clear the civil service examinations. Unsure of what to do next, Sukesh enrolled for a PhD at Allahabad University, but quietly moved to Delhi.

'Most of my friends were clearing the civil services,' recalls

Sukesh; it had become too difficult to face failure in Allahabad. But Sukesh found satisfaction in the fact that he had twice reached the interview stage.

Sukesh's father reasoned that his son's move to Delhi was to make use of the better coaching institutions.

Sukesh enrolled for an MPhil/PhD programme at Delhi's Jawaharlal Nehru University (JNU) in 2000, with his civil service dream still firmly in sight. His two further attempts to pass, however, proved to be futile.

It would have been a different matter had his dreams been fulfilled.

But destiny chose a different path for him. Since he wasn't serious about his academics, he did not clear the coursework that would have entitled him to start writing a dissertation and he was asked to leave the university hostel.

'I was virtually on the streets of Delhi,' he says.

Naresh continued to send his son. Sukesh had now given up on the civil service dream. He had no place to stay in Delhi and no income either.

There was no way he could return to Allahabad. Returning to his village or his father's place in Lucknow was also out of the question.

With the little money his father sent him, he rented a one-room residence in Munirka near JNU. He would scan the newspapers for job ads every day.

He was at the lowest point in his life, feeling sandwiched between the demands of day-to-day survival and remorse at having betrayed his parents.

In 2001, Sukesh joined a company that provided breakdown assistance services on National Highway-24. If a vehicle broke down on the highway, Sukesh and his team would take a towing truck and clear the road. He was hired for Rs 1,500 a month.

'We would sit in the van for the entire twelve-hour shift and wait for calls,' he says. 'Often I would be in tears.'

Some months later, he found another job with HDFC Bank. Hired at a monthly salary of Rs 2,700, his job involved enlisting customers to sign up for credit cards.

'I would stand outside the bank and virtually beg the customers to accept credit card offers. It was a kind of hawking,' he recalls.

The next year he found a more lucrative job. The finance company he joined offered him Rs 7,000 a month as well as good incentives. He worked at the company for over a year.

One day, he happened to see his boss's salary slip, which was Rs 65,000 for the month. He thought: 'If my boss makes just Rs 65,000 a month after serving for fifteen years, what will I get after serving for that long?' He began to think of his career more seriously.

It was clear to him that he had to do something really daring. His savings amounted to only Rs 60,000.

'That's the time I started thinking of launching a business myself,' he says. The only problem was that he had no clue what to do.

Weeks went by and Sukesh kept exploring business options. One day, an idea burst upon him. 'It came as a lightning bolt,' he remembers.

In his search for business options, he was reminded of the spices his mother would give him during his Allahabad days. Since childhood, Sukesh had eaten spices that were ground on a grinding stone with a stone roller.

He was nostalgic for homemade spices. When he visited his parents during the festivals, he would complain of the powdered and packed spices in the city that he bought to cook food. His mother Shanti Devi found an answer. She would give him half-crushed turmeric, coriander and dried red chillies.

'The half-crushed spices make the gravy thicker,' says Sukesh. 'They also add to the flavour.'

For the next two weeks, he worked on a business model that involved selling spices in pouches. He acquired a mixer-grinder. He also bought a small electronic scale and spices like coriander, turmeric and dried red chillies. He would grind and weigh them and match the price with that of similar products.

During his four years in Allahabad, Sukesh had cooked his own food. He recalled that for every one student who got hostel accommodation, nine would live in private accommodation, called delegacy. He had seen students buying groceries and packed spices from the market.

He zeroed in on a one-pouch-for-one-rupee strategy. He knew it was the only way he could avoid competition. And nobody was marketing the 'rupee-one-pouch-for-one-meal' idea.

Sukesh did some research in Munirka and bought packets of spices of all the available brands. A packet of spice cost a minimum of Rs 10. He opened the branded packets to measure quantity. It was clear that a packet for Rs 10 was enough for seven to eight meals only.

He was now reasonably certain that his strategy would do well in the market. He identified his prospective consumer base as well.

He targeted students and slum dwellers as his consumer base. He bought two more mixer-grinders and an instrument to seal pouches with. He also bought 5,000 plastic pouches.

It was 26 anuary 2003 when Sukesh boarded the Lucknow Mail for Lucknow. It was very cold and Sukesh was travelling in a 'general compartment'.

'I feared it might be the last night I lived,' he remember.

'I kept thinking of my parents,' he says. 'I had shattered their dreams.'

Since he was carrying three grinders, it looked as if he had bought many gifts for his parents.

For a week, he didn't say a thing about his plans. They didn't know he was no longer pursuing the civil service dream.

He spent days finding a place to start his operations. He also looked for areas with colleges and slums.

The economic boom had resulted in a mushrooming of engineering and management colleges and rural-to-urban migration increased slums. Sukesh made lists of grocery shops in an area.

After a couple of weeks, he found an 8x8-square-foot room, roughly the size of a large bathroom, where he based his operations.

The following week, he launched his product. He crushed red chillies, coriander and turmeric using the three grinders he had.

His mother became suspicious of Sukesh as he had been asking too many questions about spices. One day, she noticed that his clothes smelled strongly of coriander. She confronted him and he confessed to her about his new business venture.

Shanti Devi took a week to tell her husband.

'My father was heartbroken,' remembers Sukesh. 'He would not even look at me.'

Along with one worker he had employed, Sukesh would crush and package spices all day, and the following day traverse the city, leaving packets with grocers.

Grocers were briefed about the merits of the product: It was homemade, it was one-rupee a pouch for one meal, and it was for vegetarian and non-vegetarian foods alike. All three qualities he boasted of were unique to the market then as there was no product matching even one of the three.

Sukesh's product caught buyers' attention in the slums first. Kids would come asking for one-rupee masala.

In a couple of weeks, he had invested all the money he had. While the product was selling well, cash returns from sales were poor.

'Grocers knew I was new,' he says. '"Come tomorrow," they would say.'

The product was a success in the slums, but it didn't quite work in the student segment.

Sukesh borrowed money from a few friends in Lucknow. But it wasn't enough. He then borrowed Rs 1 lakh from a moneylender at a high interest rate. The lender gave him only Rs 90,000 as he had deducted interest in advance.

By the end of the first year, Sukesh still had many hurdles to cross but he was no longer despondent. He was fairly certain that the road he had taken would take him somewhere that he would like.

On the first anniversary of his business, Sukesh had ten workers and a name for the business—ABS Masale. He replaced his old grinders with new, bigger ones. He rented another facility, which had three rooms.

'People around me now started noticing me,' he says. 'My confidence level had shot up.'

By mid-2004, his turnover was touching Rs 100,000 a week. He had found a trusted lieutenant who handled production. For the first time he deputed a worker with the sole mandate of buying raw material from the market. This now freed his time to look for new markets.

During his market sojourns, he saw sattoo do brisk business.

Roasted gram flour, or sattoo, is popular in Bihar and eastern Uttar Pradesh, especially among the poor, since not only is it high in nutrition, but it also does not require cooking. Workers carried sattoo to worksites and ate it whenever they were hungry.

'I sell at least ten kilograms of sattoo a day,' one grocer told Sukesh. Another grocer claimed he sold fifteen kilograms a day.

For three weeks, Sukesh conducted market surveys only on sattoo.

He was convinced that he had hit a goldmine.

Sukesh was now on talking terms with his father. The kind father had forgiven his failed son.

Adding a new product to the ABS Masale kitty, Sukesh bought a 100 kilograms of quality black gram, and roasted it in a makeshift chulha, an indigenous oven.

'We roasted five kilos at a time,' he recalls. 'We didn't have a large vessel.'

The roasted black gram was ground into flour in the nearby flour mill and brought back to the three-room masala-making unit.

'They jumped up in support,' he says about his parents' response.

Sukesh now needed a packaging machine, which cost between Rs 75,000 to Rs 100,000. The moneylender who promised to lend him money couldn't deliver—he was involved in a fight with one of his business associates and was absconding from the police.

At the last moment, Sukesh's parents came through with the money.

ABS Masale made 200 packets—a packet contained half a kilogram of sattoo. Sukesh hoped that it would be hugely successful among the migrant workers from Bihar and eastern Uttar Pradesh.

'It was very handy to carry sattoo to the workplace in packets,' Sukesh says. 'Greed is the god of grocers,' he theorizes, 'and I offered a higher commission to retailers.'

The first 200 half-kilogram packets were sold within a week.

Meanwhile, the rupee-one-pouch-for-one-meal was failing in the student segment. Students looked for higher social markers and hence preferred branded products. Sukesh was ambivalent about whether to supply sattoo packets to the middle class localities where students lived. If his masala packets had failed in the middle class localities, would sattoo sell?

The third month into his sattoo production, he started distributing sattoo in middle class localities. His gamble paid off. 'I was baffled,' he recalls. 'Do the rich also like sattoo?'

As Sukesh was to learn later, diabetics and gym-goers ate sattoo in rather large quantities. Since his was the first neatly packaged sattoo, it was an immediate success.

In the sixth month of business, he was churning out 100 to 150 kilograms of sattoo a day. As demand went up, he upgraded his facilities.

By 2006, he was producing one metric ton of sattoo every day. The next year the production went up to ten metric tons every day.

'I had to employ people to count money,' smiles Sukesh. 'A dozen workers stapled currency notes for hours every evening.'

At this point, Sukesh needed a large office as he was now employing over 100 workers.

Meanwhile, Sukesh promoted yet another company, ABS Beverages Pvt. Ltd.

In 2008, ABS Masale acquired Prime Plaza. The next year, ABS Beverages Pvt. Ltd started production of bottled water. Six months later, soda water was added to the product line.

In 2011, Sukesh launched the ambitious Ample Green Project. Expected to be ready by 2015, the experience should guide him on what to concentrate on thereafter.

'To cross a turnover of Rs 1,000 crore in the next five years is my dream,' says Sukesh. 'A packaged fruit juice business is in the pipeline.'

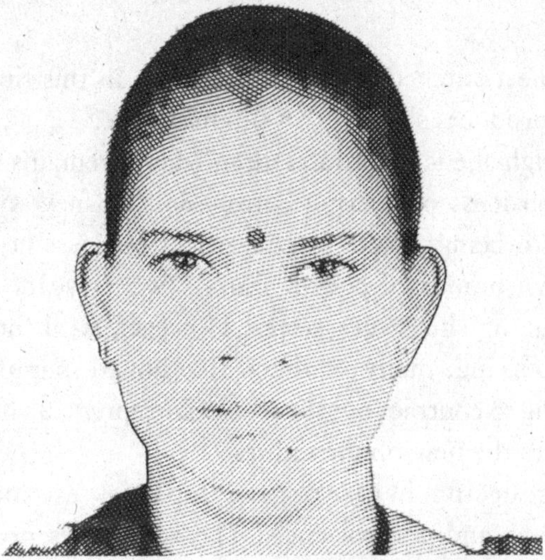

MANJU RANI

'He is a homemaker' is how Manju Rani describes her husband Mahendra Pratap Singh. 'Just joking,' she adds hastily.

Sitting cross-legged on a heap of scrap cotton pieces, Mahendra Singh nods in affirmation. He has brought lunch for her. 'She is the boss,' he says with equanimity.

Manju Rani's shirt-making unit is located in the Bapanagar business area near Karol Bagh in New Delhi. The area is a manufacturing hub for cotton and denim apparel. Manju employs seventeen workers who make over 250 shirts a day. Her factory has frequent visitors—brand owners who want her to make shirts for them, boys looking for jobs and women who collect stitched shirts for cleaning. In this tiny facility, Manju produces shirts on an assembly line.

Though she is a manufacturer, Manju remains nameless. In the business of making cotton shirts, a new system has come into being. There are dozens of business houses with their own brands of cotton shirts. Twenty years ago, they were making shirts themselves. However, with the increase in outsourcing, many of them abandoned manufacturing, preferring to contract out the work. Entrepreneurs like Manju lapped up the new opportunities.

Outsourcing helps large companies escape labour regulations and control costs. The companies provide key material inputs—cloth, thread, buttons, labels and packaging kits—to these new, small manufacturers, called vendors, who in turn deliver finished apparel, complete with price tags, to the companies.

'That's my dream,' says Manju when asked why she couldn't launch her own brand. A job provider, Manju pays nearly Rs 20 lakh annually to her workers as well as to her outsourced service providers.

Manju lives a middle-class life in Bapanagar. She has three children, all sons, and her mother, too, lives with them.

Manju was born in a slum in the same area in 1978. Bapanagar has three distinct localities—slums, a residential area and a business area. It is home to people who work in businesses, making cotton shirts and denim jeans.

Manju's father Chhote Lal was an immigrant from the Uttar Pradesh countryside, who came to Delhi in 1962 in search of a job. The son of landless Dalit parents, he had never been to school.

For the first few months, while he was trying to find a job, Chhote Lal stayed with a relative. With no work experience, he found it difficult to land a job. He finally ended up selling peanuts, an entrepreneurial activity that required little skill or capital. He would rise early in the morning, trek to Khari Baoli market, a trading centre for peanuts, where he would buy ten to fifteen kilograms of peanuts. He would hire a pushcart to transport the peanuts and hawk them on the streets until his stock ran out.

'We lived one day at a time,' Manju's mother Radha says pensively. Within a couple of years, Manju's father was able to set up a hut that was 60 square feet. It had three doors, and a roof made of black plastic sheets.

Manju had five siblings—four sisters and a brother. Around the mid-1980s her father became an alcoholic. 'He did drink before,' admits Radha. 'but he was an occasional drinker, drinking when friends came or during festivals.'

Frequently, Lal would bring home only liquor and no money at the end of the day. 'We all would wait for him,' says Manju with a tone of sadness. Things became worse when he had no money to even buy peanuts from the market.

The family would go to sleep without food. 'Sometimes the neighbours would feed the kids,' Radha says, trying to maintain her composure. She would keep a large vessel half full with water boiling on the stove. The children would be fooled into believing that the food was being cooked and would fall asleep before the 'food' was ready.

'One day, we ran out of kerosene,' recalls Manju. It was around 1986 when Radha began thinking of finding a job. A neighbour took her to a shirt-making unit where she got a job. She had to collect shirts from the factory and clean them.

'Cleaning' refers to removing lint and threads that are stuck to the shirts. The job also involved checking to see if the buttons were correctly placed. Radha began with fifty shirts a day, which eventually increased to 500 shirts a day. Soon the children joined their mother in the job. As money came into the household, Radha began to worry about marrying off her daughters.

In 1988, Manju's elder sister Saroj Kumari got married, and Manju had to drop out of school after her eighth standard to take over her sister's responsibility of cleaning the shirts.

The kids would work till they fell asleep. 'I knew I had to save money for my marriage,' Manju says candidly.

Saroj's marriage was to impact Manju's life greatly. Listening to Saroj's tales, Manju developed her own fantasies of married life—there would be a bed to sleep on, a room in which the bed would be placed, a husband who would bring enough clothes to wear, and there would be enough food to eat.

Manju was born and lived in a hut that was slightly bigger than a hospital lift for patients. The roof was made of polythene fertilizer bags that were stitched together to form a sheet. The hut had no windows, no almirah, no trunk and no water connection, let alone a toilet or a place to bathe. The eight-member family, six siblings and parents, would sleep on the floor.

'We lived in a virtual hole,' says Manju, 'and pigs lived better than us.' Bathing would be an ordeal. When one member of the family was to take a bath, the other seven would go out of the hut. The hut's floor was plastered with mud, so normal bathing was out of the question. One would have to dip a piece of cloth in the water and wipe the body clean. The bath needed a couple of litres of water, and no more than three or four minutes.

In early 1993 when she was fifteen, Manju was married to Mahendra. She was taken to her native village where relatives helped find a groom for her. 'I was excited—I had expected that with marriage, poverty would go forever,' Manju says, gasping in disbelief at her own naïvety.

Her dreams disappeared like the morning mist under a glaring sun. Within weeks, Manju realized that she had landed in another world. Her father-in-law was a low-level government servant who looked after village tube wells for irrigation. The house was fairly large and stocked with foodgrains. But, with her new life came a new set of problems.

'I was veiled,' Manju says. According to tradition, newly married Dalit women are required to wear a veil for a couple of months, especially when facing elderly men in the household. She would remain home-bound and cook food and do other chores. She would have to give her mother-in-law a massage every day. She would be veiled when she went out, irrespective of the kind of people she would come across, from the elderly to kids.

Manju had been poor but she was city-bred, and found the rural customs distasteful. But she went along with them and did what was expected of her. However, her challenges increased as she went to work in the cattle shed. Her in-laws had two bullocks that ploughed the land, a cow for milk and about half a dozen goats.

As the newest member in the family, Manju had to replace her mother-in-law in cleaning the cattle shed with her bare hands. The job included carrying dung in a bamboo basket. The basket would be placed on her head and she would have to dump its contents in a pit nearby where the dung would mature into manure. 'I vomited the first day and fell sick,' recalls Manju.

'At times, the cow dung would seep onto one's head,' she laughs. Worse still, she had to make cow dung cakes, used as cooking fuel. Once she almost froze with horror when she saw her mother-in-law placing a roti directly on the burning cow-dung cakes.

It was no fun carrying bundles of sugarcane on her head either. Unused to cooking food on burning wood, the smoke would suffocate her.

Within six months after getting married, Manju was tired of village life. She asked Mahendra to go to Delhi and find a job. He had been dreaming of a city life for a long time. It was August 1993 when he landed in Delhi. Within an hour he was at his in-laws' hut.

It had rained heavily that day and the slum was inundated. Mahendra's in-laws' hut was flooded too. Filth floated around. 'I was shaken,' he says.

He had some money with him and went out to eat. 'I would have vomited had I eaten in the hut,' says Mahendra.

Radha was embarrassed and requested a boy to take him to the nearby bus stand where he spent his first night in Delhi.

'I wanted to return to my village,' Mahendra says with a flicker of sadness. 'But I stayed back for Manju. After all, hundreds of families were living in this slum.'

His mother-in-law sought the help of a co-worker who took Mahendra to an embroidery unit where he spent the next six months learning the art.

In early 1994, Mahendra landed a job in an embroidery unit in Mangolpuri, 15 kilometres to the west of Bapanagar. With his first salary, he rented a room near the embroidery unit. He made Rs 250 a week. The room rent was Rs 200 a month. He would spend another Rs 200 on travel from home to the factory and back. Four months later, Manju joined him in their Mangolpuri house.

Manju enjoyed her life in the city. Living with her husband

without another person around was the 'first-ever joy' in her life. But this joy came at a price. Used to living with family members all her life, Manju was now lonely. Mahendra would be out of the house for over twelve hours a day. Cooking food, washing dishes, cleaning the house and washing clothes wouldn't take more than four to five hours.

Idling away seven to eight hours a day became unbearable for her. 'We didn't have a TV.'

A couple of months passed and Manju became restless. One day, she had an idea. She saw a woman selling vegetables, and others hawked other items, including household goods. What impressed her most was a young man selling rice and chhole during lunch. He sold a plate for Rs 5. His customers were mainly workers.

'Can I, too, do something like that?' Manju wondered. She thought she could sell cooked food during lunch. Their area was an embroidery workers' hub. The young workers, mostly immigrants from the countryside, did not carry lunch but would instead, buy food from roadside food carts.

One afternoon, she bought some wheat flour, mustard oil and a packet of mango pickle. She needed to work out how profitable selling parathas could be. She wanted to know if she could make twenty parathas from a kilo of wheat flour, which cost Rs 5 in those days. If she priced one paratha at a rupee, she would make a profit of Rs 15 from a kilogram of wheat flour.

'I couldn't solve the paratha puzzle,' chips in Mahendra. He enjoyed the parathas stuffed with cooked vegetable every morning, and would learn later that his wife was carrying out a business experiment.

Manju worked out how much a plate with three parathas, mango pickle, some onion pieces and one green chilli would cost. She added the cost of oil—and worked out that it would cost her Rs 6 to make eighteen parathas from a kilogram of wheat flour.

'Are you joking?' Mahendra responded, when Manju explained her business plan. 'She acted like a street magician,' says Mahendra. 'I was speechless.'

In order to sell her business model to her husband, Manju made eighteen parathas and placed them in six paper plates with three parathas each, along with mango pickle, onion pieces and green chillies. Next to each plate, she kept Rs 3 in currency notes and covered the plates with a towel.

When Mahendra finished his cup of tea that evening, Manju took the towel covering the plates off, started picking up the currency notes and rhythmically intoning 'Rs 3' six times.

'This is Rs 18,' she showed Mahendra. She took away Rs 6 as production cost, and put Rs 12 in Mahendra's pocket. 'That's our profit,' she said jumping with joy.

The couple discussed the logistics for a couple of days and, the following week, Manju took the first steps of her long journey with the slogan— 'three parathas for Rs 3 and pickle, onion and green chilli free'!

She placed the neatly wrapped parathas on a wooden plank and sat on a few bricks that Mahendra brought from a nearby construction site. She used newspapers to wrap the parathas.

'On the first day, I sold all the six plates I had prepared,' she says. By the third week, she was selling parathas made from six kilograms of wheat flour. Within a few months her output had doubled and she hired help. 'Too thick and the parathas were too cheap,' says Mahendra. 'The plate was "stomach full" for an adult.'

Mahendra was making Rs 250–300 a week, and Manju

was now making about Rs 100 a day. She would close her business by half past three in the afternoon. She was now faced with another problem—what to do with the rest of the evening?

Manju was now developing another business idea. She carried out tests at home and the model was soon ready. She explained to Mahendra that it would be easy to make five litres of tea and sell it between six to seven in the evening from the same spot where she sold her parathas. She was known in the area now. She bought a steel drum with a tap at the bottom. She carried earthen cups and sold tea at 50 paisa a cup.

'It was sheer greed,' was her take on the tea enterprise.

By the end of 1994, Manju had saved about Rs 13,000. 'I ran the family and we lived a very happy life.'

While things were humming along, Manju conceived her first baby. Six months into her pregnancy, she suspended her business activities. In her eighth month, she returned to her mother's place in Bapanagar. Late in 1994, she delivered a baby boy. A few months later, her father passed away.

Mahendra rented a room close to the Bapanagar slums and found a job nearby.

Manju soon became restless again. 'I felt as if I was losing Rs 150 a day,' she remembers. 'Away from business, I was like a fish out of water.'

But Manju's mother would not allow her to sell food. 'Street food hawkers are looked down upon,' she says. Manju was born in Bapanagar, and the locals knew her and the family well.

'I had to do something,' says Manju. She could not return to Mangolpuri because there was no childcare there, which she would need if she were to restart her business. 'My three sisters were here to take care of my baby,' she says.

Manju had tasted money; it was sweet. She wouldn't wait any longer. In early 1995 she joined the packaging unit of a shirt-making company near Bapanagar. Though officially it was an eight-hour work day, she, like many workers, would put in four more hours in overtime to make some extra money. She made Rs 30 a day.

Manju would leave her son with her mother while she was at work. With two salaries, Manju had more money at her disposal than her mother.

'Before my baby was born, my hand was always in my purse for my mother—she bore so many responsibilities,' says Manju. She was happy helping her mother.

Manju connects the purse story to her method of keeping her money safe. When she was running her roaring food business, anyone could have broken open the fragile door of her home while she was away selling food. So she developed a method to keep her money safe. 'It was to fool prospective thieves,' she says with a grin.

Manju used earthen pots for cooking. The pots also worked as storage for foodgrain. In one large pot, Manju stored yellow dal. She would hide the day's profit under the dal in the pot hoping that a thief wouldn't have the imagination to see the pot as a locker. Once in a while, she would visit Radha and leave the money with her.

Leaving Mangolpuri for Bapanagar proved to be too costly for Manju. Resuming her food business was not an option due to its 'low social marker'. Her gender, too, stifled her aspirations. Having given birth to another son, she had to focus her attention on child-rearing, though her sisters provided invaluable support. More than a decade went by with Manju being stuck in the same job in the shirt-making company.

By the turn of the new millennium, large firms were grabbing the new opportunities without increasing their workforce. Instead, outsourcing was the name of the game—it allowed firms to meet the high demand without burdening themselves with more workers who, under Indian labour laws, they couldn't fire when demand waned.

The company where Mahendra worked began outsourcing much of its work. Mahendra now had a couple of options—either to supply leather labels, which he embroidered from home, or quit the job.

Manju saw this as an opportunity awaiting the family. She accompanied Mahendra to the jeans manufacturer and sought assurance that the couple would get work. The manufacturer agreed and asked them to buy two sewing machines.

For four days they debated whether to buy new or used machines and also whether to buy automatic or manually run machines. They finally decided to buy old machines that ran manually. Their area had an erratic power supply, with nearly eight hours of 'load shedding'. It made sense to buy old, manually run machines that wouldn't need electricity.

'We each worked fourteen hours a day,' says Manju. 'To impress the manufacturer, we produced the best labels without any extra charge.' It was late 2009 when Manju bought two more machines and quit her job.

'Mahendra is shy,' she laughs when asked why she occupied the driver's seat, and after a pause, adds: 'You have to be chatty and a hard bargainer to succeed in business.'

While the couple was busy making a living, a relative from her village came to Bapanagar in search of a job. He had heard that Manju had become a factory owner and a lakhpati. He visited her unit and got in touch with them.

On his first visit home, he told the village folk that Manju worked on a leather product. The story spread like wildfire.

'It hurt us a lot,' recalls Manju, pained. 'As if we ran a tannery.'

Manju began thinking of switching over to another business. Shirt-making came to her mind as she had worked in a shirt-making factory. She knew many master tailors as well as cutters. She herself was an expert in packing shirts and her mother knew how shirts were cleaned. In early 2010, Manju decided to try her hand at manufacturing shirts.

'God is with me,' Manju reminded herself as she went to meet the shirt manufacturer. The manufacturer gave Manju a patient hearing. He asked her to buy one sewing machine to begin with. He agreed to give her the cut pieces of cloth, thread, buttons and packing material. All Manju would have to do was stitch them into shirts and return them neatly packed.

'He empathized with me because I looked so frail,' Manju smiles.

Back home, Manju called a family meeting with Mahendra, two sisters, and her younger brother who was to die later in 2010 of a congenital heart condition at the age of twenty-five.

Mahendra agreed to train himself in the art of stitching shirts. Her two sisters agreed to clean the shirts without charging any money. Her brother agreed to take the shirts to the washerman who would iron them. Manju would buy a sewing machine, hire a tailor and do the packing of the product herself.

That evening they bought a sewing machine that could run both manually and on power. The family celebrated the event. A priest was called in to solemnize the ceremony.

'In villages, Brahmin priests didn't serve us,' says Radha. 'That way, cities are good for us.'

The shirt-maker gave Manju cut fabric for twelve shirts. The family got together to produce the twelve shirts in four days.

'He was so pleased with our work,' says Manju.

The business of shirt-making was highly competitive. Manju's siblings wanted her to succeed. Her sisters didn't charge any money for cleaning the shirts. Her brother helped by taking the shirts to the washerman. Manju didn't charge for packing.

Shirt-making involves multiple processes. Brand owners procure fabric, and determine colour, design and measurements. In large units, computerized machines are used to cut fabric. Workers stitch the cut fabric into shirts and again an assembly-line process takes place.

Once the raw shirt is ready, it undergoes a few more steps. Someone makes the buttonholes and another fixes the buttons. Next, the threads left on the shirts have to be removed. The product is then sent to a washer and for pressing. Finally, the tags are attached and the shirt is packaged.

'His manager was so happy with us,' Manju says, although she did not meet the owner. 'He was abroad on a business trip.'

Manju got a repeat order for twelve more shirts. The third order was for twenty-four. The fourth order was for another twenty-four shirts.

They broke even. 'We just wanted to enter the market and have credibility,' explains Manju.

After she made over 100 shirts, the manufacturer asked his manager to call her for a meeting.

'Our story melted his heart,' says Manju. She told him that her entire family had got together to back her and her husband so that they could succeed. Upon his queries, she explained her trajectory and how from a worker, she was trying to become an entrepreneur. 'I didn't tell him my caste, though,' she says.

He asked Manju to buy two more machines. Making her promise not to tell anyone else, the owner told them how much other vendors charged for the work she was doing.

'He compensated us for our free work,' she says with reverence in her voice.

Before acquiring two more machines, Manju had to find a proper place to install the machines. Through the help of a Dalit social worker, she approached Lakshmi Narayan, who owned a property in the Bapanagar business area.

'I was so happy to learn that this lady was a Dalit and an entrepreneur,' recalls Narayan. Without even having her sign a rent deed, he allowed her to install the machines.

Within a week, Manju installed all three machines. She hired tailors on contract. 'You will not be paid by the number of hours and days you put in,' she told them, 'but by the number of shirts you produce.'

By the end of 2011, Manju had added three more machines and the number of workers had reached the double digits. In 2011, she also made arrangements for the marriages of her two sisters.

Manju now leads an average middle-class life. She has brought her mother Radha to live with her in her home. 'I am sure I will not die in a slum,' Manju says. 'God is benevolent.'

'I have realized my first dream,' Manju says about the new situation of brand owners coming to her unit. 'I no longer make rounds to them.'

Manju has two more dreams to accomplish: To touch a turnover of Rs 5 crore and have her sons launch their own brand.

Radha celebrates the triumph with tears of joy rolling down her cheeks. 'My daughter has reached the sky!' she says.

VIJAY ANAND RAO SHELKE

Ramdaspeth Pipri, a township under construction on the outskirts of Nagpur, is an easy fifteen-minute drive from both the Dr Babasaheb Ambedkar International Airport and the Nagpur railway station, which is in the heart of the city. The township is also ideally located near the intersection of the outer Ring Road and the NH-6, which slices across India, connecting Surat to Kolkata. While the township falls within the locale of Pipri village, it is also attached to Ramdaspeth, the most affluent locality in Nagpur.

On a Sunday morning, dozens of cars are already parked haphazardly outside the makeshift office. A giant billboard reads: Infratech. With ISO 9001–2008 certification, Infratech

Real Estate Pvt. Ltd is building the new township, its layout plans displayed on the outer wall.

Built on a 250-acre tract of land, the township will have fourteen sectors. Designed by architect Kuldeep Kaul, it will have flats in multi-storey apartment buildings as well as independent bungalows.

'The township will have a golf course, gyms, swimming pools, beauty salons, shopping plazas amongst a host of modern amenities, including schools and a state-of-the-art medical centre,' explains Uday Nagpuri, a civil engineer and chief operating officer at Infratech. 'Once completed, the project will be worth Rs 1,000 crore. It is expected to be completed by the end of 2016,' he says.

A perusal of the company website highlights other ongoing projects, including the construction of resorts in the Andaman Islands. Once completed, these will be worth Rs 800 crore, adds Uday.

The owners of Infratech have also diversified into agriculture with the cultivation of noni (*Morinda citrifolia*) and aloe vera. Known for its antioxidant properties, noni juice is popular around the world, and the Andaman and Nicobar Islands, due to their atypical soil qualities, are most suited for noni cultivation.

Nagpur, on the other hand, is best suited for the growth of aloe vera, whose cultivation and pulp extraction is handled by one of the sister companies of Infratech. Aloe vera is grown on 200 acres of top-class farmland in the Nagpur countryside. Another 200 acres has been acquired on which cultivation will start soon.

Once fully operational, the aloe vera line of products alone will gross Rs 300 crore. The noni juice business is also equally profitable.

'Our health products will overshadow our township business in less than a decade,' says a company official.

As Uday outlines the type of landscaping with imported grass that is planned for the township, there is suddenly a commotion among the people gathered. The company employees start dispersing. 'It's the boss,' Uday says, sounding an alert.

Vijay Anand Rao Shelke is stoutly built, round-faced and bald. Sporting a broad smile, he enters the large single-storeyed camp office. 'We have projects to enter six other cities, including Delhi,' he says.

Vijay is married; his daughter and son study in Nagpur's best public schools. Infratech is jointly owned by Vijay, his elder brother Nischay Anand Rao Shelke and Mahendra Gawai. 'Together, we have over two dozen companies,' says Gawai.

Vijay leaves after half an hour to entertain prospective buyers who wished to speak to him directly; Nischay offers to stay with us and narrates the trajectory of his brother's life.

Vijay was born in 1967 in the village of Sura Bardi on the edge of the lush green Chargaon hills in Vidarbha. The village is very near the Chargaon dam, which was built in 1983 and impounds the Chargaon river.

The tiny mud house in which Vijay was born is still surrounded by shrubs on three sides. The roof is made of locally baked clay tiles and like most houses in the village, it has no running water, bathroom, or kitchen and has just one window.

Vijay's father, the late Sayaji Rao Jawade, was born to landless and illiterate parents, but had always dreamt of owning some tracts of farmland. 'He had fantasies of farmland,' chuckles Mahadeb Bucha. Mahadeb, now in his seventies and some twenty years younger than Sayaji, was a good friend of the latter.

Married at the age of fourteen, Sayaji was restless, refusing to settle for the routine that had trapped his family for generations. India had just become independent, which provided the right setting for him to realize his dreams. The country was awash with expectations of a future without feudalism, of big landlords losing their unbridled power, and the landless, especially the Dalits, getting their share. Landlords, worried about their comeuppance, began to sell off some of the 'excess' land they possessed.

Ramji Mahar, a Dalit from Sayaji's village, owned a large piece of land on the outskirts of Nagpur. His wife had inherited it from her parents and the couple had shifted to Nagpur. Fearing a government takeover of his fourteen-acre farmland, Ramji looked for buyers.

With Rs 10 in savings, Sayaji was tempted. He discussed the matter with his wife Savitrabai and she wholeheartedly supported his venture. She had probably been worried that, like her in-laws, she too, would end up working on other people's land all her life.

Sayaji trekked to Nagpur to meet Ramji. There was a train for the 10-kilometre journey, but he chose to walk the distance as he was keen to save every paisa he had.

Although Ramji was sympathetic to Sayaji, he quoted a price of Rs 75 for all the fourteen acres. Around 1949, Rs 75 was a big amount—five grams of 24-carat gold cost Rs 5 at the time (by way of comparison, by late 2013 it cost nearly Rs 15,000).

Sayaji's dream appeared doomed.

A couple of days later, Ramji came to Sura Badi in search of buyers. Sayaji met him in a hamlet near the village and invited him for lunch. The lunch—a feast of chicken and vegetables—pleased the guest who wanted to meet Sayaji again the very next day.

Sayaji once again trekked to Nagpur and, after prolonged negotiations, Ramji lowered the price to Rs 50. Since there was no way Sayaji could pay that much at once, an arrangement was made. Sayaji had to pay Rs 25 immediately, and the remaining 25 would be realized from the harvest of the land.

How was Sayaji to raise the additional Rs 15? And quickly? Back home, Sayaji discussed the matter with Savitrabai who had the Rs 4 that her mother had gifted her. Between them, the couple had Rs 14. Savitrabai 'raised' another Rs 12 by allowing Sayaji to sell her jewellery. Within a couple of weeks, the land was registered in Sayaji's name. A celebration followed. Savitrabai brought a large goat from her parents. Sayaji invited his relatives and other Dalit families to the feast.

By 1952 Sayaji was the proud owner of fourteen acres of land. With a decent landholding, Sayaji and Savitribai led a tough but happy life despite the periodic bouts of drought that would hit Vidarbha. The couple had four children, two daughters and two sons. Their eldest son Nischay was born in 1962. One daughter would later marry a government employee and settle in Nagpur.

To Sayaji, education was the passport to success. He enrolled Nischay in a primary school in a nearby village. Nischay would walk every day, a round trip of 8 kilometres. 'He would thrash the boy if he bunked classes,' recalls Mahadeb.

'He dreamt of us becoming government officers,' says Nischay. 'He prayed we, too, would move in cars as officers do while visiting villages.'

Nischay studied till the seventh standard in the local school before moving to Nagpur, some 45 kilometres away, for further studies.

Since Nischay's sister Muktabai was based in Nagpur, it was easier to enrol Nischay in a city school. With the help of his brother-in-law, Nischay managed to get into Jeevan Shiksha Vidyalay, where he studied in residence from the eighth to the tenth standard.

In 1981 he had entered Intermediate. That same year, Sayaji brought his second son Vijay to Nagpur.

Vijay was too young to live on his own so he lived with Muktabai's family. He was admitted in the Saint Vincent Convent School located in the posh Medical Square. 'Kids of the rich study in that convent,' says Gawai, Vijay's long-time business partner.

Nischay completed his Intermediate in 1983 and enrolled for college in 1984. That same year, Vijay completed his fifth standard and went to stay with Nischay for his junior high school. Nischay lived in a two-room house and cooked his own food. He now cooked for Vijay as well, washed his clothes, got him ready for school and sent him off with tiffin.

'He was like a mother to me,' Vijay is nostalgic.

Sayaji would visit his sons in the first week of every month. He would bring rations and leave some money with Nischay.

After completing college, Nischay joined a real estate company that built apartments and commercial buildings. Being a graduate in commerce, he joined the company's finance division.

His responsibilities more than doubled. He would rise early, prepare food for Vijay and himself, and leave for office. Since he was now employed, he gave Vijay pocket money. He knew most parents with kids around the same age as Vijay would give them pocket money.

Around this time, Nischay started noticing unusual changes in his younger brother. 'So often, he would reach home late in the evening,' he recalls. Vijay would also demand more pocket money, which he would spend on grooming.

Nischay was taken aback to see his brother apply beauty cream on his face. He would try to persuade Vijay to spend more time on his studies and play at school rather than waste his time. But seeing the situation deteriorate even more as days passed, Nischay confronted Vijay, who feigned innocence.

'I was alone at home, got bored and went to a friend's house to watch TV,' Vijay said. He offered lame excuses for more serious changes in his conduct. There were complaints from the school principal as well.

'Take your brother away,' the principal told Nischay one day.

Nischay met his sister and jijaji to discuss Vijay. Muktabai called Vijay home but he dismissed the complaints as baseless.

Vijay began to disobey Nischay and Nischay thrashed him on a couple of occasions, something he regrets now. 'I did it to save him from ruination,' he says. He was not only worried that Vijay had gone down a path that might ruin him and shame the family, but he was also answerable to his father.

In July 1988, Vijay enrolled for his ninth standard after faring poorly in the eighth standard. One evening, Vijay didn't return home. Nischay wasn't too worried—Vijay had done so several times in the recent past. But when he didn't return for the fourth day in a row, Nischay became worried and took a day's leave to search for his brother. He went to Vijay's friend's homes—they told him that Vijay had gone back to the village.

'He has sold his textbooks and torn up his notebooks,' Nischay was told.

Shocked, Nischay returned to the village.

'How will I face my father?' he asked himself. 'After all, I was his guardian in Nagpur.'

Hearing that Nischay had come home too, Vijay slipped away to a relative's place in the nearby village. Sayaji found it unusual that both his sons had come home for no obvious reason—there was no festival, nor was it time for school holidays.

Vijay had not told his parents that he had quit school. He had cooked up a story that due to some dispute amongst management members, the school had been closed indefinitely.

'I had to tell our father the truth,' says Nischay.

Sayaji was stunned and Savitrabai was in tears. The entire village soon came to know what had transpired.

With a heavy heart, Nischay returned to Nagpur and resumed his duties. He would often blame himself for not being able to figure out what was happening to his younger brother.

'This is my failure as well,' was the thought that haunted Nischay. Their parents could not understand how a gentle boy like Vijay had become so aggressive.

Savitrabai approached an exorcist in the village. For a couple of chickens, she agreed to work on Vijay. She asked for one chicken as advance, along with spices and oil to cook the chicken.

'An evil sprit has entered his body,' said the exorcist. 'Unless the spirit is chased out of his body, he will not return to school. That will require many rituals,' she added.

Sayaji agreed to bear the expense.

Savitrabai had a rethink. It wasn't her dream for Vijay to become a big officer.

'So what if one son doesn't study,' she reasoned with a woman in the village. 'He could look after the farmland and cattle.'

'She was a humble woman and, as a mother, she didn't want to subject her son to torture just to send him back to school,' explains Mahadeb.

But Sayaji bought into the evil sprit hypothesis. He knew the treatment for chasing away the evil spirit involved inflicting pain and humiliation on Vijay.

Vijay learnt of the plan and disappeared from the village. He was scared of several things: he might have to tonsure his head, or blacken a part of his face and have country liquor sprinkled all over his body every day for a week. He might be asked to make seven rounds of the village bare-bodied. He might be asked to lie down so that the exorcist, in order to chase off the evil spirit, could jump on his back till the evil spirit left his body.

'How long will I be on the run like this?' Vijay finally asked himself. He returned home a determined man. He took a friend along and went to the exorcist's house with a rod in his hand. The exorcist was so frightened by them that she left for her parental home for a week.

A compromise was reached. Vijay would live his life his way and no one would bother him any more.

'Why did all this happen?' he kept asking himself. The events prodded him to introspect.

His situation was further complicated in the public school where he studied. He was a village boy and poor. He also bore the cross of being an untouchable, while most of his classmates were city-bred, rich and upper caste.

Nevertheless, Vijay found Nagpur to be a very open city and his friends accepted him as one of them. Not that they didn't know his caste. He would organize his birthday parties at his sister's house where his friends saw the portrait of Dr Ambedkar that hung in the living room. They knew who Dr Ambedkar was and who his followers were—it never caused a problem between Vijay and his friends.

He would visit his friends' houses on birthdays or festivals. Their wealth and comfort impressed him, but he couldn't be sure if he would ever possess the good things in life.

He had some relatives in the city. They were mostly government employees and none had cars or even bikes. None could match the kind of worldly goods business families possessed.

After Vijay completed primary school and went to live with Nischay, his school too changed. However, he remained in touch with half a dozen of his friends from his primary school. As he and his friends became older, they would bunk classes to watch movies. Vijay's rich friends had plenty of money and they frequently watched movies and ate out.

'True, we turned anti-school, anti-education,' admits a classmate of Vijay's now. 'We worshipped business to rationalize bunking classes.'

'We would cite examples of our parents to justify our wrong-doings,' admits another classmate.

'We subscribed to the belief that there was a conflict between business and education,' recalls Vijay. The idea of business had taken a hold of him but what he didn't realize was that his fun-loving friends came from business families and they were destined to inherit wealth and wealth-making machines. While his friends continued to live in Nagpur, Vijay had to return to the village.

In the village, Vijay lived with a guilty conscience. He had shattered his father's dream. He had seen his mother in tears. He had become an object of gossip among the villagers.

Helping out on the family farm had become his business now. He determined to give it his best.

In the second year of Vijay's return to the village, the farm output in cotton, pulses and soya bean rose dramatically as he had procured the right seeds and fertilizers. He was no longer in his father's bad books. But he kept thinking of Nagpur, and of Nischay, of whom he remained afraid.

'He will thrash me hard,' he would shudder. But he also felt stifled in the village.

'My career will begin at Zero Mile,' Vijay would remind himself.

Nagpur was known as the Zero Mile city as the surveyors of British India had identified it as the central point of India and distances were measured from Nagpur. The town was once the hub of the postal department and the people of Nagpur pride themselves on being at the centre of India.

Before finishing his second year in the village, Vijay returned to Nagpur to meet his friends.

'He didn't come to me,' recalls Nischay.

Vijay saw his classmates joining their family businesses and doing well in life. One friend drove him around the city in his car.

'Come back, I will give you shelter,' he told Vijay while they drove about in his Maruti Zen.

Afraid of Nischay and his jija, Vijay returned to the village.

A year later, he returned to Nagpur in search of his Zero Mile aspiration and stood next to the milestone inscribed with a '0'.

It was December 1991 when Vijay finally settled in Nagpur.

He had a one-room accommodation with an attached bathroom and a kitchen. As promised, his old friend supported him.

Vijay wasn't trained for any job in an urban environment. But with the help of his friends, he landed a job as a bouncer at a bar in the Mahal area. He was entitled to three meals a day plus pocket money.

He spent two years as a bouncer in the bar. Bar-owner Shailendra Jaiswal took pity on Vijay after hearing his story and found a job for him. In early 1993 Vijay joined a liquor distribution company as a sales representative.

Guarding the bar for about two years, Vijay had developed some sense of the bar industry. He also made contacts in other bars. His job involved securing sales orders from bars. He would get a handsome commission on sales generated by his efforts. He now made decent money and his family felt relieved that he was earning a living.

During his visits to bars, Vijay met Mahendra Gawai, who ran the Naga Bar. The son of parents who were both doctors, Gawai ran the bar his father had gifted him. However, Naga Bar was not doing well.

Vijay and Gawai became friends. Gawai was very happy when he learnt that Vijay was, like himself, a Dalit.

'You are not meant for the bar business,' Vijay once told Gawai. 'You are too gentle a person for this business.'

In the summer of 1998, Gawai introduced Vijay to his father, T.B. Gawai. In the few encounters that Dr Gawai had with Vijay, he was impressed with him.

'What a dashing personality Vijay is,' Dr Gawai told his son. He also asked Mahendra to see if Vijay would like to run Naga Bar.

'I jumped with excitement,' recalls Vijay. 'Will my dream come true?' he wondered.

Vijay roped in his sister's son Harsh Vardhan as a partner. They rented Naga Bar for Rs 25,000 a month from Dr Gawai. Since Vijay had worked as a salesman with a liquor distribution company, he was able to get the liquor on credit.

After a couple of months, Vijay started feeling the heat. While the bar did brisk business and there was a good profit margin, there were other factors that bothered him.

In the public's estimation, the bar business is a money-minting machine. But the police would demand their share and the mafias would demand theirs. People from the excise department would come calling. Social and religious organizations would seek donations. Bouncers would steal imported liquor.

Still, Vijay ran the show well for over a year and counted his profit. Meanwhile, something happened that would change his fortunes.

In 1999, a relative of Nischay's came to visit him. He had six acres of land near Buti Bori, one of the largest industrial clusters on the outskirts of Nagpur. The relative wanted to sell four acres. He wanted to sell the land at the earliest, but had been unable to find a Dalit buyer.

In order to protect Dalits when land grabbing was a phenomenon, the government had passed a law that a Dalit could sell his land only to a Dalit. Since there was no Dalit in the real estate business in Nagpur, Nischay's relative could not find buyers and requested Nischay to help him find one.

Thinking that his brother was doing well in the bar business, Nischay met Vijay that evening at the Naga Bar. Vijay listened to the proposal and promised to get back to Nischay within days.

'Don't miss this opportunity,' Nischay told his brother.

Vijay called Mahendra and Harsh to the Naga Bar for a

brainstorming session. 'Can we together buy these four acres?' Vijay asked. He also explained who the seller was.

They decided to meet Nischay the next day. Nischay called the relative the following morning and discussed the deal. The seller quoted a price of Rs 1.5 lakhs an acre, so the total for four acres was Rs 6 lakh.

The two brothers along with Mahendra and Harsh inspected the land that evening. On their way to the site, they saw plenty of industrial sheds coming up. Since construction activity was everywhere, Nischay hoped that the land in question would not be a prospective green belt. If it was, then the government would acquire the land at much below the market price.

Vijay and his team were excited by the location of the land. All they had to do was verify the government's master plan for the area. If the government had already identified a green belt, then the land they had just seen was safe.

The following day, Vijay deputed Mahendra to verify the master plan. By late afternoon, it became clear that the land was safe. In the master plan, a green belt had been earmarked elsewhere.

Vijay and Nischay went to a real estate expert whom Nischay knew well. He assessed the details of the deal and said, 'Go for it.'

He told Vijay, 'You will be a king soon.'

Later Vijay explained the economics of the land deal they were finalizing to Mahendra and Harsh.

'We will buy in acres, but sell in square feet,' he told them. This was the advice Vijay had received from the real estate expert.

'But where is the money?'

Vijay asked Mahendra and Harsh to arrange Rs 2 lakh

each. He knew they had the money. They agreed and assumed that Vijay would bring in the rest.

Vijay, Mahendra and Harsh told Nischay about their proposal to buy the land, and Vijay included one caveat: they would pay only Rs 4 lakh immediately, and the remaining Rs 2 lakh in instalments.

'We were speechless,' recalls Mahendra. 'But I trusted Vijay's wisdom.'

In early 2000 the deal was finalized. Naga Bar continued while the stock of liquor lasted, but it was closed within five weeks.

'We began understanding the rules of the land game,' recalls Vijay.

In the real estate business, there are a variety of business routes one can take. In their case, Vijay and company decided to build a housing colony on the land they had bought. They put up fencing around the tract of land and hired an architect to design the colony. According to the existing government rules, real estate developers could utilize only 50 per cent of the area for constructing houses. The rest had to be kept for lanes, parks and parking.

Vijay and company thus had 88,000 square feet to build up. A two-bedroom house could be built on 1,000 square feet. Vijay and company conceived of two kinds of plots: two-bedroom (1,200 square feet) and three-bedroom (1,500 square feet) units.

'With each deal, we were baffled by the profit margin,' recalls Vijay.

The first 30,000 square feet were sold at Rs 40 per square foot—it fetched Vijay and his team Rs 12 lakh. As people lined up to book their plots, the price appreciated. The next 20,000 square feet were sold at Rs 50 per square foot, which meant another Rs 10 lakh in profit. The final 38,000 square feet were sold at Rs 60 per square feet, fetching them Rs 22 lakh.

They had bought the land for Rs 6 lakhs and sold it for Rs 44 lakh. Within a year, Vijay drove a car while his brother Nischay continued to pedal his bicycle.

It was 2001. Vijay and Mahendra would roam Nagpur's outskirts looking for land. Within months, they had identified a seventy-acre tract near Buti Bori. They entered into a negotiation with the landlord. The owner quoted a price of Rs 7 lakh per acre and wouldn't budge.

'We needed Rs 490 lakh for the deal,' recalls Vijay. 'I knew we would make a profit of Rs 500 lakh in less than six months.'

Vijay approached his first mentor Shailendra Jaiswal and offered him a stake if he invested. Having long ago realized Vijay's calibre, Jaiswal immediately agreed. But that wasn't enough. The team also approached private bankers for credit, which they easily procured. One of their partners, Harsh Vardhan, meanwhile, had walked away for reasons of his own.

As Vijay and company could arrange for only Rs 30 crore, they had to follow the payment model they had adopted previously.

'That's my father's model,' says Vijay. His father had bought fourteen acres of land by paying only 50 per cent of the price up front and the rest in instalments.

The seller agreed to take Rs 19 crore in monthly instalments.

'In case of default, the landlord had threatened to charge interest as well,' recalls Vijay.

Named Balaji Township, near Buti Bori, the seventy-acre project was completed by 2002, in less than a year. The 16,00,000 square feet of land that they had carved into plots sold for Rs 80 crore.

By 2003, Vijay and company had cut three large deals and half a dozen small deals.

Vijay now aimed bigger. He acquired eighty-eight acres of prime land on which he wanted to build multi-storey apartments and independent flats even though he had no experience in this field.

'My brother will not let me down,' Vijay assured himself; he met Nischay and told him of his plan. 'Shouldn't we start building apartments and townships?' Vijay asked.

He knew that Nischay had worked for over five years in a construction company that built apartments and townships.

'Why apartments and a township?' Nischay wanted to know.

Vijay said that more than money, he now wanted to establish his own brand. He remained nameless in buying land, dividing it into plots and selling it to others. Once he had sold the plots, he was out. He remained nameless because the owners and developers of the land are the only ones mentioned in the papers.

Nischay wished his brother well. He appreciated Vijay's new dream, realizing that beyond establishing a name and receiving recognition, selling built houses doubled the profits. But when Vijay insisted that his brother become a partner, Nischay needed some time to think.

The next day, Vijay, along with his sister and jijaji, went to prevail upon Nischay to join his venture.

Nischay finally agreed in 2007.

In 2008, Infratech launched its first township on eighty-eight acres of land. Named Venkatesh City, the 900 housing units were split into two towers, and the rest were single- and double-storey buildings as well as independent houses.

'That's my business card,' says Vijay.

Prospective buyers in the Ramdaspeth Pipri township are advised to visit Venkatesh City.

Venkatesh City has all the facilities residents could seek. With a huge tank within the township, water is harvested during the rains. With the state-of-the-art water purification plant, residents get water 24x7. In addition, there are two high-capacity bore wells that draw water in case of emergencies and a high-tech security system with the entire township under closed circuit camera surveillance.

'We knew that we were competing with giants in the housing sector,' says Vijay. 'We had to be the best.'

Success has given Vijay wings. His business has expanded to as far away as the Andaman and Nicobar Islands with multiple projects that involve creating resorts, recreational and commercial complexes.

'What next?'

'To become a rupee billionaire by 2020,' predicts Mahendra Gawai.

'To rejoice in the praises customers shower on us,' says Nischay.

'To set business standards that others would emulate,' says Vijay.

KISHAN LAL SINGLA

The monsoon seems like mythic lore in the village of Nangal Nathusar in Rajasthan. The village folk often talk about it but few believe in it. Their scepticism is rooted not only in what they have witnessed but in stories passed down through generations. What is true for them as well as for a new visitor is that it seldom rains in Nangal Nathusar, a village located about 120 kilometres northwest of Jaipur.

Like many other Indian villages today, Nangal Nathusar is a chaotic mix of tradition and modernity, with one foot in the twenty-first century and the other in the nineteenth; the village exists at the fulcrum of change and resistance to change. Wobbly camel carts creak along roads only to be brushed aside by a speeding car.

Comprising about 400 households, the village is settled along a pucca road that cleaves through its centre and connects the village to the larger towns beyond. In the bustle of daily life, though, the local road is eclipsed by the encroaching shops, temples and schools and the crowds that they necessarily invite, forcing any visitor to slow down to safely navigate the village. The land surrounding Nangal Nathusar is dry and dusty, and dotted with the thorny babool trees. The week-old stubble of sprouted millets provides the eye with a welcome shock of greenery.

Kishan Lal Singla was born in this village in 1948, the year after the end of colonial rule and Indian independence. Born in a poor Dalit family in this hardscrabble environment, Kishan's future seemed bleak at best when he was sold into bondage at the age of fifteen. However, hard work and business acumen led Singla on a different path that culminated, at the age of sixty-four, in his directorship of Singla Steel Tubes Pvt. Ltd, a multi-crore manufacturing company with an annual turnover of Rs 35 crore and plants in the industrial towns of Hissar and Bahadurgarh in Haryana, and soon, a state-of-the-art plant near Jaipur.

Of medium height and stocky build, Kishan is relaxed and in his casual clothing, he easily blends in with his surroundings. When a cameraman shooting him for a documentary politely suggests, 'Why don't you wear a tie?' Kishan quips, 'I am not educated enough to wear a tie. Neckties suit those with good educational degrees.'

The lack of a formal education, however, did not deter Kishan from learning the technology of machines, which subsequently led him to ascend and master the stainless steel tube industry. Today, the Singla Group not only manufactures stainless steel tubes from steel sheets, but also makes the machines that mould and shape them.

Orphaned at the age of two, after his father, Laduram, accidentally fell to his death while trying to save a fellow passenger on a train, and his mother died six months later, Kishan was raised by his grandparents Manguram Singla and Bhuri Devi. Breaking with tradition, grandfather Manguram wanted to see his grandson educated, and decided to enrol Kishan in the village school. But he died before he could complete his task, leaving his mission to be fulfilled by his wife Bhuri Devi, who got Kishan admitted in the local school.

Admission in school was only the first of many obstacles the young boy would face.

'He was not allowed to drink water from the pot placed in the school,' recalls Pandit Jagdish Prasad Sharma, a priest at the temple Kishan built in his village.

'In those days, Harijan kids would run to their homes for water,' remembers Heera Singh, Kishan's childhood friend and schoolmate.

'In our homes, untouchables would be served water from a distance,' adds Rakshpal Chaudhary, a village elder. 'They would pluck a large leaf, roll it into a pipe, and bend, holding the leaf in both hands. Then the landlord would pour water from a distance of two to three feet.'

It wasn't just acts of individual discrimination that conspired against Kishan fulfilling his grandfather's dream; larger issues beyond his control threw him off his path. A debilitating drought struck most parts of India in 1956 and the Thar desert was among the worst hit. 'Cattle died in droves,' says a village elder. 'There was nothing left for either cattle or humans.' Escaping starvation was a priority for most Dalit families.

Seeking better opportunities, Kishan's cousins decided to move to Hissar—an industrial town some 160 kilometres north of Sikar district—and took Kishan with them.

By the time he was eight, Kishan was working at a brick kiln. 'I did odd jobs—life at brick kilns was really hard,' says Kishan, matter-of-factly.

Traditionally, brick kilns shut operations during the monsoon and workers return to their native places. Kishan, too, would follow this pattern. For years, he would migrate to towns near his village to work in brick kilns, and return home for four months. 'He would be at our house all day', says Thakur Jaswant.

Kishan's parents and grandparents had worked for the Thakur's family for generations. 'What else could he do given his age? He would remove cow dung, clean things,' says Jaswant, now in his eighties. 'He would be served food separately. Society was too conservative those days.'

For the villagers, Kishan had simply drifted to Hissar town, probably doing odd jobs for survival. What else would one expect of a poor orphan? Years passed without much update on his status or well-being.

One day, a villager spotted Kishan driving a large car in Hissar. When he reported his sighting back in the village, word spread that Kishan had won a lottery, recalls Heera Singh. It seemed too fantastic to be true and the tale was quickly forgotten, until the day heads turned as Kishan did indeed drive a car to his village.

Later, Kishan came to the village to build a house he knew he would rarely live in. The life he leads in Hissar as a rich industrialist is only a part of his persona, though. At a subliminal level, Kishan is still a Dalit boy having nobody to call his own in Nangal Nathusar. He must now meet that boy's needs, and material things he did mattered to the extent they satisfied his innate desire for recognition and respect.

It is a large house in the middle of a sprawling courtyard with a neem tree and a well. The front has two entrances, one for people and the other, the bigger one, for tractors and cars to enter. Once inside, the visitor faces a temple with a huge verandah. Behind the temple is the house for Kishan. Twenty feet diagonally opposite the temple is a modest building once used as a kitchen, now the residence for the in-house priest and his family. Every detail has been taken care of, and it is surprising that the owner spends only one day of every year in the house.

'Even that one day, sahib cooks his own food,' explains the priest who can't offer a convincing reason as to why this is so.

Employed by Kishan, the priest, a Brahmin, serves cola to guests. He is helped by Santosh, a Dalit in his late forties, who manages Kishan's farmhouse. The priest's wife, daughter and two nieces also live in the house and help with the cooking when Kishan's relatives and friends visit.

'Do these girls know that they are cooking food for untouchable guests?'

'That's past, sir. Untouchability has ended,' the priest says. 'More or less,' he is quick to add.

The meals cooked in the kitchen are a feast when compared to the daily meal of Kishan's childhood. 'Kishan lived on roti made from millet for most of his childhood, the way kids eat biscuits,' says Heera Singh. The poor would cook only once a day—often in the evening. The roti made then would be eaten at breakfast and lunch the next day. 'Usually it was eaten with raw onions and salt. Red chilli would be a luxury,' he adds.

* * *

Illiterate and unskilled, the Dalits of Nangal Nathusar usually ended up working at brick kilns. The managers of brick kilns in neighbouring towns would visit villages and give cash in advance to team leaders who would ensure the availability of workers.

In 1963, Kishan's cousin took an advance purportedly on behalf of Kishan, so that Kishan could work at the kilns as a regular labourer. Till then he was working as a helper boy, performing mundane chores. The following day he took Kishan, then fifteen years old, to a brick kiln in Hissar. A couple of days later, Kishan's cousin disappeared, without saying anything, and took Kishan's clothes to boot.

Co-workers later told Kishan what had happened. Unbeknownst to him, Kishan's cousin had contracted Kishan into a life as a bonded labourer. Kishan had only two options—either to flee or fulfil the commitment his cousin had made. He opted for the latter. 'I didn't want to breach a contract,' Kishan said. On their part, the management was kind and paid him Rs 2 a week. 'Those days, a kilo of wheat came for six paisa,' remembers Singla.

Once Kishan finished working that season, he chose not to return to his village. He had been cheated by his own relatives, but the kiln managers, who were strangers, had treated him well.

Impressed by his willingness to work hard, they hired him to work on a wall under construction, part of a stainless steel tube factory owned by industrialist Onkar Nath Mittal. On learning the boy's story and watching him at work, Mittal made Kishan an office attendant. His job involved serving water to people in the company.

But soon word spread that Kishan was a Meghwal, a Dalit caste in Rajasthan, and the ensuing disquiet reached Mr Mittal's ears.

The staff was defiant about an untouchable serving them water, but Mittal would have none of it. One day he asked Kishan to fetch him a glass of water and, as Kishan recalls, asked, 'If I can drink this water, why can't you people?'

Within months, Kishan was given the additional job of sweeping the factory floor, an occupation identified with untouchables alone. Months later, he was hired as an unskilled worker.

'I loved machines,' remembers Kishan. Now that he had become a factory worker, his life began changing for the better. Since Kishan had no place to live, he was allowed to live in the factory complex. This arrangement gave him the opportunities that led to his transformation from Kishan to K.L. Singla.

Kishan's real work would begin after sunset when work had stopped in the factory. Left alone, he would begin by cleaning the machines. He would disassemble them, cleaning every part, and reassemble them before daybreak. These were the machines that turned stainless steel sheets into tubes. He soon realized that he not only liked the job, but possessed the skill to do it well.

In 1968, Kishan was promoted to the position of supervisor. His new job required maintenance of machines, also called 'mills'. If a mill broke down, engineers would be called to fix it. However, having mastered the nuts and bolts of maintenance without any formal education, Kishan was able to replace the engineers. Soon he was also able to build new mills. By 1971, at the age of twenty-three, Kishan Lal was appointed general manager of the plant where he had once cleaned the floor. The only position left for him to aspire to was ownership.

As manager, Kishan worked on a new business model that he felt would improve the profitability of the company. The mills that helped construct stainless steel tubes were imported from Mumbai, nearly 1,500 kilometres from Hissar. In addition, when companies requested tubes made to their specifications in type and dimension, the mills needed to be modified, which required the presence of engineers from Mumbai for the completion of the tasks. Doing business long distance not only took far more time but also cost more money, which in turn cut into the company's profit margins.

Kishan had an idea. He would manufacture the mills locally, at prices that he was confident would be considerably lower than those of the mills imported from Mumbai. He would also train local technicians to undertake repairs and modify the mills as needed.

Beginning with a small factory shed in Hissar, the Singla steel factory was set up in 1979 (Kishan added the traditional business surname 'Singla' to his own). The business model worked well. Kishan's mills were cheaper, easily available and, if required, modifications and repairs were done quickly. His business grew, and within years, he had started another unit, Singla Socket Industries. The Singla Group began manufacturing stainless steel tubes in full force. To meet the increased demand, another unit soon came up in nearby Bahadurgarh.

Today, Singla devotes most of his time to philanthropic works while his two sons look after the business. He has partnered with the local government to provide half of his village, Nangal Nathusar, with piped drinking water, by installing a number of hand pumps. He has built a temple in the village and made improvements to the school building where he studied for two years. And once a year, he visits the farmhouse, his home away from home.

Kishan Lal (Meghwal) Singla is a contented man. His message for everyone: Mehnat kare aur lagan ho, to kya nahin ho sakta? (What is not possible with hard work and commitment?)

SITARAM

It is six in the morning and we are in Azadpur Mandi, India's largest wholesale fruit and vegetable mart. Over the din of idling trucks and moving handcarts and the crowds of buyers and sellers negotiating an agreeable price, conversations are not easily audible in this corner of northwest Delhi. Barefoot workers to well-heeled merchants clamour for space as they crisscross the market in pursuit of the day's mission. It had rained the previous evening and the dirt roads are awash with mud.

Unmindful of his surroundings, Sitaram (SR hereafter) makes his way to a *fad*, a business spot allotted to fruit merchants called adhatiyas in the vegetable marts of north

India. He easily navigates his way through the market, buying all that he wants. He is in his mid-fifties—he doesn't know his exact age—but has the vim and vigour of a teenager. After he is done, he throws up his hands. 'No, not any more', SR tells an agent, satisfied with his day's pick. 'The day's buying is over.'

'He is a trusted name in the mandi,' says Phool Chand, referring to SR. Phool Chand, a transporter, also hails from SR's village Vasti in district Azamgarh, Uttar Pradesh.

'Most farmers like selling fruits to fruit merchants like SR,' says Phool Chand. 'He pays on time.' Disparagingly described as 'middle men', adhatiyas are commission agents who buy fruits from growers and sell them in the mandi. They are key cogs in the fruit business. With a turnover of Rs 25 crore in the 2011–12 financial year, SR is an adhatiya of some repute in the Azadpur Mandi. He deals in apples, mangoes and oranges. His company, VK, named after his elder son Vinod Kumar, exports fruits to towns as far away as in the Northeast— Guwahati, Jorhat and Tinsukia.

'I hosted him the day he first arrived in the mandi,' recalls Phool Chand. 'It must have been either 1971 or 1972.' Neither Phool Chand nor SR can remember the exact year. 'He was good at studies, and we all hoped that one day he would become a government officer. Our village hadn't produced a single officer. The entire village was proud of him. So I was shocked when I first saw him in the mandi. And it is not that he was starving back home,' continues Phool Chand. 'I was at a loss. Aged sixteen or seventeen, what work could this boy do? Dressed in his school uniform, he stood before me almost lifeless. He looked hungry. I soon realized that SR was a runaway boy!' admits the transporter.

'I couldn't take it any more', says SR. 'I had to leave for my parents.'

SR's mother was a hawker, born to illiterate parents. She would go from house to house, village to village, peddling groceries. There were no shops in villages in the hinterland of north India in those days.

'She would place a basket full of small groceries on her head, and curl her lips, yelling in a peculiar voice while making the village rounds,' remembers SR.

That is a practice hawkers still follow. They shout in a distinctive way so that people in their homes know when a particular hawker is around.

'The occupation was looked down upon in those days, especially for women—"Where has this woman been all day?" Nasty idle minds always look for talking points,' says Phool Chand.

SR's father had no agricultural land. To feed the family, which included three sons and a daughter, he would climb the fifteen-metre-tall palm trees to harvest toddy twice a day. 'With hardly any tools, he would climb up the trees like a monkey. All kinds of rogues and drunkards would loiter around my home to get drunk,' recalls SR.

In north India, only untouchables engage in the business of toddy tapping and selling. The toddy tree belongs to the palm family, and toddy, an alcoholic beverage, is popular in parts of Uttar Pradesh, Bihar, West Bengal and south India. 'SR hated talking about his parents' occupations. He was like a volcano waiting to erupt in those days,' recalls SR's childhood friend and mentor Ram Chander, who now owns a flower nursery in the village.

'It's bloody money,' the young SR would fume. 'It's the lack of money that forces my mother to make rounds of villages! It's the lack of money that forces my father to risk his life every day. I will make money my servant,' SR would hiss in anger.

A dozen fellow Dalits from SR's village had migrated to Azadpur Mandi. These migrant workers returned to the village during the summer months every year. They would flaunt new clothes and turn on their shiny transistor radios. Tales of 'zero to hero' would make the rounds. Phool Chand, who had become a transporter by then, would be cited as an example.

'There is so much money to be made in Delhi,' migrant workers who had returned home would tell anyone who cared to listen.

These stories stirred SR's imagination, and he began exploring ways to flee the village. Ram Chander, a school dropout, also thought along the same lines.

'Money had entered his mind and heart,' says Ram Chander.

Ram Chander and SR decided to run away to Delhi. Both had saved some money. Being older than SR by a few years, the well-built Ram Chander planned the escape. Even today, he remembers the exact route they took to Delhi.

'The escape date was finalized,' recalls Ram Chander. 'SR had to be in school uniform.' He waited for Ram Chander for over half an hour.

The boys planned to walk to Rani ki Sarai, a roadside bazaar located on the Azamgarh–Varanasi road. SR's house was located on the eastern side of the village and Ram Chander had to come to his house and signal that the journey had begun.

'He walked past my house pointing to the west,' recalls SR vividly. 'I was so impatient!' he says.

After the boys had walked a kilometre and half, they reached Rani ki Sarai. SR left his school bag with a tailor whom the boys knew well. Their plan was to get to Azamgarh, from where they would catch the train to Shahganj. There was no direct train from Azamgarh to Delhi in those days. Shahganj, some 60 kilometres west of Azamgarh, was the rail junction for trains going to the eastern parts of India from Delhi.

To ensure that nobody would see them, they didn't follow their usual practice of catching a bus from the main stop. 'Many villagers hung about in the market,' recalls Ram Chander.

The boys walked for about a kilometre towards Azamgarh and then hitched a ride on a horse cart. In half an hour, they were at Azamgarh station. The train was scheduled to arrive two hours later. 'It wasn't delayed,' recalls Ram Chander. 'But we were too excited and had reached the station early.'

As the boys were anxious to avoid being spotted on the platform, they played in a mango orchard nearby. 'We feared that our parents might be looking for us,' said Ram Chander.

They had very little money, and boarded the train without tickets. 'The rail officials generally didn't bother school kids,' says Ram Chander.

At Shahganj junction, they bought tickets for Delhi. SR bought a half ticket for himself since the Indian Railways gave a discount to children under twelve years of age. Though SR had crossed that age, he hoped he could get away with a half ticket.

The compartment was crowded. 'Passengers were spitting everywhere and the toilet had run out of water. But I enjoyed the ride,' recounts SR.

By the following evening, they had reached Delhi.

* * *

Phool Chand gave the boys shelter and informed their relatives who were working in Delhi that the boys were with him. Soon one of SR's relatives took him to his home while Ram Chander went to live with a relative in Faridabad, a satellite town of Delhi. SR's relatives worked in Swatantra Bharat Mill, where mustard seeds were crushed to extract edible oil.

'Entering the mill complex was enthralling,' SR remembers. 'I had never been to any factory premises before.'

SR's idea of Delhi, though, was soon to change. 'My relatives didn't live in rooms,' he says. 'They lived in a big hall where sacks of mustard were stored.' Over a dozen workers, including SR's relatives, lived within the factory complex. 'There was no kitchen. The bathroom had a broken door. We all slept on the floor,' recalls SR.

After a few weeks, SR was hired as a grocery shop attendant. 'That's because they had heard me talking of business so often,' says SR. After a year, he lost interest—'I quit because I saw no future in continuing with the grocer,' he says.

He found work at a paan and cigarette shop near the mill, but within a year, he quit again. 'I could see my dream ending. I realized if I continued here I would never become a lakhpati.'

Hoping to find a way to strike it rich, SR reconnected with his mentor Ram Chander, who made baskets and sorted fruits at the mandi. All kinds of fruits—good, bad, rotten—came to the mandi packed in wooden boxes. The fruit sorter would open the boxes and separate fruits according to their quality. The good fruits were repacked in the same box.

'We got 25 paise per box,' says Ram Chander. 'I made Rs 20 to 25 every day.'

'It was a Sunday when SR came around noon,' recalls Ram Chander. Both discussed their past and pondered over their decision to leave the village.

'I don't want to return to the village as a failed man,' SR told Ram Chander. 'Villagers back home will make fun of me.'

For his part, Ram Chander felt guilty—after all, he had planned SR's escape from the village. He promised to help.

'Stay with me, work with me,' he urged SR.

As an inexperienced newcomer, SR was given a task considered inferior. He would unload fruit baskets from trucks and bring them to Ram Chander and his team of fruit sorters.

'I got Rs 5 a day,' remembers SR. 'The cattle in villages lived a better life than us!'

Ram Chander shared a tiny room with three fellow workers. SR became the fifth person to share it. 'The room was slightly bigger than the toilet in my house today,' says SR with a smile. Located half a kilometre east of Azadpur Mandi, the room had no electricity, cot, almirah, suitcase, or bags. Everyone slept on the floor. The room had an angithi, a coal-fired stove, and a tawa to make roti. There was one vessel in which to cook dal, and another in which to cook rice. The utensil for rice was used to cook vegetables or meat as well.

'We cooked non-vegetarian food every Sunday evening,' remembers SR. 'We had no kitchen but there were four plates. The fifth member had to wait for his turn after one of the four had finished,' chuckles Ram Chander.

'We had no toilet and used the open fields nearby. We bathed in the open air. There was a hand pump and a dozen families living nearby used it for bathing. We used water from the pump for cooking and drinking as well. We had few clothes to wash,' says SR.

Like most of his fellow workers, SR wore a lungi wrapped around the waist, a jangia (loose underwear) and a banian (vest). He would buy second-hand sweaters and blankets to use during winters. 'Kurtas were the only prized possessions we had that needed a place to store,' says SR. 'We hung them on khuntis (hooks) drilled into the walls.'

'On the first day, when he came dressed in a kurta,' laughs Ram Chander, 'some of us ribbed him.'

A tenth-standard dropout, SR was the most educated worker at the *fad*. 'He was in great demand,' says Ram Chander. In those days letters were the primary means of communication. Migrant workers would write to their families back home. When a worker received a letter, SR would read it out if the worker was illiterate and would also write the replies. 'He was a quick learner,' adds Ram Chander of SR.

Within a year, SR sat with Ram Chander and did the same job, opening fruit boxes, sorting out fruits and repacking them. 'By now we made 35 paise per box,' says SR. 'I would occasionally send money back home.'

SR recalls that it was probably 1975 or so when he moved to a new fruit company registered as Nooruddin Abdul Aziz Fruit Company. The company was owned by Abdul Rashid.

Having heard of SR, Abdul Rashid hand-picked him and gave him multiple duties. Since SR had been to school, he was given tasks that involved reading and writing, answering the phones and maintaining registers. In less than six months with Rashid, SR began to see the flowering of his dream. Rashid, impressed by SR's work and sense of responsibility, promoted SR to the position of a contractor with his company, with the task of loading fruits on trucks.

In Azadpur Mandi, the fruit and vegetable business works on a complex model. Once a truck of fruit is bought by a loader for his client, a group of workers unloads the truck and takes the fruit to be sorted, a job SR himself did initially for three years. The workers report to a thekedar, or contractor, and are paid depending upon the size of the truck; for example, they get Rs 1,200 for a twenty-wheel truck or Rs 800 for a six-wheel truck. The thekedar often works alongside the workers he has employed and receives about Rs 10 per box. Once the fruits are sorted and repacked, a battery of workers under another kind of thekedar loads the fruit boxes onto stationed trucks.

'An SC (Scheduled caste, the official name for Dalits) had become a thekedar. It was news,' beams SR. 'Fellow immigrant workers carried the news back to my village.'

Within six months of becoming a thekedar, SR visited his village. His parents had forgiven him. Now successful and eligible, SR had no difficulty in finding a bride for himself. 'On his very first visit, he had impressed our fellow villagers,' recalls Ram Chander. On his second visit, in 1976, SR married Kamla Devi.

Often, migrant workers leave their families back home in the village. SR, too, returned to Delhi, leaving his wife in the village. He would, however, go more frequently to his village—he now went twice a year.

Abdul Rashid saw virtue in promoting SR. He was now expected to answer calls from clients in places as far-flung as Assam, Meghalaya and Nagaland. 'I had to note down their lists of demands,' says SR.

Loaders like Abdul Rashid would not buy fruit for themselves. Acting as commission agents, they bought fruit for their clients located far from Delhi. Loaders like Rashid, like adhatiyas, also claimed their commission. SR was now helping his employer in a critical area of the trade.

'The phone starts ringing much earlier than when the mandi opens at six in the morning,' says SR. 'Clients place orders with loaders over the phone each morning.'

'Because he had some education, he would often be asked to handle orders from clients, arrange transport and also deal with adhatiyas at times,' says Phool Chand. 'SR was a prize catch for Abdul Rashid.'

As time went by, SR rose in status. In 1982, almost a decade after he first left his village, he brought his family to Delhi—his wife, two sons and a daughter. SR rented a place near the mandi. 'This was also big news,' remembers SR. 'There was a table fan in the house.'

SR's elder son Vinod Kumar, though, isn't impressed. 'The house had no windows, no kitchen, and no bathroom or toilet,' he says. 'All the eight families living in the apartment shared the bathroom and toilet.'

'SR can't be judged like that,' counters Avadh Narayan, a fellow Dalit entrepreneur in the mandi. 'SR's was a rare case where he bought his family to live with him, rented a brick house with electricity and put his kids in school.'

Abdul Rashid began to depend more on SR, who would directly handle clients in the Northeast and the adhatiyas in the mandi and also look after transport.

SR educated his children and expected them to lead a different life from his own. But, in October 1993, after his elder son Vinod had passed his tenth standard examination, he told his father that he had no interest in a college education. 'I want to join you,' Vinod told him one evening. 'It was very unsettling,' recalls SR. 'In my thoughts, I would often revisit my past, and think of my son's future.'

SR had dropped out of school to become a businessman. He ended up becoming a thekedar. He wanted his son to do bigger things. The question that kept nagging him was 'What if Vinod failed?'

'But I saw opportunities for Vinod as well,' recalls SR. 'After all, he was not going to start at the bottom.'

However, SR felt that he needed to secure his son's future.

'This time, I will take another plunge for my son,' he decided. He thought of two men, Suresh Kumar and Madan Lal, who might be able to help him in his new venture.

Madan Lal was a wholesale fruit merchant, based in Jabalpur in Madhya Pradesh, and a client of Abdul Rashid. He was well known and SR considered him trustworthy. Suresh Kumar owned a transport company named Anil Transport and had an office within the mandi complex. Anil Transport had a battery of trucks, a couple of which were used by Rashid's company. Since SR was a thekedar for loading trucks, Suresh Kumar would deal with SR on a daily basis.

SR devised a scheme wherein Madan Lal would order a dozen or two boxes of apples from SR's son Vinod every day, and Suresh Kumar would transport the boxes in one of his trucks. Since SR still worked for Rashid, he would not have been allowed to conduct a parallel business. For the plan to work, therefore, Madan and Suresh both had to hide the operation from Rashid.

But SR's misgivings were soon squelched when Suresh Kumar happily agreed to deliver the boxes of apples to Madan Lal and also agreed to keep this a secret. Madan Lal followed suit.

'Send me fifteen boxes of apples tomorrow,' he responded from Jabalpur. 'It would be a pleasure to promote your son.'

Back home, SR broke the news. 'I didn't really know what was going on,' said Kamla Devi. 'But I felt happy for my children and husband!'

The following morning, SR and his son Vinod reached the mandi at five in the morning. He had called one of his ablest and most trusted co-workers to the mandi. The three held a mini conference on how best to pick up fifteen boxes of quality apples.

'It was good that no one knew who I was,' says Vinod. 'Maintaining secrecy was very important.'

SR watched from a distance as his co-worker helped Vinod select a lot of good apples. Fifteen boxes were repacked. Vinod called a helper to load the boxes onto a truck belonging to Anil Transport, whose driver had been told to accept fifteen boxes of apples for a client in Jabalpur. These boxes were marked VK, for Vinod Kumar.

Madan Lal informed Suresh that SR's fifteen boxes of apples had been received. 'Anil Transport's office became my unofficial office,' said SR.

The next day, SR learnt that he had made a profit of Rs 100 per box. 'The total profit was Rs 1,500,' SR recalls. 'It was unbelievable. My God! So much money, and my employer exports thousands of these boxes every day!' On the next shipment SR realized a profit of Rs 2,000 on twenty-four boxes. After eight months in business, SR dispatched eighty boxes of apples in one day and made a profit of Rs 10,000. 'We bought a refrigerator,' recalls Vinod.

By now, the secret had spread around the mandi. When SR broke the news to Rashid, Rashid with some hesitation asked him to leave. 'Remember, a businessman can turn a pauper overnight!' he warned.

'I could understand his bitterness,' recalls SR. 'For two decades, he had depended a lot on me.'

SR and Vinod pushed ahead in their business aggressively. With a new business model, he enlisted new clients rapidly. Within two years SR had entered the markets of Northeast India where he was well known to many of the fruit merchants. By 1995, SR moved his family into their own house. 'We were making lakhs of rupees,' says SR.

SR's rise was mostly due to the business model he practised, which made his services more attractive to buyers. In the mandi, adhatiyas and loaders are critical players, and both work on commissions. While an adhatiya claims a commission from fruit growers for selling their fruit, loaders like SR claim a commission from clients located elsewhere in the country for buying fruits for them.

Adhatiyas and loaders didn't run any risk in their businesses. Fruit growers ran the risk since their product might go unsold or get spoiled. The real buyer sitting in towns located outside Delhi, too, ran the risk. His fruit might get spoiled during transportation or prices may crash locally.

As a new player, SR redefined the 'risk factor' by relocating the incidence of risk in the supply chain. When he dispatched the first fifteen boxes of fruit to the Jabalpur-based Hari Lal & Company, he had inscribed a note to its owner Madan Lal: 'Sell this at the existing market rate in Jabalpur, and keep the 6 per cent commission yourself.'

In one stroke SR had done several things. Madan Lal received a risk-free 6 per cent profit. He did not have to bear the transportation charge, and SR offered him storage and handling charges as well. SR's business model also redefined the 'trust' system. Before, clients sitting far away from Delhi would accept the rate per box a Delhi-based loader said he had bought it at. Now, a client doing business with SR would not bother with the rate at which fruits were bought in the mandi. He would tell SR the price at which he sold the fruit and SR would have to accept that. 'This system existed before as well,' says SR. 'But it was not widely practised.'

Soon, word spread and fruit merchants sitting in the northeastern cities eagerly followed the SR model. 'SR hasn't replaced his former employer Rashid in the Northeast,' says Phool Chand. 'But he has emerged as a significant player there.'

With success, SR was ready to step back and let his sons take over the reins of the business. His eldest son Vinod Kumar is in charge of the morning session, when most of the business is conducted. Later in the evening, SR's second son Vineet Kumar, with a twelfth standard education, steps in to offer logistics guidance.

'I look after the transport,' says Vineet. 'We now own a fleet of five twenty-wheeled trucks.'

'We have plans to buy a few more,' adds Vinod.

SR's third son is studying medicine. 'He might open a multi-specialty hospital,' says SR. 'That's my wish.'

SR is a satisfied man today. He says, 'Caste does matter in the mandi—from adhatiyas to loaders and transporters, all belong to the upper castes. But, when it comes to business, caste takes a back seat.'

SADHU THORAT

The Osmanabad district in the Marathwada region of Maharashtra is a remote and desolate place, a land that offers little opportunity. Sadhu Thorat's birth in this rural area went unrecorded, only to be later estimated by the keen eye of the school headmaster to have occurred in 1959.

Growing up in a large family with eight siblings, he never lacked for company. So when his father died in 1961, his absence wasn't felt acutely.

There were many mouths to feed, but the family always had enough to eat and rarely faced hunger. By tradition, all the children in their hamlet worked from early childhood.

The landlords and the landless, everyone in the village lived on farming.

Farming was done manually and tiny hands were needed for the weeding. The farming work supported Sadhu's family, whose needs were few.

Sadhu's mother wanted him to go to school as none of her other children had been educated. He was enrolled in the village school.

The first day was really exciting, and the boy, seated next to upper caste children, felt special.

The following days, however, were more challenging. The kids at school talked about the games they played at home. It was a life Sadhu had not experienced, and he felt like a misfit.

One day at school, he needed to relieve himself. As there were no washrooms or urinals in the school, the students would go out into bushes. While Sadhu was relieving himself, a group of boys playing nearby gesticulated at him, poking fun.

School no longer held any excitement but turned into a prison. To begin with, Sadhu had no burning desire to go to school, and looked for excuses to keep it from intruding into his cosy routine.

Ignoring his mother's passionate appeals, he called it a day and cried at the prospect of being sent back to school. To make sure that he wouldn't be forced to return, he threw his slate and chalk into the village pond.

Word quickly spread that Sadhu would no longer be going to school. Elementary schools in the area began their new session at the end of summer and the village landlords would keep tabs on who had opted out of school. Children who did not go to school were immediately employed.

Sadhu was told later that at least three landlords had approached his mother with job offers. Finally, a deal was struck with one who was considered to be a good employer and he was hired for Rs 5 a month. Besides the money, he was also offered one large roti, one onion and some salt at noon. The landlady also often gave him jaggery water. His main job was to take the landlord's buffalo out to graze. Sometimes, when a servant employed at the landlord's house didn't turn up, he would be required to clean the cattle stall and take out the cow dung.

Sadhu's family witnessed some improvement in their lives. During the sowing and harvesting seasons, when the entire family worked, the house was full of jowar (sorghum) grain.

In those days children were married off very young; Sadhu's three elder siblings—two brothers and a sister—were married and lived separately. The remaining five lived together with their mother. Since they all earned and cooked together, they ate reasonably well.

The Rs 5 Sadhu earned each month was used to buy clothes for his sisters. The brothers didn't require much clothing. They wore shirts and knickers that doubled as undergarments. The landlord would sometimes give them discarded shirts and other clothes that the richer villagers wore.

Sadhu worked outside of the main house—as an untouchable, he was not allowed inside the landlord's home. He got his first glimpse into the house on a dark, cloudy day. The household was frantic as it was about to rain, and Sadhu was asked to bring in the firewood that had been left outside to dry.

As he entered the kitchen, he was stunned to see all the metal utensils used for cooking. Brass and copper plates were kept neatly in one corner. The house had a courtyard, and he saw large beds with pillows.

Pillows!

What were they?

There was foodgrain kept in sacks. Sadhu watched as the landlady collected an armful of clothes hung on a clothesline. He wondered whether he would ever have the money to buy such things.

The landlord's house was a far cry from Sadhu's home. He was born in a hut measuring 10x10 square feet, with a thatched roof and walls. The family cooked food in earthenware pots, and used burnt clay plates for eating. They slept on the ground.

Sadhu was overcome with desperation. His family didn't own any farmland. Farm labour would at best get them jowari roti, onions and salt. There was no money to start a business.

The only option was to follow the well-trodden path taken by many Dalits—to go to Pune after every sowing season. They would return during the harvest sporting better clothes and build sturdier homes.

The dream of a better life in the city captured his imagination. The only problem was his age—he was only twelve.

It was around mid-June 1971 and the sowing season of the kharif crop would be over in a month. There was talk amongst the older Dalit workers about migrating to look for work. More than a dozen Dalits were planning to leave after the sowing season.

Sadhu was young. Would they take him?

Start saving some money, he told himself.

It had been dry through much of June, but started raining in July. Farm work was in full swing and the land was waterlogged. Since it was raining, Sadhu did not take the buffalo out to the fields to graze for several days.

Feed and water are not the only things desi buffaloes

need to keep well. They need to be walked for several hours. Without their walks, they become restless and cranky, and create trouble during milking. Having skipped a third day at his job due to the rainy conditions in which he couldn't walk the buffalo, he was summoned to the landlord's house.

The landlord was usually understanding but this time, he scolded the boy. Sadhu knew that he was not in the wrong and felt unjustly punished. He came back home sobbing and his mother consoled him, saying, 'Jamana aisa hi hai.'

But Sadhu saw another way out. A group of Dalits was leaving the following morning for Pune. He pleaded with his mother to talk to the group leader Shankar Girpade. She refused, saying that he was too young to strike out on his own.

Sadhu felt frustrated. He figured out the route the migrants would be taking. Most migrants carried food that would last them for a day at least. They also carried clothes and money. Sadhu, however, walked out of his hut carrying nothing but the 50 paisa that he had saved.

He didn't tell his mother that he was leaving for Pune. He sat under a banyan tree along the route his fellow Dalits would be taking. He wondered if Girpade would take him.

He decided to go even if he didn't take him. He would hop on the train they took and not buy a train ticket. If he was caught by the ticket collector, he would tell him the truth and go to jail. Once out of jail, he would again catch the train to Pune. If they caught him again, he would go to jail again.

Let that happen ten times... twenty times... a hundred times!

Going back to the village empty-handed was for him out of the question.

Eventually, the migrants appeared. The group of ten, most

below the age of twenty, walked fast. They all carried bags containing clothes and food.

'Kya re?' asked one of them. Sadhu stood motionless and let them walk past. He waited till they had walked about a 100 metres and followed discreetly behind. After a couple of kilometres, one of them stopped to relieve himself. He looked around and noticed Sadhu.

He yelled something to the group. They stopped, turned and looked at Sadhu.

Sadhu wondered whether to approach them. The group asked him why he was following them. He pleaded with them to take him along. Girpade shouted at him and told him to go back. Another one laughed at his age.

'Who will employ you?' asked Girpade.

As Sadhu stood thinking about what to do next, the group continued walking. He scrambled after them. They noticed and scolded him. He pleaded as they continued walking, and he kept following. After a while, they didn't say anything. He took that as a signal that he was now accepted.

After about an hour, the team stopped. Girpade asked Sadhu about his plans. Sadhu told him that he wanted to work with them and earn money. Girpade was shocked that Sadhu had only 50 paise.

'If I'm caught travelling without a ticket, I will go to jail,' he told Girpade. Girpade's heart melted and Sadhu was allowed to join the group.

As they walked, the group came upon a road-widening project where many trees had been felled. Sadhu was told to collect some dry wood and carry it, which he did. The group soon came across a sugar mill where many workers lived. After some bargaining, an elderly woman agreed to pay Sadhu 25 paisa for the firewood he had carried. She gave him a large roti and some salt as well. Part of the group now, Sadhu reached the Dhoki railway station from where the group boarded the Sholapur passenger train.

The train reached Kurdvadi Junction at eight in the evening and the group disembarked to catch the train to Pune at nine that same evening. The entire group had to buy tickets.

Girpade asked Sadhu how much money he had.

'Seventy-five paisa,' Sadhu told him. Girpade collected money from the group and bought the tickets.

'You owe me Re 1 and 75 paisa,' Girpade told Sadhu, who could see the displeasure in his eyes. The ticket had cost Rs 2 and 50 paisa, and he was not sure that Sadhu would be able to return the money.

The group reached Pune early the next morning and walked to the Shivaji Nagar slums on the Pune–Bombay road. At about nine, fourteen of them reached the site where a two-storey building was to come up. The digging for the basement was due to start soon. In 1971, no one used earth-moving machines in India and everything was done manually.

While the group was discussing amongst themselves the wages they should ask for, a man in his late thirties, dark and thin, arrived. Mukund Chauhan was the works supervisor.

Before anybody could say anything, he announced the wage rate per day per person.

'Male adults, Rs 3, female adults, Rs 2, and teens, Rs 2 a day,' he announced.

Sadhu was thrilled. He had worked for Rs 5 a month. He would now make Rs 2 in a day!

As work began, he was assigned very light work. He had to take care of the clothes and food packets the other workers brought with them. He was often asked to bring them water. He would also remove digging tools when asked.

During the lunch break, while the others were washing their hands before opening their lunch packets, Sadhu stood by, watching. Mukund noticed that he had no food. When Sadhu told him that there was nobody to cook food for him and he hadn't brought any lunch, Mukund lent him Re 1.

Happy, Sadhu went to a nearby food trolley and bought zunka bhakar (a spicy preparation made of gram flour and vegetables) for 50 paisa and kept the rest for dinner. In the evening, he again bought zunka bhakar for 50 paisa.

The next morning, Girpade organized a cup of tea and bread for the group. By nine, they were at the worksite. Sadhu once again borrowed Re 1 from Mukund and repeated the zunka bhakar meals.

On day three, Sadhu was asked to remove mud from the basement, which he did using a small basket. He borrowed Re 1 from Mukund again.

That day, fellow workers offered him food at noon and for dinner as well, so he saved the Re 1 that he had borrowed.

On the evening of the seventh day, the workers were paid. That week, Sadhu had borrowed Rs 6 from Mukund and so received Rs 8 rather than Rs 14, as Mukund had deducted the money that Sadhu owed him.

With Rs 7 in hand, Sadhu had to fend for himself the following week. He now spent Rs 1.50 on food and saved 50 paisa a day. At the end of the second week, he had saved Rs 3.50. By the end of the third week, he had a net saving of Rs 7.

Every Monday, a weekly market would be held near the Shivaji Nagar slums. Sadhu was told that there were vendors at the market who sold used clothing. He visited the market and bought two used knickers and T-shirts for Rs 3. He spent another Rs 2 to buy a used durry to sleep on.

One night, it started drizzling. It had become his habit to sleep outside a hut in the slum. In fact, those who had huts also preferred sleeping in the open. Now the rain pushed everyone inside their jhuggis.

Where would Sadhu go? He took a rickshaw to the nearby railway station. There was plenty of space and one could sleep anywhere one liked. He chose a place near a tea vendor and spent the night in luxury, sleeping under ceiling fans.

As it rained regularly, he continued to sleep on the rail platform. He developed a friendship with the tea vendor and did odd jobs for him. The tea vendor needed a helping hand during the early mornings when many trains would arrive.

The tea vendor would in return pay Sadhu Re 1 each day along with a cup of tea and a piece of bread for free. He declared Sadhu to be one of his employees to protect the latter from rail officials. Sadhu also kept his clothes and durry with the tea vendor.

As Diwali approached, Sadhu's co-workers from the village prepared to return home.

'Want to come?' Girpade asked him.

Sadhu had a grand saving of Rs 125 and was keen to visit his village.

Like the others, he went on a buying spree. He spent Rs 15 on clothes for his mother, sister and brothers.

Back in the village, the family treated him like a hero. They had a feast in the evening. Everyone enjoyed the chicken he had bought from a villager.

To fulfil his mother's wish, Sadhu used a part of his savings to buy her two goats. After spending four days at home, the group returned to Pune. Two among the group brought their wives along.

After Sadhu had worked for him for eight months, the

benevolent Mukund raised Sadhu's wage to Rs 3 a day. He raised the wages of his seniors as well by 50 paisa. They now got Rs 3.50. This was early in 1972 and Sadhu was thirteen years old.

One evening, a mitti (soil) contractor brought a truck full of good-quality soil. In those days builders used clay to bind bricks together. The walls would later be plastered with cement and sand. Since the truck arrived late, the contractor could not find workers to unload the soil. If the truck was not emptied within three hours, the truck driver would charge more money.

Sadhu saw the helpless contractor going from hut to hut looking for workers. It was eight in the evening and the workers had returned from work tired. Sadhu approached the contractor and asked how much he would give him if he emptied the truck within three hours.

'Are you making fun of me?' the contractor asked, livid. But he realized Sadhu was serious—the boy demanded Rs 10. The deal was stuck for Rs 7. Sadhu asked him to wait and ran back to his slum.

Many of the boys living in the slum were in school. They were the children of day labourers, and would often be in need of money. Sadhu knew one of them well and promised him that if he could recruit another three boys, he would pay them 50 paisa each for three hours of work.

The boy thought he was joking because adults were paid around Rs 3 or 4 for a whole day's work and Sadhu was promising 50 paisa for three hours of work. But he got three of his friends, all over ten years old.

The boys reached the truck and requested the contractor to pay half the amount as advance. Sadhu insisted, in case the contractor ran away after the truck had been emptied.

'After all, we are boys,' Sadhu told himself.

As they were ready to start, they realized that they had no spades and baskets with which to unload the truck. They spent half an hour getting the tools from the slum. Sadhu had to pay 25 paisa each for two spades and three bamboo baskets.

With Rs 3.50 tied around his waist, Sadhu and the boys began work. The unloading was completed before ten in the evening. Happy, the contractor rewarded the four boys by giving them 25 paisa each.

After paying Rs 2 to four boys, and another Rs 1.25 as rent for the tools, Sadhu had earned Rs 3.75.

'Can you do the same tomorrow?' the contractor asked them.

Why not? Of course!

For the next ten days, they unloaded one truck a day. Sadhu had made an extra Rs 37.50. The truck unloading business ended after ten days because the construction work was completed.

After working in Pune for nine months, Sadhu bought a 10x10-square-foot hut for Rs 50.

With a hut of his own, he was taken more seriously by his fellow workers. When he went back home for the next Diwali in 1972, he had Rs 500 in hand. He bought a buffalo, a purchase that made his family financially independent. The goats, too, were multiplying.

After returning to Pune, he decided against doing work that required digging and removing soil. He joined a construction site instead, where he worked as an assistant to the mason, a man named Raghav. At that time, a mason was paid Rs 15 a day and his assistant Rs 4.

Changing his job raised both Sadhu's income and reputation in the eyes of the slum dwellers and fellow workers from his village.

With two years' work experience, he would sometimes double as a mason as well. When Raghav was late or left early, Sadhu worked in his place.

In the summer of 1975, Raghav received a telegram from his village, informing him that his father had passed away and that he must return home immediately. The contractor was in a hurry to complete the building.

'He may not be as experienced as I am, but being young, he is faster than me,' Raghav said to the contractor, referring to Sadhu.

This was a dream come true for Sadhu. With the builder agreeing to take him on as the mason, Sadhu achieved a breakthrough. In the absence of the master mason, he worked for a full twenty days. The contractor was satisfied with his work. Raghav, too, was pleased when he returned and asked Sadhu to work under him for a month more.

Sadhu was now a trainee. Raghav gave him critical insights into the profession. On the day they were to build the roof, Sadhu performed a puja at home, seeking God's blessings. He was to measure the ratio of cement-sand-gravel and direct the workers under Raghav's watchful eye. If he made a mistake, Raghav was there to correct him. Only Sadhu and Raghav knew of this arrangement.

'You are now a mason capable of making a building,' Raghav declared late that evening. Excited, Sadhu gifted him a bottle of good country liquor.

Although he had been declared a mason, Sadhu had to work with Raghav on another site as an assistant mason until someone hired him as a mason. In early 1977, Raghav was approached by a builder to construct a small office building in a factory that made spun pipes for drainage systems.

Impressed with Sadhu's work, the contractor offered him

a deal. He promised to pay him Rs 2,500 if he took complete charge of constructing the building. That meant he had to hire labourers, pay them, manage the construction of the building and finally hand it over to the contractor. The deal was finally struck at Rs 2,700.

Sadhu was now a sub-contractor. He completed the building in fifty-eight days. After paying Rs 2,000 in labourers' wages, he was left with his share of Rs 700.

He had now saved over Rs 2,000, and returned to his village to marry. His mother had already chosen a girl, fourteen-year-old Vidya. Soon after the wedding, Sadhu returned to Pune where his wife joined him a few months later.

Near Sadhu's home in the Shivaji Nagar slum was a shop that sold firewood for cooking. The merchant stored the wood in an empty area along the roadside. One day, when Sadhu visited the merchant to purchase some wood, he noticed that he was a bit downcast. He was fed up with the business, he said; the profession didn't command respect. He was an upper caste Patil, after all. He also talked of theft of his merchandise as a regular phenomenon. He had hired two men to protect his property and they were constantly harassed by drug addicts and vagabonds, who stole his wood. When caught, they would pick fights with his men.

'This is an area unfit for business. After all, I am an outsider. Can you buy my business?' he asked.

Sadhu wasn't prepared for such an offer, and his heart raced. He was reminded of his experience in unloading sand from the truck.

'Give me a day,' Sadhu told the merchant and left. After walking a 100 metres, he went back and asked, 'How much money do you want?'

The wood merchant quoted a figure of Rs 2,000 as the

price of the wood in stock and, Sadhu understood, around the same amount for the whole shop.

'I'll return tomorrow,' Sadhu said and left for home.

'Take your own decision,' Vidya told Sadhu when he mentioned this new opportunity. She was in her sixth month of pregnancy.

With Vidya joining him and his income rising, the couple had begun to live well, eating wheat roti and rice.

Sadhu weighed his choices. He felt that he must buy the business if he wanted to amass more wealth than the upper castes in his village.

He thought that the the wood merchant might agree to a price of Rs 4,000 as he was desperate to sell.

Sadhu had saved over Rs 800. Vidya agreed to sell her silver jewellery, which would fetch Rs 200 to Rs 300. An elderly lady who had once given him shelter might loan him another Rs 100 to Rs 200. The tea vendor at the station would give him a minimum of Rs 200.

'If all works out well, I will have around Rs 1,500,' Sadhu thought, making the calculation. 'That's not enough.'

He decided to approach his guru Raghav who had certified him as a mason.

He met him the next morning and told him the story. Raghav was excited on his friend's behalf and offered to loan him Rs 300.

Next, he approached the contractor with whom he was working at that time, who eventually agreed to loan him Rs 800.

There was hope now. That evening, Sadhu went to the wood merchant and told him that he was willing to pay Rs 4,000 for his business, but would require at least three to four days to arrange for the money.

The wood merchant agreed to sell his business for Rs 4,500.

By the fifth day, Sadhu had arranged for Rs 4,000. He offered the merchant Rs 2,000 in cash on the spot.

'I can pay you Rs 4,000 right now,' he told him, 'but what about the truck that will come next fortnight demanding Rs 2,000?'

The merchant agreed and Sadhu paid him the first instalment of Rs 2,000. He further agreed that Sadhu would pay the remainder in instalments of Rs 500 on every fifteenth day. A deal was struck.

Sadhu was now a firewood merchant and proud father of a baby boy. He hired two school dropouts from his slum to protect the lot where he stored the wood.

On his third day in business, he opened a bank account in the name of Vidya.

By 1982, he had saved enough money to buy a small plot of land in Adarsh Indira Nagar. He built a single-storey two-room house with a bathroom and kitchen for his expanding family. Before shifting to Adarsh Indira Nagar, he thought of new business ideas.

'Why don't you open an atta chakki?' a friend asked. Adarsh Indira Nagar was a new locality and expanding very fast. A flour mill would be an attractive business. The residents of Pune typically bought wheat, which they then had ground into flour. Bags of ten to fifty kilograms of wheat were taken to a one-man-run flour mill and ground into flour.

'People like fresh food,' the friend reminded Sadhu.

In April 1983 Sadhu bought a flour mill for Rs 9,000 and set up the business in a house that he had rented for the purpose. It was close to his house in Adarsh Indira Nagar. He sold the firewood shop to one of his employees for Rs 10,000 on a monthly instalment plan of Rs 1,000.

With the atta chakki business, Sadhu achieved fame in his village. Within a week of setting up the mill, he opened a bank account in his name as well.

The mill did a brisk business. By 1990, Vidya's account had savings of Rs 1 lakh and Sadhu's account had another Rs 50,000.

He returned to his village and built a nice three-bedroom house for his mother and siblings.

In late 1992, another business opportunity came knocking. A middle-aged man came to his mill and asked Sadhu if he could supply him with jowar flour.

'I am building a large housing complex nearby,' the man explained. He gave his workers free food as an incentive. This saved time and the workers worked for more hours.

Sadhu agreed, and began supplying the flour. For his part, the man promptly paid the bills. He soon returned to Sadhu's mill and asked if he could also supply tur dal, salt, spices, potatoes, onions, garlic, red chillies and other food items.

'Sure,' Sadhu said.

He was now supplying raw food material for 100 to 150 workers daily. He hired two workers to procure the foodstuff.

'I must hire an accountant,' he thought. For the first time, he hired a worker for a soft job. Something big was in store.

One day, when he went to collect his payment from the builder, Sadhu took a tour of the construction site. He asked a worker if he was happy with the kind of food they were served.

'Achcha hai,' the worker replied.

'Can you supply sand to us?' the builder in charge of the project asked. 'We need trucks of sand every day.'

Sadhu saw a huge business opportunity and promised to get back to him within a few days.

Since his childhood, Sadhu had worked in the construction

industry. He knew people who supplied building material. Sand, however, falls in a different category.

After a couple of days, he was put in touch with a man who owned a licensed sand mine. He was looking for a large builder who would buy his product in bulk.

Sadhu met him and told him about the opportunity. He was thrilled. But he insisted on supplying the sand directly.

'I am a miner,' he said with pride. 'I have political connections,' he boasted. 'Since you know the builder, you claim your commission from him,' he said. 'I will give you some money per truck also,' he negotiated, appearing reasonable.

The next day, Sadhu told the builder about his meeting with the sand miner. The builder asked Sadhu to arrange a meeting with the miner. 'I will take care of your interests.'

A deal was struck and the builder started getting an uninterrupted supply of sand.

After a couple of weeks, the miner stopped paying Sadhu the money per truck that he had promised him. Sadhu complained to the builder.

'See me tomorrow afternoon in my office,' the builder told him.

The following day, Sadhu went to the office of the builder, who thanked him for finding the sand miner. He then asked, 'Can you supply me cement? Can you supply me stone gitti (gravel)?' He was unstoppable.

'I will need millions of tiles,' he said.

Sadhu started with the gitti. To supply cement, he needed a dealership with cement companies.

Sadhu bought a piece of land near the construction site. He built a storage room, an office and a room for workers. On the first floor, he built a two-bedroom house.

Within a year, Sadhu became known as the gitti-wala. Several big builders started buying gitti from him. With his booming gitti business, he sold the atta chakki for Rs 90,000 in early 1993. With the proceeds he was able to realize another desire—since he belonged to a landless family, buying farmland was a dream.

Three weeks after selling the mill, Sadhu bought two acres of farmland on the outskirts of Pune. The land was barren and dry. He spent more money to transform it into cultivable land.

Meanwhile, he got a dealership with a cement company. He started selling steel as well.

By the end of 1994, his turnover touched Rs 3 lakh a month.

'Paisa ginate ginate hum so jate the,' he says.

One of the builders with whom he had business dealings enquired about land in the area where Sadhu had his two-acre farmland. Sadhu told him about his tract of land and the builder offered him a price in crores!

'What if I sell the land, and buy property on Pune's outskirts?' he wondered. He took his wife and a friend for a long drive in the car that he had bought in 1995. The idea was to see which parts of the city were expanding the most. Driving around for hours, he got a sense about where he should purchase land.

Meanwhile, the builder who had seen Sadhu's two-acre plot of land approached him again to see if he was willing to sell the land.

A deal was stuck for a few crores. With the proceeds, Sadhu bought land in all the areas that he thought would see growth.

Having seen the vast amounts of money in the construction business and property agents driving Mercedes and BMWs, he wondered if he, too, could join that group. 'Can I become a builder?' he thought next.

Building a residential complex became his new dream. Since he worked with builders, he had an idea of how housing projects were developed.

To build a housing complex, the most critical component was land. If one had land and an assured supply of building material, constructing a housing complex was easy. Sadhu had both land and the building material. With his experience as a mason, he also had some idea of construction.

'I will create a housing complex,' Sadhu told himself. Vidya supported his dream.

Since Sadhu and Vidya were illiterate, they needed partners to help in the marketing. They found a few people who had the skills and experience, but no money to invest.

'We will build the apartment with buyers' money,' they resolved.

The first step was to form a company. They also needed to decide on a locality for the housing complex, as they had land in several places.

On 1 January 2004, he approached an agency that names companies. After many suggestions, they decided on the name Pentagon Developers.

Sadhu had asked the agency to select a name that had something to do with America, because people in Pune loved America. They sent their kids there to study.

The Pentagon project, including the land, was to cost Rs 35 crore.

By 2006, Sadhu had received the approvals required for the project. The project would have three towers, each with seven floors and 200 flats. All three towers would have escalators. A three-bedroom, 1,275-square-foot flat would cost a minimum of Rs 25 lakh.

The project kicked off in 2008 and was completed in 2010.

Today the same flats are resold for a minimum of Rs 75 lakh apiece.

***

Sadhu's company, SK Developers, has diversified its activities. One of Sadhu's sons runs a mini bank, providing credit to small entrepreneurs; the other son runs a property business. Sadhu closed down his building material business once the Pentagon project was completed. He now looks after the Land Bank.

Land Bank?

'I have 80,000 square feet of prime properties in Pune,' says he, indicating what he meant by 'bank.'

'It (Sadhu's land) is worth Rs 25 crore,' says Milind Kamble, the founder-chairman of DICCI.

What next?

'Either a star hotel or a sugar mill,' smiles Sadhu.

ACKNOWLEDGEMENTS

We embarked on this journey to inspire Dalits with their own examples of success. To the extent that we have modestly succeeded, is because of the help from many well-wishers. Foremost is the role of two people. We started the journey because of the central role played by one of us—Chandra Bhan Prasad—who first connected the dots and became the public face of the survey. All of this would have been for naught without the key role played by Milind Kamble, the indefatigable founder of the Dalit Indian Chamber of Commerce and Industry (DICCI), without whose help we could not have completed either the survey or the book.

But the process has been a mutually beneficial relationship. The media glare our survey received has mainstreamed DICCI, encouraging more Dalit entrepreneurs to 'come out' and become members. As a result, four Dalit entrepreneurs, all DICCI members, have been recognized and celebrated by the 'system' with Padma Shree awards. This owes substantially to the efforts of Montek Singh Ahluwalia, who was consistently encouraging and repeatedly made time from his busy schedule to meet with us and with DICCI and some of its members.

Identifying and surveying the thousand odd Dalit entrepreneurs across the country took several years. The initial seed money was provided by Chip Kaye and Nandan Nilekani, which then helped convince the Templeton Foundation to fund this project with a generous grant to the Center for the Advanced Study of India (CASI), at the University of Pennsylvania. The staff at the Center, led by Juliana Di Giustini, CASI's Deputy Director, meticulously and efficiently administered the Templeton grant and in this were supported by the staff at the University of Pennsylvania Institute for the Advanced Study of India (UPIASI), CASI's counterpart institution in New Delhi, under the leadership of Dr E. Sridharan.

Dr Pratap Bhanu Mehta, president of the Center for Policy Research, has been a friend and well-wisher for all of us and the title is inspired by a conversation with him. At Random House, Meru Gokhale championed this project and has steadfastly supported us while Archana Shankar tirelessly shepherded the book through the editing and production stages.

Last, but hardly least, all of us owe deep gratitude to our families who have endured our many absences with patience, fortitude and humour. Dr Sadhana Kapur read each draft carefully and edited them to make them accessible to an interested but uninformed reader.

Finally, we want to thank all the entrepreneurs who gave us their time and whose own lives are exemplars of how to succeed, no matter how high the odds might be stacked. It is to them—and the countless others who have tried but not yet succeeded—that we dedicate this book.

A NOTE ON THE AUTHORS

Devesh Kapur is Director, Center for the Advanced Study of India at the University of Pennsylvania.

D. Shyam Babu is Senior Fellow, Centre for Policy Research, New Delhi.

Chandra Bhan Prasad is a public intellectual and mentor, Dalit Indian Chamber of Commerce and Industry (DICCI).